A Hessian Report on the People,
the Land, the War
As Noted in the Diary of
Chaplain Philipp Waldeck
(1776-1780)

Eighteenth Century America

Translated from Hessian Manuscript #28
of the Bancroft Collection in the
New York Public Library

Bruce E. Burgoyne

HERITAGE BOOKS
2008

HERITAGE BOOKS

AN IMPRINT OF HERITAGE BOOKS, INC.

Books, CDs, and more—Worldwide

For our listing of thousands of titles see our website
at
www.HeritageBooks.com

Published 2008 by
HERITAGE BOOKS, INC.
Publishing Division
100 Railroad Ave. #104
Westminster, Maryland 21157

International Standard Book Number: 978-0-7884-0252-4

Contents

Chaplain Philip Waldeck may have dressed like his civilian colleagues and worn clothes similar to these.

Preface

A largely unexploited source of information on life in colonial America is to be found in the diaries of those German soldiers who came to America as the so-called "Hessians" during the American Revolutionary War. Many of those men had never before been outside their own small village, few had ever been outside Germany, and possibly none of them had ever been in the American colonies prior to sailing to America as auxiliaries in the employ of the English crown.

Upon their arrival in America they saw a new life style, new architectural styles, and even new races of people such as they had never imagined before. Just as modern soldiers traveling to new areas write descriptions of their experiences in distant lands, so the Hessians recorded their impressions of America in diaries and letters home.

In America they found workmen who considered themselves "gentlemen equal to the governor and general"; a city, New York, which several described as "oriental"; Negro slaves for whom they had much compassion as "they are human beings like we are, and Indians about whom their curiosity seemed endless.

Of all the diaries, that of Philipp Waldeck, chaplain of the 3rd English-Waldeck Regiment, contains the most thorough and all-encompassing view of life in America, as his entire diary is filled with detailed descriptions of everyday activities.

- - - - - - -

In 1975 I obtained the name of the president of the Waldeck, Germany, Historical Society and subsequent correspondence and visits turned my general interest in the so-called "Hessians" to a concentrated research into the lives and activities of the men of the 3rd Waldeck Regiment, or more correctly, the 3rd English-Waldeck Regiment. During the previous twenty years I had done research on the Hessians in an on-again off-again basis, including four years in the British Museum Manuscript Room. However, the friendship shared with my Waldeck friend, Guenter Jedicke, started my specializing in the men from Waldeck who fought against the revolting American colonists.

The more I read about the Waldeckers, the more I wanted to learn about them. Repeatedly I found references to first person accounts about the Waldeck Regiment written by Carl Philipp Steuernagel and Philipp Waldeck. But these accounts were not available in English. A version of the Waldeck diary had been published by Marion Dexter Learned as *Philipp Waldeck's Diary of the American Revolution*, Americana Germanica Press, (Philadelphia, 1907), but in German. Max von Eelking used the diary as source material for his standard reference on the Hessians, *Die deutschen Huelfstruppen im nordamerikanischen Befreiungskriege, 1776 bis 1783*, (Hannover, 1863), and modern writers who wished to cite information from the diary generally referred to the von Eelking text.

I did know that the American historian George Bancroft had obtained a copy of the Waldeck diary during his time as an American diplomat in Germany, and that the Bancroft Collection was available at The New York Public Library. Therefore, I obtained a microfilm copy, which was written in the Old German script, and written in such a hurry, apparently, that it was nearly illegible.

It then became necessary for me to learn the Old German script, and in particular to learn to read the handwriting used by the Waldeck diary copyist. I made numerous starts and stops. No one could help me, as even those who wrote in the old script had trouble deciphering the scribble. It was obviously a situation that no one before me had the time nor patience to work with the document, and each year there are fewer people, even in Germany, who can read the old script. It is no longer taught in the German schools. Finally I accomplished my goal and made a typed German transcript which, although containing many errs, was clear enough to enable a translation to be made.

The resulting translation is the basis for this book and presents America and the American Revolutionary War as a great, new adventure for the young, 26-year old, newly ordained chaplain of the 3rd Waldeck Regiment.

The version of the Waldeck diary published by Learned seems to have been obtained from a "polished" copy of the diary which Waldeck was preparing for publication. His early death may explain why it covers a shorter period than the copy in the Bancroft Collection. Even the copy in the Bancroft Collection fails to cover the final years of the war. This may be explained by part of the diary having been lost at sea, insufficient time for the person making the copy to finish his task, a period of illness while Waldeck was in America, other difficulties which precluded maintaining the diary, or an infinite number of other possibilities. Had Waldeck been able to finish preparing his diary for publication, it probably would have contained considerably more detail about the history of the German church in New York, as during the closing years of the war the Waldeck Regiment was stationed in the Long Island and New York areas.

A copy of the Waldeck diary, possibly the original, was known to be in the possession of an individual in Bad Wildungen, Germany, as late as the early 1970's. That version has since been lost. I should also note that Gisela Reid published an article incorporating the first part of the Waldeck diary in the German language *Geschichtsblaetter fuer Waldeck*, published by the Waldeck Historical Society in 1983.

The Learned version containing less detail than the Bancroft version, possibly because in his effort to polish the diary Waldeck removed most of the entries which showed him to be young, unsophisticated, and inexperienced, was translated by Dr. William Dornemann and published in the Johannes Schwalm Historical Association *Journal* (volume 2, numbers 3 & 4, and volume 3, number 1; 1983, 1984, and 1985). My translation of the portion of the final days of 1780 appeared in the *Journal* (volume 3, number 2; 1986).

I have used a letter e after umlauted vowels a, o, and u in German spelling, and used other names in the manuscript as given except where I was certain of current spelling changes. I have used parentheses when the author of the diary used such and have noted information added by me in brackets. I have changed some dates to maintain uniformity and have split some long, involved sentences and paragraphs to make for easier reading.

My bibliography contains only those references cited in the translation and my footnotes. I do not believe it is necessary to list books I have read, nor even those standard works concerning the Revolution or the role of the Hessians. Such information is available in any library.

Unfortunately I fear that mistakes still exist in my translation. If so, I must assume full responsibility. My primary effort has been, as always, to make the information written in German available to interested persons in a more readily usable volume. I recommend that serious researchers, who find worthwhile information in this volume, return to the source document to confirm that information. However, it should be borne in mind, and a comparison of the two versions of the Waldeck diary bear out, that diarists often distort facts and change their diaries depending on who may read them.

Acknowledgments

The most enjoyable part of preparing the translation and supporting information in this volume was the friendship and assistance which I have received. Guenter Jedicke and his wife, Marianne, have opened their hearts and home to my wife and me, and have provided information and introductions throughout the Waldeck area. Other members of the Waldeck Historical Society who have given me friendship and assistance are Frau Ingeborg Moldenauer, archivist; Karl and Hilda Bracht; Benno, Baron von Canstein; Linda, Baroness von Dalwigk; Wilhelm Hellwig, Klaus Peter Scholz, and Helmut and Heidi Vesper. The clergy of the area and especially Pastor Klaus Mombrei of Bergheim have opened church records to me, and Wolfgang Warnecke has provided information on men from the Pyrmont area.

No one doing research on the Hessians can give adequate thanks to Inge Auerbach, Eckhart G. Franz, and Otto Froehlich, and the Marburg, Germany, Archivschule for their contributions to the field.

Others in Europe who provided friendship, encouragement, and assistance include the Taemerich and Tichelaar families and Kerstin Hochbein.

Institutions, whose personnel have been of special value include the Library of Congress, The New York Public Library, Morristown National Historical Park, the Alderman Library of the University of Virginia, the Clements Library of the University of Michigan, the Pace Library of the University of West Florida, the British Museum Manuscript Room in London, the Hessian State Archives in Marburg, Germany, the Netherlands General Archives in The Hague, and the Dutch Army Museum at Delft.

Those in America deserving special thanks are: Mrs Arthur (Paula) Janousek, of Ludington, Michigan, who worked many hours with me on the final section of the Waldeck diary, and Mrs. Theodor (Irene)

Winkel, of Ludington, who translated the Latin passages. James Servies and Galen R. Wilson have both encouraged my efforts over the years, as have my friends in the Johannes Schwalm Historical Association.

Dr. William Dornemann's translation of the Learned version of the Waldeck diary has given me the opportunity to compare the two versions of the diary without the necessity of translating both versions.

Finally, but most significantly, my wife Marie deserves full credit for bringing my efforts to a successful conclusion. For years she has done all the time consuming errands and tasks without which a manuscript would never be ready for delivery to a publisher. She has been at my side during all my research, and has hiked, back-packed, and ridden in cars, busses, trains, and boats during our many trips to and through Waldeck, and even flown over the area in a light plane. She has read and reread the numerous copies of my manuscript many, many times. Thank you Marie.

Bruce E. Burgoyne
Dover, DE
1994

Introduction

Six small German territories sold troops into English service for use against the American colonists during the American Revolutionary War. The Waldeck contingent was the smallest, only a 670-man regiment and a 14-man artillery detachment. However, the Waldeckers served in Nova Scotia, the New York-New Jersey area, West Florida including present day Louisiana, and possibly Maine. Their travels while being transferred and as prisoners of war also took some of the men to Pennsylvania, Maryland, and Virginia, to Mexico, Cuba, and Jamaica. They were scorned as wood-cutters by the English historian Sir George Trevelyan, who gave them no credit as soldiers. Nevertheless, they fought well in the attack on Fort Washington in November 1776, on the counter-attack against General John Sullivan on Staten Island in August 1777, and in the defense of Pensacola in 1781. The commanding officer, Colonel Johann Ludwig Wilhelm von Hanxleden, was killed leading an attack on the Spanish strongpoint at The Village, near Mobile. Probably they were not much worse, nor much better, than the other soldiers engaged on both sides during the war.

The 3rd Waldeck Regiment, which was formed in 1776 with men taken from two regiments in Dutch service and a number of hurriedly assembled recruits, suffered severe losses in America due to sickness, a few battle casualties, and a large number of desertions. Many of the deserters joined the American and Spanish armies. They often deserted back to their original unit when the opportunity arose, and one man captured by the Spaniards joined the Spanish army, and then deserted back to his former unit which was then under siege at Pensacola. Several others are known to have deserted from prisoner of war status at New Orleans, worked their way up the Mississippi River, and joined George Rogers Clark's command fighting against the English in the Illinois country.

Many of the men who returned to Europe at the end of the war in 1783 remained in the Waldeck army. By 1785 the 3rd Waldeck Regiment had been redesignated the 5th Waldeck Battalion. This unit entered Dutch service in 1802, at which time it was sent to the Cape of Good Hope. The battalion commander, Colonel Friedrich von Wilmowsky, who had served in America as a lieutenant, drowned en route to South Africa. His replacement in command was Lieutenant Colonel Carl Mueller, who had served in America as a free corporal and as an ensign in the 3rd Regiment. Others in the 5th Battalion, officers and men, had fought for English pay during the American Revolution, but in South Africa they fought against their former English comrades in arms.

Others, who had deserted in America or chose to be released in America after the war, became American citizens and they and their descendants have contributed to the growth and prosperity of their new homeland. The commissary, Philipp Marc, was one of those who stayed in America after the war. For a time he was a salesman-merchant in New York and later was appointed American consul at Bamberg, Germany. His wartime autograph book is in the archives of the Waldeck Historical Society in Arolsen, Germany.

To enable the reader to better understand the events and the individuals mentioned, I have added a brief organization and history of the 3rd Waldeck Regiment.

About the Author

(Extracted from the article "Deutsche Soldaten im Amerikanischen Unabhaengigkeitskrieg" by Dr. Hermann Bing, which appeared in "Mein Waldeck", Nr. 11, 1977, published in Arolsen, Germany)

Johann Philipp Franz Elisaus Waldeck was appointed chaplain of the 3rd Waldeck Regiment when it was formed in 1776 and served with the unit during its entire period of service in America from 1776 until 1783. He had been born on 9 March 1750 in Hemfurth, Waldeck. The son of a clergyman, he attended the city school in Nieder Wildungen, was confirmed in 1764, and in 1769 entered the University of Jena to study religion. From 1772 to 1775, he was a private tutor in the Waldeck village of Thalitter. In the spring of 1776 he took his theological examinations and assumed duty as chaplain of the 3rd Regiment. At that time the regiment was just being organized, as the Prince of Waldeck was one of the German rulers who supplied troop units to England for use in attempting to suppress the revolt in the American colonies.

After the regiment returned to Waldeck, Philipp Waldeck was to have taken on the duties of pastor in the village of Affoldern, but while visiting his former regiment at Mengeringhausen on 11 March 1784, he contracted a fever and died nine days later He was buried with military honors at Mengeringhausen, having died -- probably another casualty of the war -- a few days following his 34th birthday.

Chaplain Waldeck kept a diary from the day the regiment marched out of Waldeck until the close of the year 1780. Possibly a portion which would have covered the remaining service in America was lost or destroyed.

Contents of the Diary

The diary written by Waldeck gives an account of the American Revolution from the "enemy" point of view, but it contains far more than a mere recitation of military life and actions. It gives a vivid description of new experiences for a young man from the interior area of German; it is a recording of the vitality of American life and the richness of the budding American nation. Waldeck seems to have participated in most, and seen every aspect of American life. Obviously very money and rank conscious, he noted the economic and social activities everywhere he went. His descriptions are interesting, detailed, and on a wide variety of subjects. He describes fishing, farming, sporting events, schools, churches, costumes, and customs. He also com-mented on religion and religious practices and history, and upon slavery, Indians, wildlife, and nature in general. The range of subject matter seems more than one man could have recorded. His reporting of the Herrnhuter community of Bethlehem is especially interesting, not only for the description of life there, but as an insight into the character of the author.

Eighteenth Century America
Organization and Brief History
Of the 3rd English-Waldeck Regiment

According to a treaty dated 20 April 1776, the German principality of Waldeck sold a 670-man infantry regiment into English service for use against the American colonists who were in revolt. The staff and five companies were accompanied by a 14-man artillery detachment with two small field pieces.

The key staff positions and staff personnel of the 12-man staff were:

Commander, Lieutenant Colonel/Colonel Johann Ludwig Wilhelm von Hanxleden

Major/Lieutenant Colonel Ludwig von Dalwigk

Adjutant, Ensign/Lieutenant Johann Henrich Stierlein

Regimental Quartermaster, Lieutenant Karl Theodor Wiegand

Regimental Drummer Christian Glaentzer

Provost Konrad Glaentzer

Regimental Surgeon Christian Mattern

Commissary (Auditor/Paymaster) Philipp Marc

Chaplain Philipp Waldeck

Other staff positions were an assistant provost and two wagon servants.

The 1st, or Grenadier Company, commanded by Captain/Major Konrad Albrecht von Horn until 1778, and then by Captain Georg von Haacke, was organized with:

3 Officers	1 Solicitor[3]
3 Batmen[1]	6 Corporals
3 Sergeants	2 Fifers
1 Quartermaster Sergeant	3 Drummers
1 Captain at Arms	110 Privates
1 Surgeon's Mate[2]	134 Total

The 2nd, 3rd, 4th, and 5th Companies were musket companies organized with:

3 Officers	1 Solicitor
3 Batmen	1 Free Corporal
3 Sergeants	6 Corporals
1 Quartermaster Sergeant	1 Fifer
1 Captain at Arms	3 Drummers

Eighteenth Century America

1 Surgeon's Mate   107 Privates
                          131 Total

Company commanders, all of whom arrived in America with the regiment in 1776, were:

1st Company - Captain/Major Konrad Albrecht von Horn until 1778, then Captain Georg von Haacke

2nd Company - Major/Lieutenant Colonel von Dalwigk until March 1777, Captain Christoph Alberti, Sr., until March 1781, and later Captain Augustin Alberti

3rd Company - Lieutenant Colonel/Colonel von Hanxleden until January 1781, and later Captain Alexander von Baumbach

4th Company - Captain /Major Christian Friedrich Pentzel

5th company - Captain von Haacke until August 1778, and then Major/Lieutenant Colonel von Horn.

Other officers when the regiment arrived in America in October 1776, and their company of assignment, were;

Lieutenant Wilhelm Leonhardi - 5th Company

Lieutenant/Captain Lieutenant Gerhard Henrich Heldring - 4th Company

Lieutenant Wilhelm Keppel - 2nd Company

Lieutenant Friedrich von Wilmowsky - 3rd Company

Lieutenant Karl Henrich Strubberg - 1st Company

Ensign/Lieutenant Andreas Brumhard - 5th Company

Ensign/Lieutenant and after January 1781, Adjutant, Henrich Jacob Knipschild - 3rd Company

Ensign Friedrich Noelting - 2nd Company

Ensign/Lieutenant Karl Hohmann, Sr. - 4th Company

Other officers subsequently assigned to the regiment as ensigns and who served in America, were:

Friedrich von Axleben	Theodor Ursall
Karl von Horn	August Mueller, Jr.
Christian Schmidt	Franz Philipp Wirths
Karl Mueller	Bernhard Schreiber
August Hohmann, Jr.	

The regiment arrived at New York with the second division of troops from Hesse-Cassel on 18 October 1776, and landed two days later. The regiment suffered its first casualties in a skirmish on 27 October 1776 and then participated in the attack on Fort Washington on 16 November 1776. The Waldeckers were praised for their conduct under fire during the attack, although they lost six men killed and seventeen wounded.

After Washington's army was driven out of New Jersey, the Waldeck Regiment was part of the force assigned winter quarters there. Two separate commands were overrun by the Americans in early January 1777, resulting in Captain von Haacke, Lieutenant Heldring, and about eighty men being made prisoners of war. The regiment was part of the force which repulsed an American attack on Staten Island in August 1777. The men held prisoners of war were exchanged in July and August 1778, and the regiment then sailed for West Florida in November 1778.

En route to West Florida the regiment visited Jamaica where the transports were reprovisioned. Once in Florida the regiment's suffering really began. Following the Spanish declaration of war, part of the regiment was captured at Baton Rouge and the rest of the regiment was captured at Pensacola. Prior to the fall of Pensacola, Colonel von Hanxleden had been killed leading an attack on The Village, also known as Frenchtown, a Spanish strongpoint near Mobile. Battle deaths and disease decimated the regiment.

The articles of surrender signed at Pensacola in May 1781 enabled the regiment to return to New York, but fifty of the men chose to join the Spanish army instead.[4]

Many men had deserted during the war, and following the end of hostilities in 1783, other men were released from the regiment so that they could remain in America. As a result, of all the Hessian contingents which served England, the Waldeck force lost the greatest percentage of men. Of the approximately 1,200 men, including replacements, who served in the regiment in America, only 505 returned to Germany.[5]

EIGHTEENTH CENTURY AMERICA

(A Hessian Report
on the People, the Land, the War)

As Noted in the Diary
of Chaplain Philipp Waldeck
(1776-1780)

Eighteenth Century America

A Hessian Report
on the People, the Land, the War

As Noted in the Diary of Chaplain Philipp Waldeck

The Month of May 1776

The 20th - The 3rd Regiment of the Prince of Waldeck marched from Korbach. The weather was very pleasant. The throng of people along the road, all the way to Arolsen, was unbelievable. The first night's bivouac was at Cuelte.

The 21st - At four o'clock march was sounded. The crowd of people who stood on the right and left was as great as yesterday. I wished the Herr Fector Stoecker of Herbsen and my many other good friends a good morning. Night bivouac was at Borentrik.

The 22nd - We arrived at Beverungen in good time. The regiment immediately boarded the boats which were waiting there for us. We ate in a group in the city, took our farewells from friends who had accompanied us to this point, and departed at seven o'clock. We traveled no further than Blankenburg.

The 23rd - At eight o'clock we came to Hoexter, at nine to Corvey, at ten to Holzminden. Here we grounded hard, and the sailors from the other boats had to help us to get free. This region, especially near the Weser, is somewhat hilly, and many cliffs rise near the river. We passed very close to one of these cliffs which was steeper than the others. From the midst of the cliff a spring ran, which powered a mill built close to the cliffs, which was named the Devil's Mill.[1]

The 24th - At eleven o'clock we arrived at Hameln. Two things were worth seeing here, the locks and the strong point, which is now called Fort George. I went into the city. The streets were in part deserted, because everyone had gone to see the regiment, which here also, received everyone's approbation.

The 25th - Early in the morning we passed the pontoon bridge at Rinteln. The sky again cleared and the weather was good. Today a man fell into the water, but was saved by a sailor's quick reaction.

The 26th - Because we were in such a hurry, and could not stop along the way, the Whitsuntide service was celebrated with only a singing of hymns. The boatman, himself, fell in the water today and was saved by some timely help.

The 27th - We stopped in Hoya, a most pleasant locality, at midday. Two soldiers fell into the water, and one swam over three hundred yards before being noticed, but no one drowned. The hills which have confined the stream of the Weser, disappeared, and we saw nothing but flat lands. We bivouacked in the Verden area..

The 28th - We passed through Bremen in the afternoon. Ensign Knipschild and I were transferred ashore and went through the city. Unfortunately there was insufficient time to see anything here. But even in our haste, we took time to enjoy the taste of several glasses of eighteen groten beer.[2]

The 29th - We arrived in Vegesack early. Here we already noticed how oceanlike it seemed. We received larger boats. The transfer of men and baggage took so long, that we were able to eat our noon meal on land.

The 30th - Early in the morning we arrived at Bremerlehe. Here the Weser was so wide that we believed we saw the open sea before us. The regiment landed and was mustered by Colonel [William] Faucitt. After the muster, the oath of allegiance to the King of Great Britain was cheerfully taken. The regiment again boarded the previously mentioned boats. In the evening I went to Bremerlehe in company with several of the regimental officers, and we had a pleasant time. I wrote another letter which Herr Stieglitz took with him.

The 31st - Today we boarded our transport ships.

1st of June 1776 - The regiment had three Dutch ships: *Jacob Cornelius, Benjamin,* and *John Abraham.* The ship captains were three rough Dutchmen. Obviously they administered discipline with an iron hand.

The 2nd - We lay at anchor and lived under pleasant conditions. The ship's fare which we had on the Weser had not tasted all that good; still it was something different.

The 3rd - Very early in the morning we upped anchor and sailed out to sea.

The 4th - 14th - We had only set sail when most of those on board got seasick and only a few persons were to be seen on deck. During these days we had to pass dangerous sandbanks. This travel was very slow as the wind was quite calm. We saw many brown fish which waltzed about near the surface of the calm water in brilliant sunshine.

The 15th - 19th - The sea was especially calm and the travel very slow. We had not seen the ship *John Abraham* for a long time and believed it must have sailed ahead or run aground and be sitting on a sandbank, till on the 19th when our ship's captain again saw it and at once fired a cannon shot as recognition.

The 20th - At eleven o'clock we lay at anchor at Spithead. The last division of Hessians arrived during the evening.

The 21st - 23rd - The ships were resupplied with water and other necessary items.

The 24th - We received an additional transport in order to have less crowded conditions and to have more comfort. It was an English ship, *Adamant*, to which were transferred Captain Alberti, Lieutenant Keppel, Ensign Noelting, and me, plus 126 men.[3]

The 25th - We held a secret kitchen session and decided what we should buy. Lieutenant Keppel undertook the task and went to Portsmouth to buy ten guineas worth of goods. I went with Captain Alberti to conduct religious services on our other ships. As they had changed anchorage, we traveled about for two hours without finding them.

The 26th - We finished preparations for sailing.

The 27th - The captains received orders that at the first cannon shot they were to hoist sails.

The 28th - We sailed from Portsmouth with a fleet of 66 ships.[4]

The 1st - 2nd of July 1776 - The wind was not as good as earlier and we remained since yesterday in the same place.

The 3rd - 4th - The sea was violently stormy and foggy and the motion of the ship made many people seasick.

The 5th - We asked our ship's captain if he knew where we would land. He assured us that except for the commodore, no one in the entire fleet knew. However, each captain had sealed orders, which were not to be opened until he had been separated from the fleet by a storm and had not seen the commodore for 24 hours.

The 6th - A contrary wind and very stormy. We were driven into the harbor at Plymouth. Two ships had lost their masts in the storm and one had begun to take water, and had, at this place, to be repaired again.

The 7th - I was taken to the staff ship *Jacob Cornelius* in order to conduct religious services and from there to the grenadier ship, *John Abraham*.

The 8th - Communion was celebrated on the *John Abraham* with one hundred persons partaking thereof. This morning the sea was so rough that it was nearly impossible to travel in the boat. [Philipp Henrich] Volcke, who sat in the boat with us, fell in the water when attempting to leave the boat. This afternoon we went to Plymouth. The fort which faces the sea is built on a cliff with three hundred cannons, and definitely worth seeing. The city is rather large, the streets narrower than in Portsmouth, but full of people. The buildings are mostly of stone. The market, especially now that the fleet is here, is filled with an over abundance of foodstuffs. And nowhere have I eaten better cherries than here.

The 9th - I went to the *Jacob Cornelius* and held services.

The 10th - We were quite comfortable aboard ship. We opened our wine and made punch according to the English practice, no longer warm, but cold. Everyday boats came to our ship with all sorts of merchandise to sell.

The 13th - Our ship's captain took us to the great warship *Royal George* which lay in dock being fitted with rigging. It carried 124 metal cannons. On the bow of the ship was an exceptionally beautiful sculpture of a white horse. On one side of the horse sat the king, on the other, the queen. Near the horse itself, was a rather roomy cabin in which three people could sit.

The 14th - I again held service on the other ships and I thought a long time would pass before we could speak to one another again.

The 15th - The wind was still not favorable for our departure and we traveled to Plymouth again in order to enjoy the firm land, at least as long as possible. We met many Hessian officers who told us various unpleasant experiences of their journey. Among others, one of their ships developed a leak and, despite continuous pumping, the water in the ship rose half an inch an hour. Another lost its mast in the storm and had to be repaired here.

The 16th-17th - We could get everything in Plymouth and therefore lived completely contented aboard ship.

The 18th - Captain Alberti, Lieutenant Keppel, and I visited the park which lies on the opposite side of the city and which belongs to Lord Edgecomb. This was a most pleasant woods with thousands of species of trees and charming pathways, shaded by overhanging, well-trimmed branches, where either an advantageous view presented itself, or where some other sight caught the eye. Herds of sheep and game grazed undisturbed. These and more things held our complete attention. In the middle stood the summer house, one side of which overlooked the woods toward the city of Plymouth and the surrounding region of the harbor, and the other side the open sea. A most philosophical garden, where one saw the English taste clearly with one glance.

The 19th - In the evening a sign was given by a single cannon shot to raise the smaller anchor.

The 20th - Live well Europe! We sailed at seven o'clock with a good wind. However, by evening the wind changed and was against us.

The 21st - Very strong winds which rolled the ship from one side to the other. We lay in bed the entire day because, except for the sailors, no one could move about, let alone stand. And those were the worst kind of days, when no one could remain on deck.

The 22nd - 23rd - Bright weather and contrary winds.

The 24th - Still only west winds. At noon a ship passed so close to us that we feared a collision. Fortunately, it turned aside. Two other ships passed so close to one another that each lost its foremast.

The 25th - We saw land at a great distance, which we assumed to be the outermost point of England.

The 26th - Bright weather and no wind at all.

The 27th - All of us recovered our well-being by the calm weather, as the stormy sea had made many people sick. They had to exercise an hour every day in order not to spend all their time within the stuffy ship. Toward evening the wind improved but was very weak.

The 28th - Beautiful, bright weather, and we held our customary divine service. The wind was favorable until about seven o'clock.

The 29th - The soldiers conducted shooting exercises.

The 30th - There was a thick fog. The wind good, but weak. We saw six ships of the fleet in our vicinity, and the captain had to shorten sail because the fleet was scattered. We saw a lot of birds about the ship today, which were about the size of a hawk. In the evening, about six o'clock, the wind began to pick up so that we traveled four and one-half English miles per hour.

The 31st - Favorable winds with which we covered five and one-half English miles per hour, although under trimmed sails, because the Dutch ships could not keep up.

The 1st of August - Bright weather and good wind. At eight o'clock we traveled two and one-half English miles per hour; at ten o'clock, three; and at two o'clock, three and one-half.

The 2nd - Morning windy. Later it became somewhat stiller. We traveled two and one-half miles in one hour.

The 3rd - It was completely calm. The soldiers were made to exercise at four o'clock. Today our beer ran out and from now on we must drink rum with water. Our mess began too late to use the beer properly. Only in the last few days had we begun to enjoy warm beer with a little wine in the evening.

The 4th - We held church. At noon it became very stormy and this unpleasant weather continued the entire week until

The 9th - when it became calmer. This morning at seven o'clock, the captain noticed, at a distance of about six miles, a ship which did not belong to our fleet. He noticed that it sailed far to the side and therefore determined that it must be a French ship with cargo for the Americans. We had hardly noticed it, however, when we saw a frigate sail off in pursuit. About noon we lost sight of both, the stranger as well as the frigate. By evening the frigate was again with the fleet.

The 10th - This evening we noticed a strange peculiarity of the seawater, which we had previously, to be sure, already noticed in the North Sea, but certainly not as clearly. The saltwater, especially when set in motion at night, gives the impression, an appearance, that one notices streaks of light and sparks being pulled along behind the ship.

The 11th - The wind was completely calm. A ship's captain from a Hessian ship came on board our ship. He believed that we must land in the West Indies, if we did not get favorable winds soon. A soldier fell from the deck into the deepest hold, but did not hurt himself.

The 12th - An unbearable heat. The sky cleared and the wind died.

The 13th - The wind was still calm. At nine o'clock a dreadful storm arose in the west, from which however, we received only a little rain.

The 14th - The sea was rather rough.

The 15th - During the night, rather stormy.

The 16th - Again very warm and absolutely no wind. Our captain, [Josias] Walker, went to a Mr. Mille,[5] the inspector, to show him that some casks of cheese were spoiled. According to the English custom, three disinterested captains had to inspect the goods, which, according to the findings, were then thrown overboard. He brought the news that we would land in New York, not in Halifax as we had supposed until now.

The 17th - We saw various flying fish and during the evening one flew onto the deck. It was one of the smallest species, the mouth about one inch long.

The 18th - We had a strong wind which was directly against us however, and, because of the stormy movement of the ship, we could not conduct church. In the evening we received a heavy rain and the wind seemed to increase in force. We saw a two-masted ship which had lost its foremast as a result of the strong wind.

The 19th - At six o'clock in the morning we received a most favorable wind with which we sailed at four and one-half miles per hour. At nine o'clock we saw the island of St. Maria. A cannon was fired to signal the frigate *Unicorn*, which at once spread full sails and sailed toward the coast to reconnoiter. At midday our captain caught a 24 pound dolphin with a fishpole. In the water it had a sparkling color which, however, changed as soon as it became dry. The head in the upper part is very broad and flat. According to the captain it is dangerous to eat because of the many copper deposits which are found in the Azores. As an experiment, some silver coins were cooked with it. Our captain thus convinced us to eat it. It tasted twice as good because we had had nothing fresh to eat for such a long time. The taste was like that of Eder salmon. Puppy dogs would have tasted just as good at this time.

20th - We had a good wind, which we could not use as well as we wished because the Dutch ships all fell far behind on this night, and all the English ships had to shorten sails and wait for them until three o'clock. The frigate *Unicorn*, which had sailed ahead yesterday, returned and had another ship with it which we initially took to be an American. Both ships drew nearer to us and we saw a boat from the frigate *Unicorn* sail to the commodore's ship, *Diamond*, where it remained a good two hours. From there it sailed to the new ship with a guard force of soldiers. Captain Walker spoke to another ship which passed near us. This one supposed it might be that the captain of the ship, who was an American, had some evil intent and had planned to use the ship's powder and balls against us. On our right we saw the island of Tercera, whereon we noticed many cliffs and mountains.

The 21st - An exceptional wind which drove us six English miles in one hour. We saw the island of Pico and the surprisingly beautiful mountain of the same name, whose peak rose very darkly above the clouds.

The 22nd - We had a very heavy rain and gathered all the empty casks to fill with rain water. This water was a special refreshment; everyone drank his fill and felt much better. The wind was not as good as yesterday. In general we traveled about two English miles an hour.

The 23rd - Completely windless. .

The 24th - Still the same.

The 25th - The heat was so great that during the prayer hour, three persons passed out.

The 26th - No good wind.

The 27th - We saw three Greenland birds which are called burgomasters. They were as big as, and flew like, herons. They must have gotten lost in flight or somewhere in the area there must be an uncharted island where they stop. The wind improved. However, we had to wait for a warship which was towing another ship.

The 28th - Again we saw a strange ship in the fleet. A frigate raised the English flag and sailed to investigate. We noticed nothing further, however, except that it sailed on uninterrupted.

The 29th - The wind was good, but weak.

The 30th - Early this morning, we noticed a special fish, which is called the devil fish, close to our ship. It can not see and therefore nature has given it small fish which serve as pilots and which swim in and out of its body without harm. It had the form of a stretched-out horsehide. The captain threw the harpoon at it, but missed.

The 31st - The sea was very rough. During the evening the wind improved considerably.

The 1st of September 1776 - The wind was relatively calm. Our troops for some time had had no tobacco. Our captain put a boat over the side and sent the ship's quartermaster to the ship *Unicorn* to get some. He returned with twenty pounds. The quartermaster had learned that the supply of water on the frigate was running low, and that one ship in the fleet had only one cask of water left. Once again all was well because the soldiers could smoke a pipe of tobacco. They had helped themselves up to this time, and the least quantity of tobacco that one or the other still had hidden, when it became known, would then be smoked. Then the ashes would be given to those accustomed to the use of snuff, for that purpose.

The 2nd - Beautiful, bright weather and almost no wind. We saw one of the *Benjamin's* boats steering toward our ship, in which I was to be picked up to conduct a baptism aboard the *Benjamin*. The captain was the godfather and named the child Benjamin after his ship. I had the pleasure to meet all the gentlemen there. They entertained the same wishes which we had, of reaching land soon. According to the reckoning of our captain, he assumed that we would see land on the 20th of this month. I believed it could be no other date than the 20th, because so many noteworthy events had happened to us on the 20th. On my return trip, I only spoke with our grenadier ship because the boat was like a leaf and I feared trying to board the ship.

The 3rd - Beautiful weather. Captain von Horn and Lieutenant Strubberg visited us. Except for a bottle of wine and some simple cakes we had nothing to offer our guests. The captain, however, treated the entire mess to royal punch and spread a sail over the deck. We sat in comfort as if we had all one could wish. However, the gentlemen had a stormy return trip that evening.

The 4th - The sea was especially stormy. The waves beat against the deck and there was no way to move except on hands and knees.

The 5th - 6th - Still the same.

The 7th - The sea was a bit calmer.

The 8th - It will be a long time before there is another such night. At nine o'clock in the evening a terrible thunderstorm arose in the west. The entire sky was frightfully black. The lightning flashed across the sky from morning until evening, from midday to midnight.

The thunder crashed without let up. The ships lowered their sails and sailed widely separated from one another in order not to break up by ramming. Everything possible was done to protect against the storm. In order to keep out of the way of the sailors, we remained in our dismal cabins. Lightning, thunder, rain, and the beating of the waves, which threw the ship from one side to the other, combined to present us on this night with all the frightfulness of nature. In our cabins everything that was not fastened down, tore loose. Chairs, tables, bags, kettles, everything mixed together, and we needed all of our ability to keep from falling out of the beds, where we had fled, as either the back and forth rolling of the loose baggage or some other object could break our neck. And I firmly believe the overall movement of the ship was comparable to being rolled down a mountainside in a barrel. At four o'clock in the morning the storm passed and with it all the resulting fears. The sea was still rough, the wind, however, favorable, and moved us five and one-half miles in one hour. By the same opportunity one can learn something of the difficult tasks of the sailors. And by this occurrence I thought of Gellert's, *Thoughts*, and found at once how true is said:

Fear not in this life

Bold deeds undertaken, etc.

The 9th - The wind was still rather calm. Toward evening the *Unicorn* frigate fired a shot. It did not please us especially as it sailed opposite us and if it had fired again, a broadside would have given us the first compliment.

The 10th - Very little wind. Captain Alberti went to the staff ship. In the afternoon the grenadier ship passed next to us. Lieutenant Strubberg called to us through a speaking trumpet to ask if we knew of the incident on Captain Pentzel's ship, And the ship quickly passed us, without giving him the opportunity to explain what had happened. The good Lieutenant Keppel and I, one as curious as the other, guessed first one thing and then another, but we were unable to guess the right one. A fire had broken out on the ship. The misfortune was very great. The ship was leaking and everyone was in danger of drowning. The misfortune was still less in our eyes than in theirs. Captain Alberti came back toward evening and bought the explanation that the ship had caught fire. The Englishman who passed out the provisions held a burning light in a rum keg, which at once caught fire.

There was even a good fortune by this misfortune. The ship was sailing in the middle of the fleet and the sea was completely calm. And in a moment, fifty English boats were standing by to rescue them. The fire had already spread to the bread storage where fifteen rum kegs were. A ladder on the ship, which became overloaded by too many people, broke and two soldiers and the ladder landed in the sea. Both held fast to the ladder, however, until help from a boat was hurried to their rescue.

The 11th - A very good wind. We traveled four and one-half miles in one hour.

The 12th - 15th - Nothing new.

The 16th - An especially strong storm came out of the west. About four o'clock we saw lightning in the distance, and about seven o'clock the storm was upon us. The thunder could hardly be heard, however, because of the howling of the wind and waves. The sailors had to work throughout the night. The thick crossbar, which held the largest sail, broke, and one piece of the crossbar and the sail lay in the water, and the other piece on deck. The wind drove the ships so close together that the captain had to use the speaking trumpet because the broken crossbar prevented his being able to move out of their way. The full distress lasted until morning. One became accustomed to the frightful events. We were not allowed to get in the way on the deck. We remained lying in bed and calmed ourselves as best we could.

The 17th - The sea was still rough with contrary wind.

The 18th - It became calmer and the wind improved.

The 19th - A beautiful day with gentle winds, with which we covered 43 miles in a day and a night. We sat on deck half the night under a bright sky and beautiful moonshine. Nowhere does man place a higher value on moonlight than at sea, and it is a special treat when a part of the night can be spent outside the stuffy cabin. For me, especially, it was the most pleasant part of the day, when I could leave my cabin in the early morning and, undisturbed, occupy myself with a walk about the deck. In this way I passed many hours before the other people awoke and came on deck. Then coffee was served, without sugar, brandy was issued to the men, and a prayer service was held.

The 20th - Again a storm, which passed after a few thunder claps, leaving behind a very favorable wind.

The 21st - With a fresh wind we sailed five miles an hour. Following yesterday's storm, the day was very cool.

The 22nd - A good wind drove us ahead, at times at six miles an hour. During divine services we saw the frigate *Unicorn* pass by with all sails set and, as she passed within four miles of us, we heard two cannon shots. This was the signal for a strange ship to identify itself and to hove to. The sailors on the mast however, noticed that it sailed away. The frigate followed and by evening had still not returned to the fleet.

The 23rd - A gentle wind and very warm. The frigate *Diamond* sailed away quickly, from which we gathered that another strange ship had been observed. *Unicorn* returned to the fleet.

The 24th - Little wind and very warm. The commodore gave an order to all ship captains that no one should sail apart from the fleet because many American frigates had been seen during the night. Each captain was to pass this word to other captains whenever their ships passed. This caused more joy than fear as it gave us hope. We could not be very far from the American coast. The captain assured us that soon we would see more English warships than American warships. At evening the fleet drew closer together. We went to bed content, having seen that the commodore had the situation well in hand and we had nothing to worry about. The commodore led the way with *Unicorn* on the right and *Ambuscade* on the left. Let the Americans come.

The 25th - Stronger winds, very foggy, and rain. About noon the winds became so strong that the grenadier ship *John Abraham* lost its middle mast. As unpleasant as the storm was, and as many difficulties as the rolling ship caused, nevertheless these were minimized by the sight of the flying fish which we saw by the thousands today. They do not fly from the water until chased by another fish, which the English call albacore. The blessed nature has given every animal a means to defend and protect itself, otherwise the flying fish could never elude the albacore. The albacore is four or five feet long, and in stormy weather remains near the surface so that it can be seen when the waves break over it. It is as swift as an arrow. As soon as the flying fish senses danger, it knows no other way to save itself than to fly fearfully from the water. The albacore then makes a hump-like lunge after it, often clearing the water by a man's height, but seldom catching its prey. My good companion, Lieutenant Keppel, and I watched this hunt the entire afternoon. For our evening meal we ate a burnt soup, over which we had a hearty laugh, as the oats settled to the bottom, leaving only water above. The surgeon Herr [Karl Friedrich] Pfister sat beside me and as the ship rolled a great deal, everyone had to hold onto his plate. Like a flash of lightning , a wave struck the ship, the soup flew from my bowl onto Herr Pfister, top to bottom, and I was left with only the soup bowl in my hand.

The 26th - Still strong wind. This morning we had our usual storm, however it did not last long. This morning the frigate *Unicorn* sailed in the van and in the evening, *Ambuscade*.

The 27th - The wind was a bit lighter and a person could partially recover. The commodore hung out a flag and indicated therewith that the *Unicorn* should sail ahead to examine an enemy ship. The strange ship could be seen from our mast.

The 28th - Bad winds. Another strange ship was seen and as the *Unicorn* had not yet returned , the *Ambuscade* sailed away.

The 29th - We held religious services and were disturbed during our devotions by a very heavy rain. During the night a Dutch ship fired three cannon shots. The commodore sailed off to assist and in the morning we saw the pumps on the ship being worked very hard.

On the ship *Adamant* - Early this morning the commodore raised signal flags to warn of the presence of strange ships near the fleet. Our captain climbed the mast, saw four strange ships, and immediately reported to the commodore with flag signals. They continued to draw nearer to our ship and were apparently English ships from the coast of America. One sailed through our fleet and quickly departed. The commodore expressed his thanks with a cannon shot. Our frigates returned in the evening and the *Unicorn* brought an American ship of ten cannons and a ninety-man crew. The sailors were taken off by the warships and the ship was required to return to America with us. It had received three shots through the mainsail.

The 30th - Although yesterday was Michaelmas, still it was quite warm today. This noon on our ship there was some commotion, and all the ships stopped because signals were made by the warships. They had no other meaning than that the American prisoners were to be put on other ships. They have been very well received by the English and have had friendly treatment. They came from Boston and had been at sea for twelve days. This ship brought the news of a battle at New York, much to the rebels disadvantage, and that the Americans had set fire to the city before evacuating it. In the Carolinas however, the American weapons were victorious and the English had to leave the coastal area.

The 1st of October - Very warm with favorable winds.

The 2nd-4th - The wind was favorable and we sailed seven miles in an hour.

The 5th - This morning the soldier [Friedrich] Teigtmeyer, from Goettingen, died of scurvy. I had served him communion yesterday and one could hardly stay by him half an hour due to the terrible smell in the stuffy ship. He was sewn in a hammock, a song was sung, and the words of the twentieth chapter of the Apostles, thirteenth verse, struck me. "And the sea surrendered her dead", on which I gave a short sermon. I do not believe a funeral sermon has ever before been based on this text, in my country. The body was lowered into the sea from the right side of the ship.

The 6th - A beautiful, bright fall day, and a fresh northeast wind with which we sailed seven and one-half miles an hour.

The 7th - Very little wind.

The 8th - Still the same. O that we might soon see land! We spit on our evening bread - slush and spider webs, and with it drink water filled with unknown insects.

The 9th - The ship's lead was cast, but without finding bottom.

The 10th -Traveled with Lieutenant Keppel to the *Jacob Cornelius* to baptize a child. During this time the sea became so stormy that we were obliged to remain until

The 15th - when the sea became somewhat calmer.

The 16th - We saw several signs of land. The water had a different color. There was floating grass. We saw many birds, including three ravens. The lead was cast and we found bottom at 35 fathoms. Soon land could be seen from the mast, and about noon it could be seen from the deck. I will write nothing more of our joy. This the pen can not describe but the heart beat faster. God be praised and thanked, that was the expression used by every soldier, even those who seldom had used this language.

The 17th - The thick fog hid the land from our eyes and caused us to sail more toward the Jersey coast. The fog lifted and we saw Long Island close at hand. At ten o'clock we dropped anchor.

The 18th - We raised our anchor at four o'clock in the morning. Every ship raised the English flag and all about us we saw land. At twelve o'clock the warships gave a signal, with two cannon shots, to drop anchor and wait for the tide to enter New York harbor, which was still twelve miles away.

The 19th - We raised anchor. Because of the sandbanks the ships criss-crossed so close to one another as to frighten us to death. Nevertheless, we had to laugh at the fearful Hollanders. They could not maneuver their clumsy ships out of the way as easily as the skillful English could, but hastened in as if chased by ghosts. At evening we dropped anchor.

[1776 - New York - New Jersey]

The 20th of October 1776 - On a beautiful Sunday morning we sailed between Long and Staten Islands into New York. This same afternoon I went into the city. The fire had terribly devastated the beautiful New York. The rebels had set it afire before they evacuated it. A fourth of the city lay in ashes. The streets are rather wide, especially the so-called Broadway, where the King's statue stood. High trees stand before the houses. But on Broadway stands the beautiful Paul's Church, which is copied after the St. Paul's Church in London. In peacetime it was the most rapidly developing commercial city in all of North America, because it was the middle point thereof. The plan of the city is laid out in a broad area, of which only a fourth part is yet developed. It lies on a tongue of land between the Hudson, or North, and the East River. In the East River ships can sail right up to the city to be loaded and unloaded. Among the most impressive buildings one must consider the college. More about New York will follow, when I get to know it better.

The 21st - The sick were landed and sent to the hospital on Long Island, and the order was given that we should be prepared to land.

The 22nd - All the troops were debarked and sailed up the East River in small boats. I went into the city to buy some things because it was apparent that we must spent the night in the boats. I returned and my good Captain Alberti had departed.[6] I remained the rest of the day in the city and was quite at ease as I felt that the regiment would go no further than Long Island, where I could go the next day. I was so fortunate as to find a German inn. I ate my evening meal with a large clientele, among whom was the German Lutheran preacher of the parish. This man asked about my background and told of having studied at Goettingen with a person of similar name, and that was my brother. His name was Prell. The inn was so full that I, and also two Hessian doctors, had to sleep on the billiard table.

The 23rd - Now for the first time I realized my embarrassment. No one could tell me where the troops, which landed yesterday, had gone. I asked at General [James] Robertson's headquarters, at the Hessian port company, in short, everywhere. At evening I could not find my inn and had forgotten to ask the name of the street, or my host, as I had expected to join my regiment. An old woman

18

approached me in the street and spoke to me in German. Who was happier than I, when she offered me her home as a place to spend the night? Her friendliness and her excessive concern awoke my mistrust. There are no witches in America, otherwise I am sure she would have been one. I patiently followed her, although I thought she would deliver me to the rebels. Finally, we came to her house, situated in an out-of-the-way alley, which only increased my fear. She busied herself preparing my evening meal. She asked what I wished and I said boiled eggs. She gave me her own bed on which she put a lace spread, and slept on the floor with her husband. This politeness awoke another feeling in me. Could it be there were kidnappers here? To this point my hostess did not know who I was. I pulled off my overcoat, and my dress caused her to ask my title. I was the field chaplain of the Waldeck Regiment. "O, a holy man", she said. She would have kissed my feet, believing her house thus blessed. How unjustly I had treated this good woman. She was a woman full of loving kindness. That night I slept well.

The 24th - My honorable countrywoman bought thirty oysters for my breakfast, fried them in butter and pepper, and felt bad that there was nothing more she could do for me. I could not adequately appreciate her kindness. She accompanied me over the East River to Long Island.

The 25th - Even here at the ferry, no one could tell me further news of the regiment, except that all the troops had gone down the river. I decided it best to follow the river as long as people could tell me they had seen the boats. Need teaches prayer, but it also teaches one to use English. I could express myself to the extent that I could ask if a boat with soldiers had been seen, what their uniforms were like, etc. Mainly our guard caps served as a distinguishing characteristic, as these had caught everyone's eye. Night overtook me and I turned in at the house where a true Hollander lived. Fortunately, unbelievably fortunately, live the people on Long Island. They live in the middle of their farm. They have the best meadows for their livestock, the most beautiful estates. A man who owns one hundred acres only pays the King thirty shillings for it. My host led me into a nice room, in which was a comfortable bed, and because I was still distrustful in this strange land, I took my purse to bed with me. God, in what a flourishing condition these people have lived!

The 26th - I continued my journey. I passed through some abandoned rebel defenses. Twice I had to cross over water inlets, where I nearly drowned, as the boat was so full of holes. A black boatman. I arrived at Flushing just when a single-masted ship was preparing to sail to the army. The commanding officer could speak some Latin and had the kindness to offer to take me with him. My companions were 24 oxen and a Hessian regimental quartermaster, [Johann Andreas] Ungar. The space was very crowded and we both had to sleep on a sailcloth. He had a bottle of wine and I had a loaf of bread. One shared with the other, and thus we had an evening meal. The ship sailed at nine o'clock, and very early in the morning we were at the place where the troops were landed.

The 27th - The Hessian guard post was still by the river bank. We went to the guard and were shown the way to the camp. I came to a Hessian regiment and a Major [Johann Philipp] Hillebrand assured me that the Waldeck Regiment was no longer with the army, but along with several other regiments, was on the march to Philadelphia. This report, as doubtful as I considered it, struck me down. General [Johann Ludwig Friedrich von] Stein, Count of Basswitz, who rushed by on his way to General [Leopold] von Heister's headquarters, also was unable to give me more exact information. It so happened that on his return trip we met again and he at once said, "Your regiment is on the right wing in the brigade of Lord [Charles] Cornwallis." I thanked him for this information and immediately set out through the whole army, until I came to the regiment at one o'clock. Lieutenant Keppel offered me lunch. The region is called West Chester. Many already were of the opinion that I had fallen into the hands of the rebels, which easily could have been the case.[7]

The 28th - We held church for the first time in camp. We lived well and happily. Fresh meat was delivered and well-baked bread, chickens, and geese. Eggs were available at a ridiculously low price. Complete herds of fat oxen followed the army. Our baggage was so limited, however, that no one had more with him than a servant could carry in a knapsack. We did not have our tents with us. The regimental surgeon and I shared a soldier's tent. The adjutant, Lieutenant Wiegand, the regimental surgeon, and I set up a household and lived very well after our 22-day sea voyage.[8] We received orders to march in the morning.

The 29th - We marched from West Chester to New Rochelle. The region is very flat, well-developed, and fruitful. By one o'clock the new camp was already set up. It was possible to buy wine, coffee, and tobacco as a ship had just arrived from New York. A half-gallon of beer cost one reichs dollar.

The 30th - The nights were growing rather cool.

The 31st - There were few occupied houses, because the people had abandoned all their property and were with the rebel army.

The 1st - 4th of November 1776 - We lay in camp at New Rochelle. Occasional alarms at night, which had no significance. It required only that we dress and then lie down again on the hay. The nights were getting rather cold, so that a bottle of water froze in my tent. I find the present life in the company very pleasant. Currently we go for a week at a time without spending any money. We wrote our first letters home. My good Captain Alberti and I wrote at a house situated near our company. In this house was an old family consisting of a great-grandmother, a grandmother, her daughter, and the daughter's many grown children. The location here is on the coast and the ground is fertile. We encountered many barns full of wheat, corn, etc., which the owners had deserted, as well as several fine houses and gardens, and especially orchards. Next to our camp was a field of excellent flax, which was carried to our tents to use in making fires.

The 5th - We broke camp and marched nine miles further. The weather was very pleasant, such as on a beautiful fall day at home. Along the route one could get apple cider and milk. At two o'clock we arrived at our destination camp, called the Sun Redoubt. All the tents had not been put up before we received orders from General [Wilhelm von] Knyphausen's headquarters to continue our march to another strong point, which was called Fort Independence. We arrived after dark and the tents could not be set up. On the march we had heard heavy cannon fire, which reportedly came from White Plains. The lieutenant colonel had a meal prepared, of which I had the honor to partake. We lay down to sleep in a stall which still had some hay. We slept well, but from our lodging we collected so many lice that it took all of the next day to pick them off.

The 6th - Two companies were posted inside the fort and the others outside. The view was as good as that from the castle at Waldeck, although the fort is not so elevated.[9] In the fort lay many

21

cannons, cannonballs, and chain shot, which the enemy had left behind. The Jerseys and Fort Washington could be seen from here. Water had to be carried a great distance. Captain Alberti, I, and others put our noon lunch and a bottle in our packs, went to a fresh spring on the other side of the hills, and drank, with pleasure, all kinds of toasts, as if we were enjoying the best wine, because we tasted the heavenly pleasure of health and contentment. We had tasted just such a glass of water during our 22-week long crossing. Also, we had often gone to sleep at night, still hungry. Fortunately, those times were past. Our table was again delicious and expensive, a good piece of beef with soup, that was all, and this was delivered to us.

The 7th - Still pleasant and quite warm during the day. The leaves in the forest began to fall. Several sales persons came from New York with coffee, sugar, and tobacco.[10]

The 8th - We were all on foot, except the lieutenant colonel, who had obtained a horse. I, too, received forage money, but have been unable as yet to get a horse.[11]

The 9th - The regiment sent out strong patrols in the region of Fort Washington, where our outposts were always under fire.

The 10th - Twenty-four of our men returned to the regiment from the hospital.

The 11th - Commanders of regiments were assembled at General Knyphausen's headquarters. At eight o'clock Lieutenant [Colonel] von Hanxleden returned and gave the order for our regiment to assemble at three o'clock in the morning, leaving our tents and knapsacks behind. Everyone grasped this meant an attack on Fort Washington, because the artillery was ready and the bridge had been strengthened to support the heavy guns. During the night such a torrential rain fell that nothing came of all the planning.

The 12th - The rains continued.

The 13th - Generals [William] Howe and Heister returned from White Plains with the entire army, and gathered at our camp.

The 14th - Pleasant weather and, as we are part of the army, there were many changes.

The 15th - Orders were received to assemble the regiment as quietly as possible at three o'clock tomorrow morning.

The 16th -The regimental surgeon and I took our places with the regiment. We passed Kingsbridge while still not daybreak and arrived at our assigned positions. We marched through a ground where the cannonballs screamed terribly overhead. Fortunately, they were aimed too high. A Hessian Lieutenant [Georg Wilhelm] von Loewenfels, that I had met in Bremerlehe, shook my hand as we passed near a woods, and we expressed our pleasure at having arrived in America in good health. Half an hour later his body was brought back. O fate of mankind! He had to make such a long journey in order to find his grave at Fort Washington. The English batteries had found the range so exactly that shot after shot burst among the advanced enemy and they were finally forced to retreat.

Our flankers, commanded by Lieutenant Leonhardi with such honor, and the Hessian Jaegers suffered heavy losses. The rebels posted themselves behind trees and boulders and always took careful aim at their targets. The flankers kept pushing forward under the covering fire of the cannons and the firing could be heard steadily nearing the fort.

The abatis was amazing to see and one would have thought such a thing could not be surmounted. But then it happened, but not without difficulty and the loss of many good Germans. It was nearly impossible for one man after the other to get over the interlaced trees. One held the hand to help the next man, and in this way, the passage was forced. About twelve o'clock the hill had been climbed, all the rebels had pulled back into the fort, and they capitulated. A frigate sailing up the North River received a heavy cannonade from Fort Lee.

As I went forward I saw many dead and wounded; among others, a Hessian jaeger who had just been shot through the head. His brother stood over the body, complaining that he could not be buried. Another jaeger had both eyes shot out. He still lived. Further along, the rebels lay packed together like herring. The capitulation was completed toward evening. The prisoners, who numbered about 2,000, were led through the regiments, and had to stack their weapons. For a dollar it was possible to buy a beautiful box. Despite the strictest orders, the prisoners received a number of blows. Especially comical, I watched the treatment handed out by a Hessian grenadier. One of the rebels being led through looked around proudly to the right and left. The grenadier grabbed him on the ears with both hands and said, "Wait a bit and I'll show you the big city."[12] Another tied him up with his scarf. Two others hit him on the sides of his head.

A third gave him a kick in the rump so that he flew through three ranks. All of this took place in half a minute. The poor guy never knew what hit him, nor why he had been hit. About nine o'clock we marched back to our camp, hungry and still thirsty, arriving at eleven o'clock. Our regiment had six killed and seventeen wounded.[13]

The 17th - The following letter from General Heister to General Knyphausen was published.

> Your Excellency, I should not fail to bear witness of the innermost joy for the well-earned praise and thanks from General Howe, which you and the troops of your command merit for your proven courage and determination in yesterday's affair. Neither can I neglect to extend my own appreciation to General [Martin] Schmidt and the troops engaged in yesterday's attack. They accomplished a thing which by rights seemed nearly impossible, and did it in such a manner as could only be expected from the best soldiers, and which speaks well for our future undertakings and reputation. This I will convey to our Prince. Be assured that I wish my good comrades the best of luck, with all my heart. I earnestly wish to have my most sincere pleasure and appreciation conveyed to the troops who have been ordered to march tomorrow morning, before their departure, and that I will do all that is in my power to seek the reward and recognition which is due to you and the troops under your command from our most gracious Prince, and which you have earned with glory and honor. With the greatest respect, etc., your,
>
> von Heister

The 18th - We received orders to march. We finally broke camp about three o'clock because of a delay by the command which was to occupy the fort. We moved to a camp on a height this side of Kingsbridge.

The 19th - The Hessian grenadiers marched past our camp in order to be carried across the Hudson River to attack Fort Lee.

The 20th - We began to dig in as it began to get really cold. We had hardly gotten well started when we had to break camp and march to General Howe's headquarters, near Delaney's Mill. On the march we met General Howe. The regiment came to present arms and the officers led with drawn swords, until he had passed.

The 21st - Foggy and rainy weather. No one was dry day or night and our boots nearly rotted on our feet. Another thirty men, who had regained their health, returned from the hospital. We received the news that Fort Lee had been taken without the loss of a single man. The rebels fled at the approach of our army, after having lost their greatest hope, Forts Washington and Lee. General Howe had a beautiful concert, which we could hear in our camp. We all long to go into winter quarters.

The 22nd - Still bad weather. The region here about is well-developed.

The 23rd - The light dragoons passed our camp on the way to winter quarters.

The 24th - Orders to march tomorrow.

The 25th - We broke camp very early. Underway we met the army, all of which was on the march today. We marched over Kingsbridge, passed Fort Washington, and about four o'clock, arrived at Harlem. No camp was set up here, rather the companies were assigned to houses and barns which were scattered about the area.

The 26th - The most pleasant area that we have yet seen, nicely developed, with many smooth, level fields. The road leads to New York and is never empty.

The 27th - I held communion in the hospital, which was in the city of Harlem, a small place where ships arrive down the East River, and which has a beautiful church.

The 28th - Dysentery spread among us and even I was not completely healthy, which prevented me from enjoying this pleasant region as I would have liked. It is possible to get everything from New York, such as wine and coffee.

The 29th - The weather began to improve again. We had a good herd of livestock. Several animals were slaughtered every day for the camp.

The 5th of December 1776 - We struck camp in order to go into the long-wished-for winter quarters, which had been designated for us at Amboy, in the Jerseys. This march did not make me happy, as I still did not feel well. We marched through New York and embarked on the North River, where we had landed. The embarkation lasted until four o'clock, during which time I drank a bottle of Madeira wine, and a very old, special one it was, which was all the better, as I did not feel up to par, and had no opportunity to get any other medicine. We sailed at four. I had the pleasure once again to sail with my good traveling companion, Captain Alberti.

The 6th - Toward evening we arrived at Amboy, but remained on board overnight as it was so late.

The 7th - Early in the morning, the debarkation began. The regiment formed on land and marched, with flags flying, through the city to the barracks. Our quarters were very tight because the barracks were equipped to handle only 300 men. The lieutenant colonel allowed the regimental surgeon and me to find our own quarters in the city. We took quarters with a widow, who was happy that we were so good, went to bed early, and were advised as to how to keep this room neat and orderly. Just then the lieutenant colonel entered

The 8th - the room and said that we must leave at once and march to Elizabethtown. We quickly packed again and departed our quarters for this night, which we had expected to occupy for the winter. The regiment had received no provisions. Therefore the lieutenant colonel decided to have some bread baked for the men and we marched at three o'clock. Our canons and other wagons were short of horses. Therefore we could not reach Elizabethtown, which was fifteen miles distance, and had to spend the night out under the open sky. We had to be especially alert as there were reports of 400 rebels being on our flank. There was a hard freeze at night.

The 9th - We resumed our march early. The pleasant land appeared to be well and thickly settled, with orchards on every hand and the fields well-fenced. The route was mostly level and easy. At one o'clock we entered Elizabeth, a village that right from the start was a source of special activity for us. We met the Lossberg Regiment here. Captain Alberti, Herr Noelting, and the regimental surgeon took quarters for the night in the home of a lawyer, as no quarters had been assigned as yet. All the rooms of the house were papered. The house was absolutely perfect, furnished throughout to my taste, and exactly as I would build a house if I could afford it. Herr Noelting prepared a good evening meal which tasted delicious, as we had lived on bread and schnapps for the last six days.

The owner of the house, like many other residents, had fled with his entire household, but had been so friendly as to leave behind a cellar full of potatoes, squash, beets, and an ample supply of cider. We knew how to use all of these things. I did not begrudge the private soldiers all these things, as they needed beef, potatoes, and cider in order to recover from a long sea voyage and an autumn campaign. Besides, the rascal was reportedly an arch rebel.

The 10th - The Lossberg Regiment departed from Brunswick and we immediately moved into their former quarters. Elizabethtown is a charming place. The houses are scattered and widely separated, and between the houses are large orchards and vegetable gardens. The entire region seems fertile and level. Indian corn, here as in most parts of America, is widely cultivated. Through the city flows a small river, called the Elizabeth River, which above the city can only be called a brook. Small ships, sloops, and boats can sail up to the city, as the tide from New York Bay extends this far. There are two churches here, one very large with vaulting made of wood, another built of brick, and it also has an organ. The houses here have fine wallpaper, as a rule. From here it is possible to travel to New York by water. This is the only way to travel to Staten Island and Bergen, and the region provides a very pleasant view from the ship. The generally splendid, well-situated houses, which are always pleasing, bear witness to the good taste of the inhabitants. The wood-work which one sees in nearly every house, shows us there is no scarcity of skilled artisans and craftsmen in America.

The 11th - I had no quarters and Captain Alberti was so kind as to put me up for the night. The captain had quarters with a coppersmith, and the room was furnished and papered in a manner not to be expected from a man of his class. The man supported the King; his wife supported the rebels. But she was a good cook and, in her way, very good. Toward midnight there was an alarm when the rebels attacked our pickets, and three men were wounded. There was no rest for the remainder of the night.

The 12th - The regimental surgeon and I obtained quarters with good landlords. It snowed for the first time.

The 13th - 14th - Very cold and water froze in the room.

The 15th - The large English church was swept out after the troops which arrived yesterday departed, but a company of light dragoons arrived, causing such a disturbance that no church service could be held. Many rumors circulate. [General Charles] Lee is captured; Washington has quit his command. But one allows himself the freedom still to doubt such tales.

The 16th - The spoiled Sunday was recovered and I preached in the large English church. Our officers were very gallant and escorted the ladies from their quarters to the church. We brought the year to a close in fine quarters with many pleasures. The many inhabitants, who had fled from fear, now returned again because of the reports of good conduct of the regiment. We celebrated Christmas in peace and quiet. On both the first and second holiday, communion was served as there had been no time to do so during the autumn campaign, and many now took part. On the second holiday a very heavy snow fell.

Eighteenth Century America
1st of January 1777

The entire officer corps went to congratulate the staff officers on the New Year. The lieutenant colonel allowed us to draw our forage money for the new year, for which I received my pittance of 39 Spanish dollars. From here everyone went to church.

The 2nd - With the new year, new disturbances for us. Our outposts were attacked and several men wounded.

The 3rd - The bad news from Trenton spread more and more and could hardly be doubted any longer. Our pleasure in Elizabeth has passed. One can no longer lie down to sleep without thinking this is the last night, the last night of freedom. Instead of undressing in the evening as usual, one becomes accustomed to dress completely, and to go to bed in this manner. Here, except for rest, we have everything. Only none of this.

The 4th - The light dragoons ride out, and suddenly one is wounded, the other shot dead. These are victims of the war, who are shot dead in a dastardly fashion by the rebels that had hidden behind bushes and houses. This evening our regiment sent out a strong patrol. It captured a few prisoners, but on the return took a heavy fire from the enemy, who had taken a position in the nearby woods.

The 5th - Captain von Haacke and Lieutenant Heldring went out with a fifty-man patrol and several light dragoons. A few hours later, the dragoons returned at a full gallop. Their horses were in part wounded and all had been ridden so hard they could hardly go further. They brought the sad news that the patrol, after suffering a visible loss in dead and wounded from an enemy which outnumbered them four to one, had been captured.[1] Today we did not feel secure enough to hold church services and the entire regiment had to be on the alert. Everyone had a feeling of loss concerning the fate of both men, not knowing if they were dead, wounded, or still alive. Man is inclined by such misfortune always to fear the worst; such was the case here. As we were not safe from an enemy attack at any moment, three regiments of Scots were sent to our assistance.

The 6th - We were ordered to pull back to Amboy, as quietly as possible, in order to have the shelter of Fort Washington, which again held 20,000 men from New Jersey. But then received counter orders and the regiment occupied all the entrances to the city. Everyone moved to the neighboring places at the same time.

The 7th - We broke camp early, but marched only at eleven o'clock. It was a very cold day and we arrived at Amboy at dusk. There were no quarters, no shelter. The barracks, which was the English hospital, were quickly evacuated. The rooms were so filled, that the troops could hardly lie down. The officers were all assigned in two rooms. How unbearable this was compared to our Elizabethtown quarters, which were so comfortable, so pleasant. Here was neither bed nor space, also no fire, also no wood with which to make one. I went with some others to the best restaurant in the city. And in this establishment there was not a single piece of bread and butter to be had. Finally, after a hungry four-hour wait, we got a bone from which all the meat had been scraped four days earlier. We returned to our barracks and, fully clothed, laid down on the cold, dirty floor.

The 8th - Nothing was available here. Everything had to come from New York. In addition, we had the tension which results from never getting a full night's rest. As soon as one would lie down, he would be turned out by shots fired near the outposts. And this happened repeatedly.[2]

February 1777 - The winter was quite severe throughout the month. Our rations were nothing but the royal issue which was fed to the ordinary soldiers. Toward the end of the month much sickness spread, especially high fever. Eventually, one became so accustomed to the firing near the outposts, that he would not even bother to get out of bed.

March 1777 - The weather became more pleasant day by day. Our main diversion was riding, which we did every day.

April 1777 - The bushes and woods began to turn green. Walking, especially in the morning and evening, was made even more pleasant by the singing of the birds. Most of our time was spent bowling, as the place was very near to our quarters. Many foodstuffs were now brought here from Staten Island.

The 21st of May 1777 - The garrison moved again to a site without quarters and the Waldeck Regiment was assigned on the right wing, half an hour from the city of Amboy. This was the assigned site developed later into a very pleasant camp in a pleasant grove of trees. I continued, while camp was so near, to live in the barracks. Captain

Pentzel, because of a leg injury, Lieutenant Wiegand, and the regimental surgeon did likewise. And this time, I can honestly say, was the most pleasant period that I spent in America. Captain Pentzel, who was always the life of the party, would entertain us with his stories, often until after midnight. We were ready to move from this location at a moment's notice. The rooms were no longer straightened out, no longer swept, and everything began to pile up in a heap. At this time, the colonel traded me a fine brown horse for the one I owned, which was nice also, but for a rider who was a member of the clergy, too wild; and when riding, had several times put me in danger of breaking my neck. Mine was a spirited steed of four years, which I had purchased during the winter for one guinea. After the affair at Trenton, the servants of the Hessian officers fled on their masters' horses. Their masters were in part captured, in part killed, in the battle. They had no fodder for the horses and could not take them into New York. And this was the basis by which a horse could often be obtained for next to nothing. Mine was too spirited, and for me, too wild. Therefore, the colonel traded with me.

The 25th - Generally speaking, the weather was becoming rather warm. Grass and other growing things grew with a surprising swiftness. In the woods, now and again, asparagus and other plants which could be used as vegetables were to be found. Our camp was in an open space with many and various trees growing thickly nearby. The melodic songs of an uncountable number of birds increased the charm of this already most pleasant campsite. The songs of these birds are comparable with the songs of various birds in Germany, such as the nightingale, the finch, and the canary. These last fly wild, but are smaller and a brighter yellow than those which our people keep in cages. In appearance their colors are more beautiful than one can imagine. Those which belong to the thrush family have a variety of colors, completely black, black with red wings, black with a red head, and gray. Another sort, whose song compares with that of the chickadee, is the prettiest, which only the skill of an artist can describe. Head, breast, and tail are a shining black, the wings a dark red. Still others are yellow, black, and speckled with red. There are also many turtles which the soldiers catch and make into butter dishes. Many snakes have been killed near both our and the English camps. The English, and especially the Americans, are very adept at catching them.

31

They quickly step on the head, tear out the tongue, and strip the skin off, which is then used as a covering for staffs and sword sheaths. The color of the snakes vary, as does their size. The black snake is by far the largest. The tiger snake, as I call it, is red and white flecked, but here the flecks are black, those there red. These flecks are separated by a completely white stripe, and when the snake is alive, and the sun shines on it, appear as if the flecks are enhanced with silver.

The black snake shows no fear of people, and if not disturbed, never attacks. The bite of the other snakes is considered very dangerous, and the bite of the rattlesnake is deadly if not tended at once. At the same time, I happen to know from my Elizabethtown host, who lived there 36 years, that in those 36 years he only knows of two instances of the rattlesnake, as he calls it, doing any harm. But a person must be alert when he hears the snake's rattle. He still has the rattle of a snake which he killed some years previously, behind his house. The snake had drunk milk together with his child. The child was not happy with his uninvited guest, and went into the house to complain to his father. This one, not understanding what the child wanted, followed him out and saw the rattlesnake drinking from the child's bowl. Whereupon he immediately killed the snake. The savages have a certain and completely sure cure for rattlesnake bite, which is extracted from a weed which they squeeze on the wound. Therefore the Indians do not fear this poisonous snake, because they have an antitoxin.

The savages who live on Long Island are very different from the others in that they have become more civilized as a result of association with the local residents and learned their customs. Their usual way of settling differences legally and protecting their custom is very special. The eldest in the tribe makes the judgment, which must however, be based on a previously established precedent. There is no appeal from the decision. Even a death sentence is carried out without opposition.

All laws and customs are passed down within the tribe by word of mouth. Nothing is recorded in writing. When a new law is decreed, the eldest of each family sit together as a court. To each is told what he is to remember and he dare not forget it for fear of death. And, if after many years, he is asked about the law and has forgotten it, he is executed without hesitation. No vice is more prevalent among them than drunkenness. Their appetite for rum and other strong drink is unbelievable. And in their drunkenness they revert to the savagery of their wild nature, and are capable of the most terrible acts, limited only by opportunity. This weakness of their race is so well known among them, that they have taken steps to prevent the drunkenness from immediately leading to excesses. Certainly a much needed requirement. A resident of Long Island told me, in New York, that whole tribes assemble and if they want to do something up right, without being forced, they all get drunk together on rum. However, one member of each family must stay sober and watch over the others. This is such an unpopular position among them, that it is rotated among them and only lasts from one feast to the next. Whoever has the unrewarding pleasure of getting intoxicated today, must give his sober attention to looking out for his drunken brothers tomorrow to insure that they do not lose all control of themselves. They adhere closely to the bidding of their supervisor and what he decides is done, even in their foggy-minded condition. He has the right to use the strongest punishment. Therefore the supervisor of the drunken mob must have the gift of maintaining complete temperance. He can not allow himself to have a drink. If an excess occurs under his supervision, which generally would end with cruelties, he is responsible, and he alone. The others go free.

Men do absolutely nothing in the house. Only on Long Island do they plow and tend the fields. The other wild Indians live by hunting and fishing. The colonists who live nearby trade with the savages to get the most beautiful hides. Among them are to be found the best marksmen, and when they shoot at something, they seldom miss. In addition, they can run exceptionally fast. They leave their huts and travel into the furthest depths of the wilderness without getting lost as others would, never to be seen again. But they know, if they have only a glimpse at the stars, how to find the way, go directly to their destination, be it over mountains and valleys, hill and dale. And, if by chance, which seldom happens, they get lost, and a dark cloud hides the stars, they feel the bark of a tree and so find their way home. Instead, as in Germany, of bundling a child up and protecting it from every draft, the savages tie the naked child to a board and let it toughen up in frost and heat. The main object which they seek is to raise children who are strong and patient, and they have grown really strong and big. Because the children are plagued with mosquitoes, of which there are a great many, the children are smeared with oil. This smearing accomplishes a secondary purpose of giving the children a dark brown color, which is considered a sign of great beauty.

June 1777 - One hears nothing but of war and the rumors of war. The army is in the Jerseys. My primary diversion is to ride through the camp, mornings and evenings, when everything is alive, the roads are full of people, and the meadows and gardens are full of horses. The soil in the Jerseys is truly productive and fertile, although not nearly as rich here near the sea as further inland. Along the stretch of Woodbridge, Spenton, Elizabethtown, through which we have already traveled, everything grows which is put in the earth as seed. An especially large amount of Turkish wheat, or Indian corn, is grown. From this grain, especially when mixed with wheat or other grain, the whitest bread is baked. But mostly this grain is used as fodder for the horses and pigs. The farmers grow more of this than of any other grains because it gives a higher yield. The situation is different in Germany, as the autumn weather is not as good as it is here.

It would be difficult to find orchards in any part of the world more beautiful, larger, better laid out, and thickly planted than here in the Jerseys. Only a rare and sensitive poet could describe, with all its stimulation, the spring which presents itself to us after having experienced a disruptive and miserable winter. He would have to call on all his talent, apply with feeling all compulsion and help, all assistance and inspiration, and still, to the stranger, who has never been in the Jerseys in springtime, not describe it with enough zeal and enthusiasm. But truly, all his pictures depicting nature itself will remain as only a sketch compared to a painting for one who has seen and enjoyed the natural beauty which makes such a strong impression.

When one stands on the height between Amboy and Woodbridge, to the right and left are to be seen rivers covered with sloops and single-masted ships, which currently bring provisions from New York up the Raritan River to Brunswick. Further back one can see the channel made by the merging of the Hudson and Raritan Rivers, and still further in the distance can be seen the profusion of blooming orchards. At the foot of the hill lies the widely scattered buildings of Woodbridge, and further off, because of their red brick, the easily distinguishable farm and manor houses. The houses however, are not set in the middle of the artistically laid out gardens, but on green places which are the meadows for their livestock. The inside of their houses is furnished with the most expensive tastes. It appears as if the occupants of this fools' paradise do not enjoy their pleasure gardens, but prefer to raise vegetables, or even more so, turn their efforts to raising fruit. They certainly deserve criticism, when nature has provided them such bounty, for not improving upon it with some skill. As great as the surplus of fruit in bountiful years may be, still there is no great amount of fruit dried. One would believe, since there is enough wood everywhere, that there would be a lot of dried fruit, but this is not the case, and the greatest amount of fruit is stored as cider or vinegar. This is accomplished using a large wheel which is rocked back and forth in a groove by two people, and crushes all the fruit. The juice flows out of the groove and directly into a keg. Fresh from the cellar this drink tastes just like the fruit. The fruit is exceptionally sweet and pleasant. When it is aged, however, it is very similar to our Rhine wine in color and taste.

The 29th - We were busy packing this entire night. We were ordered to ship over to Staten Island at six o'clock in the morning. It took somewhat longer, and the transfer across took the entire army until toward evening. Our march was not overly long, only about three English miles, and we halted in a level area of oak woods. It took so long to bring up the tents that we barely had time to set them up. Our camp was alongside the main road on which the entire army passed by.

The 30th - We were undisturbed in our camp. In the afternoon I visited Chaplain [Johann Christoph] Wagner from Ansbach.[3] In the evening we received orders to break camp early tomorrow morning and to continue our march.

The 1st of July 1777 - I drank my coffee at five o'clock. The bags were still packed from yesterday. The tents were knocked down, I stuck a pipe of tobacco in my face, and mounted my horse. The normally rather wide roadway was, for so many regiments, too narrow, and each regiment often had to halt in order to let another march pass. At two o'clock we arrived in camp, which is part of the defenses for New York.

The 2nd - This night there was a terrible storm. Lightning lit up the tents so much that no light was needed. The day was rather cool, such as we often have in Germany following a storm.

The 3rd - Rather warm.

The 4th - Again we were a bit disturbed not to have boarded ship, but will remain here. The regiments which are to remain were assigned to fatigue details, with the task of improving the so-called defenses.

The 5th - During the evening we saw many fireflies, which have a much brighter glow than those in Germany.

The 6th - I have never experienced a more unpleasant change of weather than last night. Our church services began at seven o'clock because of the heat. Yesterday evening it was still astonishingly hot. At twelve o'clock the wind blew so cold through the tent that it was necessary to use an overcoat as a blanket. By midday it was again hot enough to cause a stroke.

The 7th - In the cool of the evening I rode in company with several others through the entire camp until we came to the Flagstaff where the Knyphausen Regiment was camped and where we had acquaintances. The Flagstaff is a height facing the sea, and when ships enter, two flags are raised as a signal to New York. From this hill the view is as exhilarating as one could wish. One looks out over the open sea, where just now, in the offing, a fleet numbering thirteen ships from England comes into view. The ships must pass close under this height, and only three ships can pass abreast through this narrow. Opposite lies the magnificent Long Island. Across the Raritan Bay, Perth Amboy and the beautiful Pharaoh's Tower can be clearly seen. Behind the height is the camp of the entire army. Currently we have a very pleasant life on Staten Island. I stay in my tent during the morning. After lunch I ride out, if only through the camp, to the water's edge. Still, I have enjoyed a pleasant afternoon.

The 8th - In the evening, a quick passing storm. Today the embarkation began and that creates a sharp increase in the cost of foodstuffs.[4] A pound of meat already costs a shilling.

The 9th - We again took a pleasure ride to the other side of the island, along an even, sandy path. This entire side is built along Dutch lines and most of the inhabitants are Hollanders. Every farmer has his estate, meadows, fields, a fenced in garden, and a woods which sits behind all this. In front of his house he also has a river flowing which is rich in fish and on which he ships his wood and other products easily, and at almost no cost, to the markets in New York. What he pays the King is next to nothing. A boat load of fish or of wood, sold in New York, gives a greater return than his outlay.

The 10th - A trial was conducted at the parade ground for a deserter named [Christoph] Cleeman. He did not take into account the need for a ship to effect his flight.

The 11th - Together with Captain Alberti and the regimental surgeon, I rode to a house on Newark Bay. The man, named Nosehor, was the brother of Captain Alberti's landlady in Elizabethtown. We spent a most pleasant afternoon.

The 12th - Lieutenant Colonel von Dalwigk left the regiment to return to Germany.[5]

The 13th - It rained through my tent and the continuous rain prevented us from holding church services today.

The 14th - Today the heat was tolerable.

The 15th - Two women, wives of English ships' captains, came into our camp. One, a pretty young woman, saw the son of the wagoner of Captain Pentzel's Company, took him in her arms, and showered him with kisses. She wanted to take him back on the ship. She offered the mother twenty guineas and the father two guineas, and promised to give the boy a good upbringing. Only the mother wanted to keep her child. The good woman had recently had a child, which had died. The following summer the child of the wagoner died and the wife believed, according to the common Waldeck superstition, that the good English lady had somehow put a curse on the child.

The 16th - Yesterday the recently captured deserter was punished by running the gauntlet twelve times. During the afternoon, we broke camp and moved a quarter of an hour higher up the hill. I entertained my catholic colleague from the 2nd Ansbach Regiment.[6] We drank very often to the good health of the Jesuits. After lunch the tents were quickly taken down. Before we could put them up again, and while our baggage lay on the ground, we were suddenly struck by a downpour and everything was thoroughly soaked. The 52nd Regiment is on our right and the 2nd Ansbach Regiment on our left, and we are in the middle. During the evening the rain ceased and we lay in our wet tents, rather damp.

The 17th - What was soaked yesterday was dried today in the sunshine. So it goes during a campaign; even the heavens which make us wet, make us dry.

The 18th - We are still puzzled where the fleet, which lies just behind us, will sail. The frequent cannon shots from the warships alert us, but still they remain at anchor. Both Admiral [Lord Richard] and General Howe are aboard the *Eagle*. a b c cannon.[7]

The 19th - We sent eighteen sick to the hospital in New York.

The 20th - Church was held at seven o'clock and many Ansbachers attended. A large part of the fleet departed.

The 21st - The rest of the fleet and five warships followed.

The 22nd - The heat was exceptionally strong. The air, however, was cooled by a heavy rainstorm. The rain beat through my tent so hard that I had to lie soaking wet all night long.

The 23rd - Cool and windy.

The 27th - Church at seven o'clock with the Ansbach Regiment also present.

The 28th - I was asked to visit several German soldiers of the 52nd Regiment in the hospital.[8]

The 29th - Unbearable heat.

The 30th - Now all sorts of rumors are abroad. Philadelphia has already been occupied by our army, and all such tales.

The 1st of August 1777 - This month began, as is common throughout the temperate world, with hot weather.

The 2nd - A summer storm, followed by a warm day.

The 3rd - At seven o'clock church; then I went to the regimental hospital at an hour's distance and visited the sick. This afternoon, one shower after the other. Rain and lightning alternated, one with the other. Living in a tent is miserable during such weather.

The 4th - I took leave from the regiment and, with the regimental surgeon, traveled to New York. We stopped at midday at Mr. [David] Grimm's, where many Ansbach and Hessian officers visit.[9]

The 5th - We went to the hospital and saw two from our regiment who were dead and two who were near death. The hospital was in a beautiful and splendid house. The room where our sick lay had been a ballroom in peacetime. I bought a new saddle, bridle, halter, and everything that goes with riding. The saddle alone cost five York pounds.

The 6th - We traveled back to Staten Island with a good wind in 35 minutes and were in camp by one o'clock.

The 8th - I visited my catholic stepbrother whose tent stood not far from mine, having been invited to lunch. He is a good man, with no special opinion on the present rebellion and no desire to influence anyone to his ideas. That is the least of his ambitions. His servant, who is also his cook, is smarter than he is. He has vowed never to marry, but is rather tight-fisted except where his desire for good things to eat comes into play. He does not preach at all, but holds private religious services in his tent. His regiment attends our religious services.[10]

The 9th - At the request of Colonel [Friedrich August Valentin] von Voit [von Salsburg], I visited the Ansbach hospital and served communion to the sick.

The 10th - After conducting church services in the camp I rode to my branch establishment to conduct religious services at the hospital. Captain [Philipp Friedrich] von Seitz, who commanded the picket in this area, invited me to lunch, where among a large group from the Ansbach Regiment, I spent a pleasant afternoon.

The 11th - I was called to the ferry early today to serve communion to Lieutenant [Maximilian] von Streit, who lay near death.[11] No one can remember ever having seen a more violent storm. Lightning, like glowing chains, continuously flashed across the sky.

The 12th - In Germany a cool day follows a thunderstorm. Here it seems to be reversed, as today is hotter than yesterday. Free Corporal [Schoenberg] von Spiegel died in the hospital from a burning fever, from which many others are suffering. Toward evening another storm arose, which lasted throughout the night, and until morning. I thought the wind would blow the tent away.

The 13th - Early this morning it was foggy and cool. Toward noon it became hotter again. The newspapers from New York inform us that at the capture of Ticonderoga, the savages sold a horse for a bottle of rum. The war chest of the rebels was captured at the same time, but consisted only of paper money and a few thousand pieces of Spanish dollars. The Germans, who best know the value of paper money, lit their pipes with thirty dollar bills.

The 14th - Again a storm.

The 15th - One storm after another and the lightning lit up the tents all night long.

The 16th - Very windy. The wife of [Friedrich] Otto had twins, which I baptized today in my tent.

The 17th - Church at seven o'clock, and during the sermon, such a rain came that services were interrupted.

The 18th - There is still doubt as to where the army has landed, in New England or on the Delaware.

The 19th - Rainy weather.

The 20th - The colonel, who returned from New York yesterday evening, told us that within two days the uneasy public would be informed where Howe and his army have landed. Colonel von Voit let me know that his regiment desired communion Sunday. I visited Lieutenant Strubberg at the outpost and, in his company, amidst old tales about Waldeck, wasted a most pleasant day.

The 22nd - The general ordered the regiment to be under arms. At the set time, it was ready at the gate. Suddenly there was an alarm that the rebels were at hand and the regiment had to move out. During the previous night the rebels had crossed over to plunder and quickly to storm the defenses. They began to cross by boat at midnight and by three o'clock in the morning already had 2,000 men and three generals, [John] Sullivan, [William] Smallwood, and [Prudhomme] DeBorre, on our side. A battalion of provincials, who were first attacked, suffered heavy losses. Two alarm guns were fired by the defenses and two by the warship *Centurion*. The 52nd Regiment and ours marched down to the waterside and fortunately were able to cut-off the rebels' crossing point. Our cannons and the English cannons were brought into play and ours, in particular, earned high praise. I rode along the way some hours later and met a group of prisoners. The number of prisoners amounted to more than 260 and 21 officers. In dead, the rebels suffered a noticeable loss, as many drowned while attempting to swim to safety. The rebels, who were now completely disorganized, ceased firing and were taken prisoner from behind every bush.

We suffered no one killed and no one wounded in the action, although three men were struck down by the heat.[12] I would never have believed that this heat, and the strenuous marching, could have such a result. Youths, as strong as trees, crashed to earth and showed no signs of life, but nevertheless, soon recovered. Still, in this manner, four men of the 52nd Regiment died, including one who discovered a pail of cool water, drank, and fell dead. To this was added that the men were hungry and had marched off without taking anything with them. I had considered this and sent my messmates some cold snacks and wine. The servant did not reach the regiment until midnight, however. The Ansbach Regiment had the duty of maintaining the defensive posts at our camp.

The 23rd - Because of the unrest, neither communion nor church services were held. The prisoners were loaded aboard ship and sent to New York. They were, as is to be expected, treated with kindness. Not one was deprived of his possessions. A lieutenant colonel of theirs still had his watch on a silver chain. This lieutenant colonel had two brothers who served as good officers with the provincials, and today they conducted themselves very well, fighting against the rebels. Even the close ties of brotherly love can not drive away the spirit of the rebels.

The following congratulations were published in official orders:

General Campbell desires to express his recognition of the 52nd English and the 3rd Waldeck Regiments, the detachment of artillery and the provincial troops for their display of unexcelled and determined courage in pursuit of the rebels, as well as their efforts to attack, as proven when the opportunity arose. He is pleased to have the honor to command troops who possess such determination to do their duty and to serve when called upon. At the same time, he feels compelled to state his appreciation to the honorable von Voit, for his attention to the duty and alertness while commanding the rest of the troops in the camp during the general's absence.

I wish to share in the reputation and good name of our regiment and therefore record the following friendly comments of General [Henry] Clinton, concerning the previously mentioned regiments.

The general wishes to acknowledge his great respect for the extensive military abilities and the true soldierly determination displayed by Brigadier General Campbell throughout the affair. The conduct of Lieutenant Colonel Campbell of the 52nd Regiment merits the warmest recognition. The general extends to him and the officers and men of his regiment, his heartfelt thanks for their efforts, which are yet one more example, among the many called forth by this war, that no power can withstand English troops when they seriously engage the enemy. The general wishes to thank Colonel von Hanxleden and the Waldeck Regiment, also, for the dispatch and courage demonstrated when this opportunity arose. The conduct of the provincial corps reflects to its credit and the general desires that they receive his strongest expression of appreciation. The general awaits more exact details from Brigadier Campbell concerning the still unspecified individual exploits so that special appreciation may be extended to them.

The 25th - During the past night, there was again an alarm. The regiment turned out and the unrest continued until eight o'clock in the morning, when it was apparent that there was no cause for alarm.

The 26th - Again, a restless night.

The 31st - Communion was served today; confession was held at seven o'clock, and at nine o'clock our church services began, which lasted until twelve o'clock. There were 302 person all told who partook of communion. The sun burned down on my bare head so strongly that I developed a severe headache and was indisposed for eight days.

Eighteenth Century America
[The Close of 1777]

The 1st - 11th of September 1777 - Absolutely nothing of consequence.

The 12th - During the previous night the 52nd Regiment and our and the Ansbach Grenadiers marched to Elizabeth Point and crossed over. General Vaughn crossed the North River near Fort Lee.

The 13th - 14th - The troops in Jersey broke camp again today and marched further.

The 15th - A fleet arrived from England, bringing some recruits.

The 16th - Our generals returned today. They were frequently engaged with the enemy, but could not bring on a battle.

The 15th - 21st - The best of news has arrived from our army in Pennsylvania, and the army is now only nine miles from Philadelphia. We were out for a pleasure ride and met a funeral procession, which, because of its composition, is worth noting. The corpse was on a wagon, with four young men riding ahead. Behind the wagon, on horseback, were thirteen or fourteen women and at least twenty men. Immediately behind the wagon rode two matrons in deep sorrow, and they seemed ordered on occasion to shed a few tears. The procession wound its way directly past us.

The 22nd - Today it was cold and so windy that no sailor would risk sailing to New York. The news is that Philadelphia is in our hands. It was the King's birthday and all the cannons on the warships and at Fort George were fired at twelve o'clock.[13] Because of the raging waters and the strong wind storm, we could not hear them.

The 23rd - A warm and pleasant day. His Excellence George Washington supposedly has had to transfer his headquarters to Trenton on this side of the Delaware.

The 24th - Unpleasantly warm.

The 25th - Again cool, windy, and rain during the evening.

The 26th - An officer from the warship *Centurion* ate with us. He told us that General Lee, who is a prisoner aboard his ship, is very unhappy with the present state of the rebellion, and has openly stated during his captivity that Washington need only move from one province to another until the English are exhausted. The land is so extensive that England can not outlast the colonies. Since Washington has abandoned Philadelphia, he begins to develop a different tune. Washington is clever, who knows why he has done that!

The 27th - A very pleasant fall day.

The 28th - Once again our church services begin at ten o'clock, after parade formation.

The 29th - The newspapers boast continuously about the progress made by our weapons in Pennsylvania.

The 30th - The 52nd Regiment received orders to be prepared to travel.

The 1st of October 1777 - Warm weather. Commissary Marc came from New York with mail from home.

The 2nd - The newspapers report that [Lieutenant General John] Burgoyne defeated the rebels and that 700 men were buried in one place.

The 3rd - The 52nd Regiment embarked, reportedly to go up the North River for an attack against Fort Montgomery.

The 4th - There are already fifteen ships in the mouth of the North River this morning, and we have the strongest hopes that we too will soon leave this island. It appears that something of consequence will happen this fall. Among others, I was invited to dine aboard the warship *Centurion*. At twelve o'clock a sloop came to pick us up. We were given a tour of the ship. We made our compliments to General Lee, a man of medium height, very thin; his nose is so large that its shadow darkens the other half of his face. One reads sincerity, thoughtfulness, understanding, and a complete reflectiveness in his appearance. He is very clever and spoke only of inconsequential things. No one, who has not seen it for himself, can picture the order and cleanliness aboard a warship. Every weapon, every line, of which there are many hundreds, has its proper place; every hand knows what it must do, every sailor and soldier knows his station, every cannon has its crew, and when battle sounds, everyone, in an instant, is where he belongs. At two o'clock we sat down to eat and many flags were displayed on deck. On our table everything was to be found that anyone could expect in the best restaurant in a great city. On such a ship, and by such a well-laid table, one can forget that he is on the water, and instead, without effort, think he is in a beautiful house rather than aboard ship. After dinner we were served punch and remained at the business of drinking until our departure. At six o'clock we entered a beautiful boat and sailed away.

The 5th - At nine o'clock church, and the entire Ansbach Regiment was present. We have fewer sick now than at any time previously. It was a pleasure when I entered the hospital today and found all but two of our men up and dressed. At the present time we have only eighteen men sick. We were still eating when the regimental drummer brought us letters from home. I went into my tent and quickly read them with pleasure.

The 6th - Warm weather. At eleven o'clock in the evening there was an alarm when a ship on the side toward Jersey attacked. But as the staff officer of the day received no report, we lay down to sleep. Our picket, commanded by Captain Alberti, Sr., returned and all was quiet. Supposedly the shots were from a warship which lay near Amboy.

The 7th - On a beautiful afternoon and in good company, I rode to Richmond, the main city on the island. Here is a church to which most of the inhabitants belong, and about twenty houses. Behind the church stands a pretty height on which a defensive point has been set. The ground here is stony and the most infertile on the entire island. This disadvantage is offset, however, by an incomparable growth of trees. About two English miles from the place is a schoolhouse situated at a crossroads, where all the children of the area are taught. The furnishings of a table and benches were exactly as by us in Germany. On the two long benches sat the boys, and on the other, the girls. They gazed at us with unabashed curiosity. The number of children was between fifty and sixty. The youngest wrote already, and with very large letters; the older ones, however, wrote normally.[14]

The 8th - News was received that General Clinton had taken Fort Montgomery by storm, during which we lost 300 men. The enemy had 500 taken prisoner and the rest were massacred.

The 9th - Now one piece of good news follows another. We have opened the Hudson River as far as Albany. General Burgoyne has again beaten the rebels in a major battle and made 1,777 prisoners. Philadelphia has been greatly strengthened.

The 10th - 11th - Warm weather.

45

The 12th - At nine o'clock church. As we were still standing together after church, the long-awaited order came to prepare to move up the North River.

The 13th - At daybreak we struck our tents and the regiment marched toward Jersey, in order to embark at that place. It was a most beautiful day and instead of being aboard ship by evening, as we had hoped, at three o'clock the brigade major arrived in all haste with orders that everyone and everything was to be off-loaded and the regiment was to return to camp. It was impossible to unload all the baggage and tents from the ship this evening. Therefore, everyone had to seek out his own lodgings as best he could. The two grenadier companies of Waldeck and Ansbach had to take their knapsacks and everything back from the ships, also their canteens filled with water, and we really thought that they were chosen for some special task. We arrived back at our camp late at night. Old [Claude] Prieur, the regimental surgeon's servant, offered me a piece of cheese, but instead of cheese, he gave me hair wax, which he had in the same bag, and which, because it was dark, I did not realize until I had bitten into it. That caused me to lose my appetite for cheese, but not for something else. And Herr [Henrich] Beck did me the greatest favor which I could expect this evening, considering my day. He provided me with a good piece of roast. Next we discussed where to sleep. There were several small huts, previously built, which we took over. However, these were not the best of lodgings, and because they were damp, I saw the need for some other quarters, and found truly the best that I could hope to find. The servants had brought a wagon filled with hay and tied all the horses to it. I did not hesitate very long, but climbed in and crawled under the hay. I had hardly gotten warm, when I felt the wagon start to move, which was caused by the horses tied to it. The wagon stood on a slight elevation and did not dare to start to roll or it would have rolled into the ocean. What could I do? I climbed out and laid large stones around all four wheels. Then I climbed back into my bed with much effort and slept more comfortably than I had during the entire summer.

The 14th - We made preparations to bring the tents and other belongings from the ship back to camp. I had my tent set up at once and we thought we would remain here in peace. The regimental surgeon sent old Prieur out to get something to cook for our noon meal. He brought back beef and potatoes, and as we had had nothing adequate to eat for several days, we prepared to cook our meal immediately. At twelve o'clock our meal was ready and as we were about to sit down to the table, we received orders to strike the tents quickly and to march. We just could not bring ourselves to leave our potatoes, but quickly wolfed them down, Here there was no one who would buy our horses and we could not take them aboard ship. We found it necessary to turn them over to the care of the general quartermaster. The embarkation went rather quickly and by ten o'clock in the evening we were all on board. The major and the grenadier company, Captain Alberti, Lieutenants Strubberg, Brumhard, and Wiegand, and Regimental Surgeon Mattern, and the Field Chaplain Waldeck found themselves aboard the ship *Klenehorn*. That evening aboard ship we drank to a good voyage and sailed at twelve o'clock.

The 15th - In the early morning light we passed New York and entered the North, or Hudson, River. A very beautiful, bright day, just as I like when traveling on water. The ship makes a minimum of movement, but goes steadily onward so that one barely notices the progress. It is beautiful to see such a large ship under sail on a river. We drank our coffee in the cabin early, then took seats on deck, watching the bank to right and left, which gradually held our attention. At nine o'clock we were between Forts Lee and Knyphausen, the most dangerous passage on the river. The rebels have made such a row of submerged hazards across the width of the river here, that only the most careful pilot can conduct a ship through. Two of our ships became stranded and had to await flood tide to be floated free.[15] One other ship, with Ansbachers, passed so close to land by Fort Washington, that a person could have jumped ashore. The submersible hazard has been made in this manner: Thick beams with sharpened iron points mounted thereon are fastened on a boat. The boat is loaded with stones and sunk so that when a ship runs against the hazard, the ship is caught or sunk. Toward noon we arrived in the region of Kingsbridge, where we saw our camp of last year's campaign, and which reminded us of many things of the first campaign. Now we came to Connecticut, where we saw the finest gentlemen's houses from the ship. The most magnificent of all, laid-out so tastefully and with large gardens surrounding it, was Philipsburgh, which belonged to Colonel [Frederick] Philipse, and lies close to the bank of the North River. Not far from there, is an especially beautiful church with a leaf tower, in which all the Germans of the region worship. To our left lay Jersey, which the high walls of the river bank prevented our seeing beyond. At ten o'clock in the evening we came to West Point and anchored after a 54-mile trip up the river. It was in this region where the rebels strung a terribly thick chain across the river in order to hinder the ships. We still had seventeen fathoms of water here. There was beautiful moonlight and Lieutenant Strubberg and I sat on deck gazing on the area as we smoked our pipes until midnight.

The 16th - We hoped at any moment to debark. We suggested to ourselves that we would now march by land to Albany to join with Burgoyne' army. Our suggestions and dreams of the broad and pleasant expanse of land through which we would wander were interrupted by an order from General Clinton, which commanded our immediate return down river. We did not yet know the reason for this order. We ate our noon meal in disgust, because of the retreat. The rebels fired at our ship from the shore with small arms, but to no effect. We sailed down the Hudson River at about four o'clock. Some, in disgust, lay down, while others discussed the present situation of the war.

The 17th - Before noon we dropped anchor near Fort Knyphausen, previously Fort Washington.

The 18th - We remained aboard ship, not knowing where we should go. Our ship's captain returned aboard ship from New York in the evening with the good news from our army in Philadelphia, and also that General Vaughn's army had pressed on as far as Aesopus. This evening over a glass of wine we made our plans of what would be most favorable to us. But to this came the order that tomorrow at daybreak we were to disembark, leaving all baggage aboard ship. Now new plans had to be made and Major von Horn was in high spirits. We believe we are being landed in order to proceed to a union with the army from Canada. Under this supposition, to which each added his opinion, we spent half the night in discussion.

The 19th - In the early morning light we began to debark and as all the baggage remained aboard ship, we were quickly finished. We marched to Kingsbridge and by two o'clock had a new camp standing.

The Hessians, who were next to us, had just beat church parade, and as we were unable to conduct services, I attended with them. Our old Prieur, who cooked for his master, Lieutenant Wiegand, Adjutant Stierlein, and me, prepared a rather good meal. It was necessary here to carry water a half hour's distance, and even then it tasted like manure drainings. Otherwise, it was possible to get everything here that a soldier needed. But there was no further similarity with solid ground. It is a sorry place for the army to have been during the entire year.

The 20th - For me at least, this was a restful day. Commissary Marc had brought us letters, which until now, because of the continual unrest, could not be answered. I had already written several letters and had just unpacked everything that I had with me, when the order came to strike our tents and return to the ships, which were still waiting for us on the North River. I was rather annoyed with this order. Everything was in complete confusion and it was evening before we arrived near Fort Washington, where the ships lay.

This was as disadvantageous a point for embarkation as could be found on the entire river. The small boats could only approach the shore under a steep cliff, which it was necessary to descend in order to enter the boats. To further complicate things, it started to rain and the wind blew continuously. The night was so dark that the ships were indistinguishable, and the water became so rough that the sailors were able to row the boats between the ships and the shore only with the most strenuous effort. I still find it difficult to understand why several hundred men were not drowned. Already on a number of occasions the 20th of the month had had special meaning for us. We arrived aboard our ship late, had nothing to eat or drink, nor even a blanket to lie down upon because our servants were still on land, and the wind was so strong that the small boats could no longer travel back and forth. We sailed at ten o'clock in a strong, driving snowstorm. At three o'clock we were opposite Greenwich, which consists only of garden and summer houses. Opposite, in Jersey, on a very high cliff, stood a summer house. I have never in my life seen a more pleasant place. The gentleman who owns it, looks out of his window over the river to the city of New York and the entire surrounding area. He sees the ocean and all the ships coming and going. The eye can never have a larger and more pleasant panorama. Toward evening we dropped anchor at Staten Island.

The 22nd - We landed on an unusually cold morning and entered the camp where the 52nd Regiment had been stationed. Bringing the tents and other baggage to the camp was a slow process because we had given up not only the wagon and cannon horses, but our riding horses as well.

The 23rd - Colonel von Hanxleden assumed command on the island. Reportedly, Burgoyne and his entire army have been captured. We do not believe this in the light of his recent great victories.

The 24th - General Vaughn withdrew from Aesopus and this is not a good sign.

The 25th - Foggy weather, and foul weather for campaigning now sets in.

The 26th - It was cold and damp and after church it rained the rest of the day. A fleet, which had on board regiments from Ansbach, came out of New York bound for Philadelphia.

The 27th - Continuously rainy weather. It rained through the tent making the bed and everything else wet. A regular river flowed under my bed and during the night my slippers and other things, which I kept under my bed, floated to the front of the tent. It was impossible to make a fire and therefore impossible to cook.

The 28th - It continued to rain and a windstorm sprang up as well. The tents of the grenadier company, which sat more exposed than the rest, were all blown down and torn to pieces. Few tents of the other soldiers remained standing. It was necessary for the soldiers to seek shelter in the bakery and in several other small houses in the area. I was soaked to the skin and had not been dry for 24 hours. My bed was wet, which I nevertheless had to lie in, but I took the precaution of checking that the tent was securely fastened, otherwise the wind would have blown it down about my head. There was not much sleep during the night and I finally got out of my wet bed and went to the ferry house where there would at least be a fire. But it was so crowded, there was not even room to stand. Therefore we continued on our way and turned in at a house where at noon we could also get something to eat.

This was possibly the most difficult day which we had in America. It rained day and night and the wind turned as cold as in the middle of winter. No one in camp could light a fire. Several of us slept in a farmer's house, on this night, where we made a good fire in the stove, drank good punch, dried our clothing and boots, and forgot as much as possible the unpleasant conditions which we had to tolerate during the last few days.

The 29th - I returned to our camp early and was glad that my tent was still standing. The strong wind and rain continued unabated. Until now, the colonel's tent had withstood the wind, but this afternoon the wind tore it into a thousand pieces. My tent still stood and I again slept in it on this night.

The 30th - The rainy weather eased somewhat, but the wind blew so cold that while everything dried quickly, it was nearly unbearable in the tent. Once again we could cook in camp. It was much easier to put up with the cold than with the rain.[16]

The 31st - Our regimental horses and the artillery horses were delivered to us. The riding horses which had been taken to Long Island to graze were returned, also. Unfortunately however, through a mistake by the commissary, my horse was not returned with the rest. I turned to the general quartermaster for help. He promised to do all he could to get it for me, and offered me another nag, if mine could not be found.

The 1st of November 1777 - Because the tents were all in tatters, the colonel quartered the regiment in houses in the neighborhood. And we, that is Lieutenant Wiegand, Adjutant Stierlein, Regimental Surgeon Mattern, and Chaplain Waldeck, were quartered in two rooms at the ferry. The colonel took quarters in an adjoining house. If we were in rather tight quarters, still it was better to be a little crowded than to spend this time of year in a tent.

The 2nd - General Campbell returned and assumed command.

The 3rd - No one any longer doubts the unfortunate defeat at Saratoga.

The 4th - In the neighborhood of the Jerseys, forces are being consolidated, and because the general does not believe our quarters are secure enough, today our regiment had to return into the camp.

The 5th - The great success of General [Horatio] Gates has occasioned a disunity among the rebel generals. It is certainly a condition from which many evil consequences could result for our army. And this could be the reason General Clinton brought us back down the river. It had apparently been his intent to move toward Burgoyne to provide him relief. It reminds me of when the doctor goes to visit a sick patient who died the day before.

The 6th - 8th - Once again there is beautiful, pleasant fall weather.

The 9th - At ten o'clock, church in camp.

The 10th - Our army began an extensive retrograde movement. True, General Howe has Philadelphia, but nothing more, and is surrounded by rebels, so that in looking back, the consequences seem disadvantageous to our army. General Gates is now moving down like a flood which has burst through a broken dam. In the previous night, when it was foggy, 100 rebels crossed over and attacked the sentries at Elizabeth Point. Presently we are so uncertain that we never feel safe from an enemy attack at night.

The 11th - There was a hard freeze.

The 12th - The first snow fell, which melted again after sunrise. Our soldiers were occupied, since it began to get cold in the tents, building huts.

The 13th - Now that winter has actually set in, block houses are being constructed for our regiment, and there is a dread that we must spend the winter in huts.

The 14th - I and the regimental surgeon went to dinner with the colonel. While we were still at the table, a letter came from the general in which he wrote that the rebels were expected to attack. The colonel left at once to command preparations of the regiment and to tell the sentries to be especially alert.

The 15th - We were awake during the night but the threatened attack by the rebels never came.

The 16th - In very wet and cold weather, we held church services in the camp.

The 17th - General Campbell mustered our regiment.

The 18th - Now the soldiers all live in the ground.

The 19th - Once again a corps of rebels made an attempt to cross over to attack us.

The 20th - 21st - Mild and pleasant weather.

The 22nd - During the previous night we had another alarm.

The 23rd - At ten o'clock, church in camp. The weather was pleasant and warm.

The 24th - Heavy firing heard this night at one o'clock. A corps of provincial troops had been transferred across the water to attack a rebel outpost, which was going to visit us.

The 25th - During the night, at twelve o'clock, there was an alarm again. The regiment was alerted and the picket moved out. About two o'clock we lay down to sleep again.

The 26th - Bright, warm weather.

The 27th - At daybreak the regiment stood to arms because a strong rebel formation had crossed over. Our regiment was divided into several corps which marched there by separate ways. On the firing of the alarm guns from the fortifications and from the warships, two frigates came from New York and landed their crews, also. But the rebels had again withdrawn. In the beginning the situation appeared very serious and the inhabitants fled with their best and most precious belongings into our camp. The loss on our side amounted to a few rangers being wounded and captured. The rebels suffered several killed and ten taken prisoner, of whom some were wounded.

The 28th - Once again all was quiet and the frigates departed.

The 29th - Rainy weather, and a continuous storm which prevented the ferry boats and mail ships from operating to New York. The tide forced two foolish, single-masted ships to land; also another ship was torn loose from its anchor and stranded.

The 30th - The wind and rain continued so that church could not be held. The captain of the warship *Centurion* tried to return to his ship in a small boat with a good crew. He was prevented from doing so by the wind and the rain, which threw the boat against the cliffs and the captain and his men had to swim to save themselves.

The 1st of December 1777 - The storm and rain had severely damaged our huts, which partially caved-in, and once again were in need of repairs. We lived at the ferry in a wretched house where it rained in and where the construction was so bad that we expected it to be blown down by the wind at any moment.

The 2nd - Because the tents no longer provided any shelter, the colonel allowed them to be taken down and sent to New York, where the rest of our baggage was stored.

The 3rd - The rebels in Jersey are concentrating and want to make another major effort against Staten Island in order to cut off the shipping approach to New York. I fear the worst this winter. Here we lay in the greatest discomfort, while the soldiers in Philadelphia live it up every day and play the fools. An astonishing amount of money disappears there and all these lovely guineas eventually reach the rebels. This is to their political advantage, so they let General Howe remain undisturbed in Philadelphia, provide him with the products of the land, and in exchange take the money from our army. Today a fleet of twenty ships came in.

The 4th - 13th - It was still rather unpleasant weather.

The 14th - Church in camp, and afterwards I rode, with several other friends, to the wedding of the English Commissary Osstin [Austin?], who lived about one and one-half hours distance from here. This man had previously asked me to perform the marriage ceremony, but his bride was too anxious and in the meantime had gotten herself a bit pregnant. This necessitated a slight delay of the ceremony until today, when both the baptism of the child and the marriage ceremony took place. I performed both services. It is customary among the English, and therefore among the Americans, also, for the minister to kiss the bride at the conclusion of the ceremony. Then she kisses the groom and the rest of the guests. We ate a good meal and then drank port wine followed by punch, until evening. It was already night when we mounted our horses, and coming home we had to cross a bridge which had been partially dismantled. We could easily have had an accident, if we had not had good, sure-footed horses. On this occasion I was again riding my own horse, which I had gotten back through the efforts of Captain Robotson [Robertson?].

The 15th - There has never been so much reason to talk of peace. In Congress, which has reassembled in Bethlehem, there is talk of repealing the Declaration of Independence, and, as the newspapers report, Mr. [John] Hancock has gone to Boston and other members of the Congress have resigned. I do not believe this.

The 16th - A fleet arrived from England and another departed.

The 17th - Nothing is mentioned about winter quarters. Our huts are called [Waldeck Town - a portion of the German manuscript apparently was not copied], but appear more like an Indian village.[17]

The 18th - 21st - Still quite pleasant weather and the autumn is as nice as it was during our first campaign in 1776.

The 22nd - The troops from Kingsbridge moved into winter quarters in New York. We had delightful letters from Waldeck to read.

The 23rd - Although we are not in winter quarters, there is still one advantage which we enjoy common to those in winter quarters. The regiment receives spruce beer. This is a fairly good drink made from certain burnt roots. Candles are also issued. The colonel gets two pounds every week, the major two, the captains one each, subalterns a half each, the regimental surgeon and the chaplain one each, and the Regimental Quartermaster Lieutenant Wiegand and the adjutant a half each. At the same time, we have hopes of being paid our forage money. This amounts to about fourteen and one-half pounds sterling for me, which compares with the utensils money of two pounds to be used for buying cooking implements each campaign. We call it table money.

The 24th - It is so cold that I do not think we will be able to have divine services on Christmas Day.

The 25th - It turned warm and such pleasant weather that we could hold church services in the camp, and it was the first Christmas that we celebrated under the open sky. Ships arrived from Philadelphia.

The 26th - It snowed.

The 27th - Six hundred Scotlanders, who had come from Philadelphia, moved in here.

The 28th - True winter weather. I held communion in a room at the ferry.

The 29th - It remained unusually cold until the end of the year.

1st of January 1778

The ground was snow covered but the weather was quite pleasant. We held church in the camp. I had the honor to be invited to lunch by the colonel, in company with Major von Horn and Captains Pentzel and Baumbach. We had a very pleasant get together, talking about home. In the evening I was invited to dinner by Lieutenants Strubberg and Brumhard. Captain Pentzel was also present. We drank warm punch until eleven o'clock.

The 2nd - Lord Howe arrived with a large fleet from Philadelphia.

The 3rd - Unpleasant, foggy weather.

The 4th - We again had the pleasure of reading letters from Germany, of which most had been written in September.

The 5th - 7th - Beautiful weather. Our recreation consisted of a few hours of riding for pleasure.

The 8th - A fleet arrived from England. The traffic at New York is very heavy at present with ships coming and going daily.

The 9th - Beautiful, mild weather.

The 10th - Today it is cold again. The weather on the ocean is so changeable.

The 11th - 15th - Mild, winter weather. Currently everything is so peaceful that it is difficult to imagine that there is a war on.

The 16th - I was asked to conduct communion services for the Hessian regiments in New York as their Lutheran chaplain had gone with the troops to Philadelphia. So I departed under good weather today for New York. My companions on the ship were our regimental surgeon, an American doctor, who had been a barrel-maker in his youth, and two ladies from Brunswick. We asked the latter, as is the American custom, what was new in Jersey, as the Americans after the first exchange of pleasantries, ask what is new. They knew nothing special other than that at the moment everything is very quiet in Brunswick and Amboy, and there are no rebels occupying either place. In order not to just sit in our narrow cabin, I told them that I remember having read in travel magazines that the most clever women in all America were to be found in Brunswick. They believed, however, that in these unsettled times, the most clever women had already flown to Philadelphia or New York. During this exchange, the sails were already being lowered and we climbed ashore. The

56

regimental surgeon and I at once visited Captain Pentzel, who because of indisposition, had transferred from Staten Island to New York and lived in our baggage house. He asked us to lunch and we accepted and remained there.

After lunch, Captain Alberti and Mr. Grimm, our former host, whom we visited whenever we were in New York, stopped by. The church elder was a really fine man and I very much liked his equally fine wife and well-raised, but more clever than beautiful, daughter. During the evening a large number of Hessian officers visited the Grimm home. Therefore, we ate in a separate room and Captain Alberti had our countryman, [Wilhelm] von Leliva of the Hessian corps, as a guest. We went to bed late.

The 17th - It snowed all day today and was the first winter weather. I went to visit Chaplain [Johann Georg] Hausknecht early, and after we ate breakfast, I visited Colonel [Carl Ernst] von Bischhausen, as he wished to have communion. He invited me to lunch, but because confession was at two o'clock, I asked his permission to put it off to a later date. From here, we went to General Schmidt to offer my compliments. The general asked me to dinner for tomorrow evening. At two o'clock I held communion at the Lutheran Church. I drank a glass of punch with Mr. Grimm and went to my room.

The 18th - Religious services started at ten o'clock and the number in attendance from the Hereditary Prince, Prince Charles, Stein, and Truembach Regiments was nearly 300. The church was surprisingly full and the singing quite good. What a difference, preaching in an open field and in a church. It struck me that I had not preached in a church since Elizabethtown. At General Schmidt's I met more people, including Lieutenant Colonel [Carl] von Kitzel and Major [Johann Georg] von Selig. We drank port wine at the start, good French wine in the middle, and the truly good Madeira at the end of our visit. We remained together until dusk. From the general's, I dropped in for a moment with Captain Pentzel, and then went to my quarters. Here I met a leader of the German Lutheran community ... began, she took me with them to baptize a child of the parish this evening.[1] The people pleased me very much and I remained until ten o'clock in the evening. I took this opportunity to learn something of the history of their church. Twenty years ago there had been only one German Lutheran parish here in New York, which met in the large Holland church. A large portion of this parish consisted of Hollanders who desired that their services be conducted in Dutch. But the number of High Germans was always larger and they desired to have a German minister, and even prevented the Hollanders appealing to the church authorities.

About thirty families decided to build a church, but without success, as the others of the parish put many obstacles in the way, which stopped progress and the parish developed only slowly. The true cause of the separation appeared to me to be dissatisfaction with the preacher, and they could not agree on the selection of a replacement. The new parish took Mr. Muhlenberg as their preacher and set his salary at 150 pounds. This step set in motion an unexpected growth for the parish. He worked diligently teaching the school children, and teaching the adults in church on Sundays. This unexpected exertion gave the parish great joy, and gave him the trust of all the parishioners. The mother, who already sent her daughter to the English school, took her personally to Mr. Muhlenberg's instruction, and the father encouraged his son not to neglect the church. The adults set the example for the children and in a short time the parish had grown to more than 200 families. Then came this war, and as it hindered the growth and prosperity of America, it hindered the growth of the church even more. Mr. Muhlenberg resigned from his position in New York and moved to Philadelphia, where his wife had relatives, who at that time were still living undisturbed. Since that time the church has been without a preacher. They tried very hard to convince me that I should like to take over their church, and that they would give me the position, even allowing me to make some changes. I countered that I could not leave my regiment. As long as the church continued, they offered to leave the position open for me until after the war. I was convinced, however, that being their preacher would not be as pleasant as my position with the regiment.

The 19th - I have been in a variety of tea-drinking situations. I would bet everything in the world that it is impossible in traveling through North America to find a single house, from that of the fanciest gentleman to that of the oyster digger, where the people do not drink a cup of tea at midday. The men could sooner get their wives to give up their finery than to do without tea. And if a law were passed making tea-drinking illegal, I do not doubt for a moment that the entire population would take up arms and begin a rebellion such as now exists. It is not only the ladies who are so addicted to tea, but also the men who break from work at three o'clock in order to sit down to a cup of tea. We drink it, however, as a courtesy to the society in which we find ourselves, or for fear that we will be served coffee, which the Americans make in a strange way. They only color the water brown. The ladies in these social situations are generally clever, and those raised in Philadelphia, the most clever of all. The German language, however, apparently will soon be completely forgotten by our landsmen, and in a single generation will cease to be spoken at all. The parents speak English with their children, and this is necessary as they have no German schools, and must send their children to English schools. Even in their discussions with Germans, the young people find it necessary to use English, and generally claim their German is inadequate for polite conversation. And it is true, that they speak German only when necessary.

The Germans in New York are industrious and good people who follow the middle ground between Dutch coarseness and the easy going way of the English. They stick to their trade, although not as bold as the English. The craftsman is hard-working and makes certain that by his unceasing industry, he accomplishes what the Englishman, who looks down on him as if his birth guaranteed his success, accomplishes by his cleverness. Nevertheless, in the present war, all are getting rich. The scarcity of hard money does not hinder trade, but does prevent the growth of trade. They are all like children who would rather have a single coin than twenty times as much in paper money. At present an unimaginable amount of money comes from England for our army, and from the army it goes to New York and Philadelphia, and these cities return it to England for more manufactured goods. And so the money circulates in the states here until it returns to its original source. And during this movement, the so-called merchants profit, as the English trade is conducted with paper money, which is to the advantage of the English.

During this month there was no difference between the winter here and ours. The ground was covered with deep snow. The rebels often disturbed us, to no serious end, in that it was often only a single boat which came over. We shod our horses with rough shoes and occasionally rode along the road to Amboy. Once we went this way with a sleigh. Ensign Stierlein was the driver and the regimental surgeon was talked into riding as a passenger. Lieutenant Wiegand and I, and several others, who rode ahead, saw the sleigh come crashing along.

A spirited, unaccustomed-to-harness steed, an inexperienced driver; soon we were riding hard, and they were trying to catch up to us, but changed their places before they overtook us. The sleigh swung around and the men found it necessary to leap clear. The horse came up to us, still attached to the shaft of the sleigh. We hurried back and met the uninjured, who were in the process of brushing snow off one another. The group continued on until we arrived at our so-called Fourteen Pence House, where the sleigh was repaired. This house is so-named because the woman there charges fourteen pence regardless of what one orders. Good "egg punch" was available here, which we called by this name as it was good for "breaking sorrow". It was made from sugar, beaten egg yolk, rum, and water, and is a good winter drink.

The women keep themselves busy during the winter primarily with spinning, and the care of the cattle is turned over to the Negroes. The cattle graze throughout the winter, let the winter be ever so bad. The cows and sheep go into the wild and fend for themselves, return in the evening of their own accord to the house, where they have a shed or merely a fenced area with some straw or corn put out for them. In the same manner, the young colts must fend for themselves during the winter, which causes them to have a coarse appearance, but later they are horses of great endurance for riding. Understandably there is no better horse to be wished for than those in America. They can be ridden over hill and dale without fear of stumbling or falling, and while they are not as large as the English, they are fast and durable. In summer they have the finest grazing land in the forest, as well as in the enclosed pasture. Pigs are raised on corn in a very small enclosure, and on this diet they grow extremely fat. Nothing has disturbed me more than that the Staten Islanders have so neglected sheep raising when every advantage is so abundantly present near their houses. Few, very few, sheep are kept and the person who has the means of grazing 400, never has more than three head. O the foolishness, of so wasting the advantage which the all-providing nature so abundantly offers. They do not know how to treasure the blessings their land has above all others, which are over-populated and where with little effort one reduces the nourishment of another. That the rich live well throughout the world is well-known. But the land is to be venerated where the poor, by hard work alone, can earn a rich reward, where there is no shortage of opportunity nor choice of means of supporting oneself, where he seldom, almost never, can be pressured or down-trodden by the rich, but can enjoy all the freedom and advantages of a gentleman, this is America. America has no shortages, only an over-abundance. It knows nothing of the concept of sub-missiveness, nor even of suppression, and therefore, it has been necessary to find means to offset the ravages of war. America was fortunate, and grew more so year to year, but the fortunes of war might change all this.

March 1778 - During this month it snowed occasionally, but on the whole, there were often very pleasant days. Our diversions were still the same. We arose at the usual time, drank coffee together, then rode into camp where we would have breakfast. After that one would read a book or maybe write a bit until lunch. Immediately after lunch, the horses would be saddled and we would take a ride. During the evening we would drink a glass of spruce beer and enjoy a pipe of tobacco while reading the English newspapers. And so the time passed pleasantly enough.

April 1778 - The days are becoming more pleasant and spring has broken out with all its beauty.

The 11th - I was called to New York to conduct religious services for the German Lutheran parish. I departed at ten o'clock and my traveling companions aboard the ship were the not-so-pleasant wives of English soldiers, and a few rangers. No people in the world love to sing more than the Americans, let it sound as it will. The whole group pressed one of the soldiers to sing a hero's tale of General Howe at the Battle of Flatbush, as several knew the soldier to have a good voice. I would have liked to have run away. If he, like a new hand aboard ship, had to learn everything new, so I had to remain there. The song was similar to the singing in Cologne about the three wise men. He received the applause of all the Americans, but I could not add mine. I arrived in New York at about two o'clock. My quarters had already been arranged at the home of Mr. Fink, who met me at dockside and invited me to his home. After a cup of coffee, my friendly host suggested a pleasure ride, with which I was agreeable. However, I thought it best to hold confession first, which I did. After church we drank a glass of wine, set ourselves in a carriage, and rode the most pleasant route that I have ever seen, to Harlem, and then returned along the North River.

When we arrived at his house, a woman of the parish was waiting for me and requested that I go visit her sick husband. I enjoyed a pleasant evening with my host and hostess and went to bed late.

The 12th - Church started at ten o'clock, and I got revenge on the Hessian chaplain for his sermon. The church attendance was exceptionally large. I had taken Adam Schmidt with me as song leader. After eating, I visited Mr. Grimm and then went for a walk with his family. And this was the occasion on which they clearly let it be known that I could have the position of preacher in their church.

The 13th - I wandered about the streets of the city and in the afternoon drank coffee with the church elder Grimm. He showed me the parish house which, if I left the regiment and became their preacher, I could occupy immediately. I excused myself, thanked them for their confidence in me, and put off a decision until after church.

The 14th - I rode again with Mr. Fink along the pleasant route to Harlem, where in the previous year we spent fourteen days in camp after the capture of Fort Washington. This region is beautified by the East River which flows by, and all the local produce can be shipped to market in the city by boat. We stopped along the way at the "kissing bridge", which gets its name because each gentleman of the city, when he crosses the bridge with a lady, always kisses his companion on the bridge.

The 15th - The people tried to get me to remain here over the holidays. I excused myself, however, as I had to preach to the regiment, and at twelve o'clock departed by the ferry boat for Staten Island. We had very little wind and our crossing went very slowly. Here on the slowly sailing boat, I reviewed all that had happened and all that I had heard in New York. It really caused me an internal struggle as to whether I should deny myself the opportunity of again seeing my native land by assuming the position of preacher offered by the German Lutheran parish. The primary factor in my decision always turned on the regiment. And in the end, it would be impossible to find as much pleasure in preaching in the city of New York as I would find in the regiment. With these thoughts in mind I arrived at Staten Island on the ferry boat. I kept all these thoughts to myself and never made them known even to my most trusted friends. I made my compliments to the colonel and reported that I had returned to duty. What a change! I had been gone barely five days, and in this time all the trees had turned green, which were not so when I departed. And in the garden a miracle was to be seen. I remained to dinner with the colonel, where there was already fresh lettuce on the table, which had not sprouted when I left. The industry of my staff comrade, Lieutenant Wiegand, had provided a garden at the ferry where we lived and asparagus was already starting to grow. The entire earth, in a few nights, turned green. Our horses now had wonderful grazing and I believe that in the period of my absence, my horse had visibly filled-out. It now became exceedingly pleasant.

The 16th - On Maundy Thursday we held church services in our camp.

The 17th - I preached from Jesus' last sermon from the cross.

The 19th - We celebrated Easter with church services.

The 20th - The unpleasant weather prevented our holding religious services.

The 21st - Now all of our thoughts were on the new campaign. Everyone wanted to see the newspaper, which often told us less than nothing.

The 22nd - We took a ride along the shore to Elizabethtown, where we had not been for a long time. During this recreation, I again forgot New York and I became even more attached to the regiment.

The 29th - The colonel went to New York and from there wrote back to Major von Horn that General Schmidt desired that I cross and hold communion for the Lutherans in his corps. The major passed the order onto me and I prepared to cross this coming Friday.

The 1st of May 1778

It was my intention to go to New York. However, the wind blew so violently and the water was so rough that no boatman would risk sailing.

The 2nd - There was still a strong wind but the boatman considered it possible and despite the terrible weather, contrary winds, and rough water, I departed at nine o'clock. While underway, the wind died down and the water became calm. However, I did not arrive until one o'clock. I immediately made a courtesy call on General Schmidt and remained there to dine. The general at once sent word to the regiments of my arrival and that confessions were to be held at five o'clock. The number of participants was exceptionally great, including General Schmidt and his two sons. I took my residence with Mr. Fink.

The 3rd - Church began at ten o'clock. General [Werner] von Mirbach sent word to me that he desired me to serve communion to him in his room. I went there at eight o'clock. For my trouble, the general paid me one guinea and invited me to eat my noon meal with him. There I met many others, including the worthy [Lieutenant] Colonel [Henrich] von Borck. I doubt it there is any place in the city where one can eat as well as by General von Mirbach. It was not required of anyone to drink, but for those who wished to do so, there was enough to please everyone. After dining, tobacco and coffee were set out. During the afternoon I took a walk along the East River where the ships are repaired. Here I saw an anchor that weighed 300 weight, and a chain which was stretched across the Hudson River near Kings Ferry to prevent ships sailing up the river. This was surprisingly heavy. On each link there was an iron barb.

The 4th - I dined at noon with General Schmidt, drank afternoon coffee with Mr. Grimm, and spent a pleasant afternoon in the company of his family. I had already been invited, together with Chaplain Hausknecht, to lunch with Mr. Grimm tomorrow, as well as with General Schmidt, and although the idea of eating with the general pleased me, I would rather spend the afternoon with Mr. Grimm and his family.

The 5th - At eight o'clock I went to the general and made my apologies for not accepting the honor of dining with him, as there was a ship waiting and a good wind blowing to take me back to Staten

Island. This was only an excuse and I remained here the whole day with Mr. Grimm.

The 6th - I departed at eleven o'clock and because the wind was weak, the ferry did not arrive at Staten Island until three o'clock. When I departed New York the Regimental Quartermaster Ludwig told me that General Howe had been recalled and that General Clinton would take command of the army. A frigate which arrived yesterday evening from London had brought the news.

On this trip, as I was alone on the ship and could not converse with anyone, I tried to recall what had transpired during my stay in New York. First, I recalled the surprisingly rich fish market. Everyday more than fifty fish boats go out, which return in the evening fully loaded. This is the primary means of earning a living for those persons who are not land owners. People who have nothing for capital, who do not have enough to acquire a fish net nor a little boat, make a canoe for themselves from an oak log or cut out a nut tree, and using that, fish along the shore from Bergen and Long and Staten Islands. They earn a reasonably good income, which I believe amounts to about two dollars, that is four guilder, each day. In the fish markets of New York can be seen most clearly how rich in all species of fish the surrounding waters are. The least valuable sort is used to provision the army, which buys them at a rock bottom price. This is a specie of fish that when fresh is not good to eat. However, they are, like herring, which they most nearly resemble, salted, and then they are a delicacy which I prefer above all other fish. They are most valued in winter when few fish are caught. In New York I have always had them for breakfast, and seen them by the thousands being salted down, before every door. Fish at this time of year is the usual ration. Of all the nations of the world, America is so accustomed to fish, that in the morning, when he drinks tea, the American must also have baked fish available.

It is also the case, that the American can make no less expensive meal than one including fish, which he can buy so cheaply that is hard to imagine. America is a wonderful land, where the industrious hand of the worker never goes unrewarded, and those who work need never want. The boats, which the farmers use to catch fish during the summer, are used in winter for another purpose. The farmer has a woods not far behind his house. Before the door he loads his boat with wood and, with very little effort, sails to New York, where he sells his wood for a good price. On the other hand, a man in Germany must work very hard just to earn enough to cover his labor, as he must then send the wood to market. So two men with their own boat earn the same profit as is earned by us using a four-wheeled wagon, and instead of needing eight men working 24 hours, here it requires only two men working four hours, and I am sure there is still a difference in the amount of production, and the greater profit goes to the American. No land in the world is better situated for conducting trade than America, and there is no country in which I would rather travel than in America. Of course, I mean during peacetime. During a war, travel is more difficult throughout the world than during peacetime.

Between all the most important places, a person can travel either by land or water. From Charleston to Philadelphia, Philadelphia to New York, from here to Boston, to Halifax, to Quebec, all these trips can be made, on land or on water, as I may choose.

The 10th - After church we rode, those of us who had or could rent a horse, to a horse race, which is a common event during this month all through America. At these events, one can truly get to know the Americans, who even surpass the English in the love of gambling. The Americans, from their youth on, participate in vigorous body exercises, and when nothing else is to be done, they hit a ball. Therefore, it comes as no surprise to see an old man playing ball with young people. This activity would be considered beneath the dignity of the old man in Germany. The Sunday recreation of the young people consists of riding and other pleasures. And the ladies join in as readily as the men. We go in gigs, ride like hussars, and go as fast as we possibly can. And I would never give an American woman a handicap in a horse race.

We rode ten miles from our camp to where the races were held. Here most of the residents of the area were to be seen, all on horseback, and there was no horse of reasonable quality from the whole island that was not there. Even the cream of the black society was in attendance, with the permission of their mistresses, and so made up that when first seen from the rear, they appeared to deserve a compliment from every gentleman. Accompanied by their gallants, who were clad in the discarded clothing of their masters and their masters' sons, they held a ball which was worth seeing, if only for the music. A Negro scratched on a violin which had only one string.

However, this is not only the music of the slaves, but even the white gentlemen enjoy this violin. No nation is the world loves music more than the American, but no nation in the world loves it with less taste than this one.

Now to return to horse racing. Both horses in the race are decked out with all sorts of decorations and paraded back and forth to get the audience worked up and ready to bet. Hardly had this occurred for the first time, when twenty were ready to put down a wager, the one on this horse, the other on the second horse, and shook hands to seal the deal. Others were explaining the entire blood line of each horse and checking to see if they really were of English stock. One praised the virtues of this horse, which the other failed to appreciate because the first one praised it, and that was enough ground for a wager. Two others heard the bet of these two and wagered as to which of the two would win. And they're off! Everyone is watching. The riders barely reach the mid-point before one horse falls back a stride. Now many long faces were to be seen. Both could not win a race. And the horse that was beaten was no longer of any value, even though it was much more beautiful than the other. When this was finished, all the other betting on races began. One says, "My horse can beat your horse. Come, one, two, yes, ten dollars!" They jump on their horses and race to settle the bet. It is easy, and often happens, that someone breaks his neck. We rode back to our camp at four o'clock.

The 18th of June 1778 - A fleet arrived from Philadelphia. Troops could be seen on board, which strengthened our belief that the army in Philadelphia was being withdrawn and that all Pennsylvania would be evacuated.

The 19th - We were cheered up with letters from Waldeck which were the more welcome as we had not received mail from home for four months. These letters had come to Philadelphia first and came here with yesterday's fleet.

The 20th - We exchanged news of home with one another.

The 21st - At seven o'clock we had church in camp. I climbed aboard my nag and rode to the Flagstaff where our grenadiers were stationed and conducted church services there at ten o'clock. I spent the rest of the day there enjoying myself. It is possible to look thirty miles out to sea from here, to watch the continuous in and out movement of large and small ships, to view the beautiful Long Island opposite, and the fertile valleys of Jersey behind the point, to see the great New York, the Hudson River, and all the things which keep the eye fully occupied. I returned to camp late, through a thick and lonely, heavily planted, but level woods, which extended as far as Cole's Ferry. Not only the pleasant and strong aroma of white clover, which covered all the earth like snow in winter, but also the flickering of many millions of glow worms, which are much brighter and larger than ours, made this way very pleasant for me. It was to me as if one were traveling through the heavens and saw about himself all the stars in motion. And this enjoyment makes a hungry attack of the innumerable mosquitoes nearly unnoticeable.

The 21st [sic] - The weather was more cool than warm. We received the general order that no one was to leave the camp because a visit from the enemy was expected.

The 22nd - The rebels are concentrating in our area and a part of our army began to march out of Pennsylvania, through the Jerseys.

The 23rd - Each month brings its own special type of fish on the coast. I watched a fish catch where sea carp of thirty pounds, sea crabs, and sea spiders were caught in a net. The spiders have a shape like those on land except they are a hundred times larger. We usually have fish for our evening meal.

The 24th - An eclipse of the sun which lasted from eight until eleven o'clock and caused a considerable darkness.[2]

The 25th - A boatload of rebels landed during the previous night but did no damage other than wounding a few men.

The 26th - The order of the 21st was canceled today.

The 27th - A violent storm directly over New York. It is a very beautiful sight when the water is calm and the lightning flashes are simply doubled by the reflection.

The 28th - At seven o'clock we held church in camp. Another fleet arrived from Philadelphia. Now all our ships have been removed from Philadelphia and the Delaware, and the entire army is on the march to New York. Amidst a group of others, I was at the Flagstaff where we saw a whole fleet sail in beneath us, as from the Kohlen Hardt.[3] When we returned to camp we found the order for the regiment and all the troops on the island to be prepared to march on a moment's notice.

The 29th - The army is still in the Jerseys, where, during the night, we heard heavy firing.

The 30th - A packet boat arrived from England. There was an alarm this evening. A heavy fire was heard in Jersey, both cannons and small arms. Our regiment was put under arms and remained on the alert all night long. The artillery drove past on the way to Elizabeth Point.

The 1st of July 1778

The heat is much greater this year than last year in 1777 and the mosquitoes have never been more unbearable than during these hot days. The inhabitants light fires on all sides of their houses and smoke in their bedrooms in order to drive these insects away with smoke, but nothing can drive them completely away. They are ever present in the tents and a person can go wherever he pleases, but nowhere can he escape their attack. I saw a cow come running today which surely had as many mosquitoes sitting on it as it had horn. And on several places they were as thick as bees swarming about a hive at swarming time. There were so many in the swarm that no more could light. They completely covered the animal. The cow ran into the water until completely submerged and some were surely drowned. The others continued to swarm over the water, like bees, as if only waiting until the cow would again leave the water. It is worth noting that the wind blows these last guests to us. The few storms which we have had this year have generally come from the Jerseys on strong winds, and with them come the mosquitoes, thick as sand on the beach. They are, when grown, so light that they are blown like dust on the wind. When they have settled for only a half minute, they have already sucked themselves so thick with blood that they swell up as heavy and as large as a barley corn.

The 2nd - A light breeze offset the heat. Our grenadiers, who are stationed two hours from here at the Flagstaff, complain about the clouds of mosquitoes even more than we do. During the last three nights, they have not been able to close their eyes, and have burned everything which the sea has cast up in order to make smoke. It is possible to tell which of the men are good soldiers, as their hands and face are swollen.

The 3rd - Now misery sets in. Our supply of meal and bread is exhausted. The fleet from England is eagerly awaited, and further, we have nothing except what comes from England. The army receives a small portion of rice instead of bread. The rebel army on the other hand has an over-abundance of all foodstuffs, while we have a shortage.

The 4th - Our army still stands in Jersey and the fleet of 200 ships lies off shore at Amboy. Today we had the pleasure once again to have Lieutenant Heldring back in camp after having been a prisoners of war, and Captain von Haacke and the remaining prisoners are expected any day.

The 5th - At seven o'clock we had church in camp. At noon another fleet arrived. At the present time we are still as much in doubt as to what will be undertaken during this campaign as we were in the previous year of 1777. Some even believe the army will be sent back to Europe. Others have suggested another plan. In short, things appear more confused than at any previous time.

The 6th - The entire army boarded ships at Amboy. I rode as quickly as possible to the Flagstaff in order to see such a spectacular fleet sail by. This is a place comparable to looking down on the Eder from Waldeck Castle. There were over 300 ships, including the admiral's ship, the *Eagle*, of 64 guns, on which Lord Howe sailed, and which looked very good.

The 7th - An exceptionally active and disruptive day. Nine English regiments came to Staten Island and set up their camp as neighbors to us, both to the right and to the left, and thus vastly strengthened the army on Staten Island.

The 8th - I see the provisions ships with casks of flour arriving, and wish that the poor soldiers will once again receive bread.

The 9th - Admiral Howe again sailed out of port with a great number of warships, perhaps to engage the French fleet, which is generally reported to have already arrived on the coast of America.

The 10th - More warships departed and it is high time, as the French fleet is no longer only a dream, but has actually entered the Delaware. Lord Howe took all the volunteers from the merchant ships aboard the warships and sailed out to sea.

The 11th - An especially violent storm. The lightning struck an outpost close behind our camp. The cartridge pouches of the soldiers were only full of powder, however.

The 12th - At seven o'clock we held church in camp, to which many Germans came because of the so-called tailor's draft for the English regiments.[4] This afternoon Captain von Haacke returned from captivity.

The 13th - For a long time we have had our fun at the expense of the French fleet. But it is not funny any longer. Lieutenant Brumhard came from the Flagstaff as we were gathered around our horses and assured us that the large fleet which could be seen lying near Sandy Hook was really a French fleet of ten ships-of-the-line and as many frigates. Everyone who had a horse was curious and rode to the Flagstaff. From there we saw them lying in the most beautiful order and every ship showed the white French flag. The admiral's ship was called the *Languedoc* and the admiral was [Jean Baptiste Charles Henri Hector] Count D'Estaing. The *Languedoc* was a ship of 90 guns and the others had 80, 70, 74, or 64 cannons. Our admiral, the experienced and famous Lord Howe, lay with his fleet in sight of the French and we daily expected a naval battle between the two fleets, which we would be able to watch in comfort from our camp. Lord Howe sent a frigate to sea in sight of the French fleet. The frigate sailed with a full wind and full sails directly past the enemy fleet. Never in my life have I seen a ship sail so that hardly a cannon could be fired at the frigate before it sailed past like the wind. It was sent to Rhode Island and along the coast to warn our ships that an unexpected guest had arrived on the coast. It was an exceptionally clever trick as well by Lord Howe, as also by General Clinton, that they had gotten the fleet and the army away from Philadelphia. It had apparently been the plan of the French admiral, Count D'Estaing , to lie at the mouth of the Delaware and to blockade the entire fleet which lay in the river before Philadelphia. Then Washington would have pressed forward with his entire force and encircled the army at Philadelphia.

But even if Lord Howe had remained lying in the Delaware, it would have also been possible for D'Estaing to have entered the harbor at New York. In short, it was a terrible situation which had no sooner arisen that it was over. Both the army and the fleet were at Philadelphia when the plan proposed by D'Estaing had been drawn up. But England should not sink so low. It was already an unheard of insult that a French fleet should sit in the face of Lord Howe, admiral of the seapower whose flag floated in triumph over all the waters of the world, and whose fleets covered the oceans. I was at the height by the Flagstaff just when many Englanders were gathered, sputtering and cussing. I believe no bitterness between nations can be more deep-rooted than that of the English toward the French. Every young seaman volunteered to serve on the warships to fight against the French. At this time, a merchant ship, which had no fear of encountering an enemy fleet here at New York, the most important port on the American continent, came from the ocean. A French frigate broke from the fleet and, to be sure of capturing the ship raised an English flag instead of the French one. The ship drew nearer, the frigate fired a cannon, lowered the English flag and raised the French one. The ship was captured, as were eleven others, in a few days.

The 14th - At the present we are not in the best situation. It would have been much worse, however, if the French trick had succeeded. The harbor of New York is blockaded so that no ship can get in or out. A French ship-of-the-line lies in the East River and the entire fleet is at Sandy Hook. On the land side we are so completely closed in that we can not possibly be pressed more closely together. General Washington has spread his army out so beautifully that from here on the height we can see some of his positions. From Elizabethtown to Newark,[5] to Second River, Hackensack, Aquakenunk, etc. Only the water separates us from Washington's army.

The 15th - We read in the newspapers that the rebels recently celebrated the anniversary of their independence at Princeton. The cannons which were fired during this celebration could be heard clearly in our camp. The toasts raised on this occasion were the following:

1. The Congress
2. The free and independent states of America
3. General Washington
4. The American army and navy
5. Our independence, may it last as long as the sun shines and the rivers flow
6. His Most Christian Majesty, the courageous defender of our rights
7. May the united and pledged together states of America always be brave with the love of country through which they were created

8. Our envoys at the court at Versailles

9. The state of New Jersey

10. Our honorable and patriotic militia

11. All our officers and soldiers who fought in the recent battle at Monmouth where we gained a complete victory over our enemies

12. The remembrance of all our heroes who have fallen in the defense of American liberty during the war

13. May our example awaken all downtrodden in all parts of the world to cast off the day of tyranny

The 16th - 17th - Fair and not especially warm weather, much as in Germany.

The 18th - Finally, a general exchange of prisoners has occurred. We received 39 men back to the regiment from captivity.

The 20th - We have been curious as to what would take place between the two fleets which lie undisturbed beside one another, watching each others every move. Lord Howe had certainly attacked if he had only one ship which could challenge the *Languedoc*. We do not have a single ship on the coast with more than 64 guns. On the other hand, the French have many ships of 70, 80, 90, or even 100 cannons. Nothing in the world is to be more wished for than that Admiral [John] Byron, who is expected daily with his fleet, would arrive, as then we would have relief on the ocean. He has 80 and 90 gun ships in his fleet and will be able to engage the French. It appears Lord Howe is awaiting the arrival of this fleet.

The 21st - Washington is very busy transferring his army across the Hudson River near Kings Ferry, and his outposts are not far from Kingsbridge. It appears that his intention is to capture New York. If this transpires, he will lose many men, but for us, it will be the end. If the French fleet strikes the harbor at the same time that Washington attacks on land, it is to be feared that it will be a classic siege, and will starve us out. At present the rumor is that Byron's fleet has been scattered by a storm and several badly damaged ships have arrived at Halifax. It looks bad for our army just now.

The 22nd - The Americans are so delighted with the French fleet that they have sent Admiral D'Estaing 100 fat oxen by way of South Amboy, which oxen are to be divided among the ships.

The 23rd - At the moment, we have no sick in the regimental hospital and despite the shortage of provisions, we are completely healthy.

The 24th - Now the French envoy to Philadelphia has arrived and been received with every possible honor.

The 25th - At daybreak the French fleet was no longer to be seen. Until now the first object checked by our camp every morning, it disappeared as if blown away. It was a measure of the cleverness of Lord Howe, that he sent several good sailing frigates after them to observe, because if he had followed with the whole fleet, it would have been possible for D'Estaing to take a different course and to enter New York. The regiment was mustered and the muster master was much surprised at the regimental strength. I wrote a letter to Waldeck which our commissary took, as no packet was departing.

The 26th - At seven o'clock, church in camp.

The 27th - Captain Pentzel and his company relieved the grenadiers at the Flagstaff.

The 28th - One storm after another, and at the same time, very warm. Toward evening a packet boat came from England, which would not have been able to enter the harbor if D'Estaing were still lying off Sandy Hook.

The 29th - General [James] Grant assumed command here on the island. A ship arrived from Cork with 2,200 casks of salted meat. This enables one to see how much can be loaded on a single ship. This too, would have been a good prize for the French.

The 30th - I visited Captain Pentzel at the Flagstaff where we watched three large ships enter from the sea and wished that they might be the first ships of Byron's fleet.

The 31st - The mosquitoes seem fewer since we have had storms every day.

> Ph. Waldeck
> Chaplain of the Prince of
> Waldeck's 3rd Regiment

Continuation
of the diary beginning August 1778

Ph. Waldeck
Field Chaplain in the Prince of Waldeck's
3rd Regiment
then in the service of Great Britain in America

Eighteenth Century America

August 1778

From this point on, I have sent my copy back to Waldeck with Major von Horn, who was returning home. However, as we went aboard ship and sailed for West Florida, the furthest and most noteworthy part of America, the wide distance from New York has prevented my receiving an answer to these letters.

The 1st - As is customary in the whole world, the heat here increases day by day.

The 2nd - At seven o'clock, church in camp. I had the honor, together with Lieutenant Heldring, to dine with the colonel. The lieutenant entertained us with interesting tales of captivity. Among others, he told of the wonderful organization of the Herrnhuters at Bethlehem, which certainly merited our close attention. For rearing their children, especially those who have only limited means, they set up the most beautiful establishment. They built the most beautiful building, at a common cost, which is dedicated to the education of their children. As soon as a child has attained an age where he is able to profit from instruction, he is brought to this house and delivered to the care of a person selected for this task. If a boy, he is placed in the wing of the building where the males will be raised. Here he is placed under a man who never lets him out of his sight, and who is attentive to his demeanor, his destiny, and his complete conduct. This man gives the boy, according to the ability of his age, instruction in religion, reading, and writing. His parents have no need to spend the least amount on him. But he must work to earn his support. In whatever field he has an interest, in this house, he will find a master to teach him. What this group of children, boys, and young men, earns goes into a common fund which is applied to their total support. The adults, who earn more, must help support the smaller ones. There is no craft which is not accomplished here with the greatest skill. Woolen goods, silk, cotton, stocking makers, cabinet makers, sculptors, painters, artists, in short, all types of men are among them. Everyone buys with pleasure from their shops, because they sell the best made wares at the very best prices.

The raising of young girls is equally interesting. They occupy the other wing of the building and are under the care of an especially selected woman. All is activity, all is work, each one instructs and encourages the others to do their best. These young girls knit, sew, stitch with gold and silver, make silk cloth; the most beautiful and artistic seamstresses. Is it possible to find among these human seedlings a single one so spoiled that he or she would not strive to quickly learn? God bless you, you hard-working Herrnhuters, also you, you peace-loving, quiet Quakers. You are useful members of society. Through you, Pennsylvania is beginning to bloom, and you will be the ones, who will bring it to ultimate maturity, by industry, by truth in dealing with others, by thrift and tolerance, and with the protection of God, whom you also love. God will not permit these peaceful, affable citizens to be disturbed in their homes by this war.

After their evening devotions, they retire in a long well-ventilated hall, where the little ones sleep two by two and the larger ones each have a separate bed. Draperies of silk and linen, and although their dress is very simple, one sees in their homes furniture of great beauty.

The supervisor sleeps before the door. And from this house the girls marry and receive, according to their needs, their dowry.

Who is not pleased with this method of raising children? Does it not fit human nature perfectly? Is it not a move to the elimination of all slavish methods of raising children from our human society?

The 3rd - An exceptionally strong storm with hail. During the night fire broke out in New York. The fire began in a storehouse where items were made for the ships. It is assumed the fire was set by someone sympathetic to the rebels. And this disgruntled person will not rest until all New York lies in rubble. We heard that 100 houses were already lying in ashes, and the fire still has not been extinguished. We were very concerned about our baggage house, because everyone who wanted to protect his belongings, had sent them there.

The 4th of August 1778 - One misfortune after the other seems to be piling up on New York. A terrible storm gathered over the city today and from here we saw the lightning flash. During the afternoon several ships arrived, by which we were informed that the lightning had struck a warship, a sloop laden with 248 tons of powder. Although many ships were in the area, the accident had primarily damaged the houses which were near the harbor. It did not leave a single window unbroken. The damage is reportedly very great. A heavy timber from the ship flew as far as the statue of Lord Chatham, which I know for a fact, stands in the middle of the city.

The rebels will certainly consider these quickly following, one after the other, disasters to be comforting signs that heaven and all the elements are opposed to the King's army. We again had the pleasure of reading letters today from our homeland, which still have not solved the puzzle of where our long awaited recruits are, but only report that they have been gone from home for a long time.

The 5th of August 1778 - Very hot.

The 6th - Seven of our prisoners of war returned to the regiment today.

The 7th - As we thought, M. D'Estaing has sailed to Rhode Island.

The 8th - Exceptionally warm with an afternoon storm.

The 9th - At seven o'clock, church, and then followed one storm after the other until ten o'clock at night.

The 10th - A bit cooler.

The 11th - Lord Howe has also sailed to Rhode Island.

The 12th - A very strong windstorm.

The 13th - Fog and rain.

The 14th - Very stormy. The ferry boat could not run.

The 15th - We have been rather anxious to hear news from Rhode Island, what the French admiral intended to do, and if he had made contact with Lord Howe. Today we learned the following, which can no longer be doubted:

The admiral promised the rebels upon his word of honor as Frenchman, that he would silence the British batteries with his ships' cannons in 25 minutes. He asked General Sir Robert Pigot, who commanded that island, if he would surrender to the United States and the French admiral. Sir Robert Pigot immediately replied to this question from the mouth of his artillery. And after a two-hour cannonade, the French fleet was forced to depart the harbor as quickly as possible. The admiral's ship, the *Languedoc*, was heavily damaged. Toward evening all the ships put to sea. General Pigot immediately dispatched an express boat to Lord Howe, who was already under sail with his fleet to engage M. D'Estaing at Rhode Island. Therefore, Lord Howe turned out to sea in as much as his support was no longer needed at Rhode Island. A heavy cannonade had been heard, also, as our warship *Isis* was engaged with a French ship. A heavy pall of smoke had been seen to rise, which darkened the entire sky above the ocean for a long time, from which it was assumed that one or the other of the ships had blown up. We hope that it is from D'Estaing's rather than Howe's fleet.

The 16th of August 1778 - Communion service was held, but as it rained very hard, it could not be held in camp. Instead, we used a barn not far from camp, in which our hospital was also located.

The 17th - The mosquitoes, which had withdrawn somewhat as a result of the rains, returned and brought with them another insect which had been unknown to us previously, and which was most evident where candles were used.

The 18th - Lord Howe returned and lay at anchor off Sandy Hook. The especially thick fog, which persisted during the entire previous week, has been an advantage to the French fleet, which, as expected, sailed to Boston to make necessary repairs.

The 19th - A packet boat came in six weeks from Falmouth. The news which it brought caused everyone to be gloomy, and there is not an Englishman who did not exclaim his sincere God damn about the present circumstances. We have been waiting for reinforcements for three months already, and our situation becomes more desperate with each passing day, as the army must be reinforced to maintain its present posts and before anything can be undertaken. It even appears nothing will be done this campaign. The English navy can claim to rule all the oceans and her flag may wave over all the waters of the world, but the great naval hero, Lord Howe, must sit idly by and watch England's arch enemy sailing along the coast of America, and know that he can do nothing to prevent it, as the post at Sandy Hook is the key to the harbor of New York and must be protected. Admiral Byron with additional naval strength has been expected since early June and is to be followed by Admiral [Augustus] Keppel. The army awaits some sign of activity from the fleet. We openly speak of the joy we anticipate when, under the roar of our cannons, the French fleet is engaged, captured, destroyed, or driven aground. O vanity of joy, the packet boat has brought news that Byron's fleet was scattered by a storm and unable to regroup.

And that Admiral Keppel lies at anchor off St. Helens, while we fear the Brest fleet will also appear on the American coast.

The 20th - Surprisingly hot and a very strong thunder storm, which failed, however, to break the heat. Even though it is so hot during this month, and seldom rains, the farmer has no need to fear that the heat and drought will be disadvantageous to his meadows and other crops. There is such an unusually heavy dew at night, that even when the day is ever so warm, the next morning all stands fresh and grows as well as if nourished daily by the most invigorating rain. The farmers know examples of times when there was no rain for a month, but of crop failure and unfruitful years, they can not remember a single instance. The fruit trees bear every year, some years more than others, but no year do they fail to produce an abundant yield. I am surprised by the fields which I saw being plowed and made ready for planting, and now see covered with the richest produce ready for harvest. The slaves till the land and till it so badly, three times worse than the farmers by us. It is immaterial to them if the rows are one or two feet apart when planted, or if the seed is scattered on the ground or covered over. If there is a stone in the way, they plow around it to one side. As wild swine would tend the land, so the blacks tend it, and so it is planted, grows, and produces the most wonderful fruit. Many have planted their farm with fruit trees, but the crops grow as well under the trees as if there were no shadows there. Indian corn, or Turkish wheat, grows better than all other crops. The Germans in Pennsylvania reportedly are more industrious in working their farms, and in general, one can see the results of their exertions in their fields. The plows, harrows, wagons, and all other farm implements are made according to the usual German practices. They have stalls for their stock in winter, wherein they are fed and cared for. Especially Germantown is said to be a place worth seeing. Every house stands widely separated from the others, and behind every house is a barn, stalls, and a garden. The Americans leave their stock outside winter and summer. The German farms are above all noted for being well-tended, and a traveler has no need to ask whose farm it is. It is especially easy to tell the difference from the farms of the Irish. These are lazy and inept about the house, and are satisfied to live by trade rather than to engage in any manual labor. Anyone who settles in Pennsylvania and wants to work, receives a good return for his effort, and soon a surplus. Staten Island can not be compared to Pennsylvania, Maryland, and other provinces, and yet if it rewards the lazy farmer so richly, how much more must the other provinces do that.

The 21st of August 1778 - A soldier on detail at the Flagstaff, who would bathe in the sea, drowned.[1]

The 22nd - The detail at the Flagstaff was relieved by Captain Alberti, and a soldier named [Valentin] Stein died of the heat.

The 25th - It is as hot here as it is said to be in the West Indies, because the sea breezes temper the heat there.

The 26th - A bundle of letters was sent to Waldeck.

The 27th - A ship from the Cork provisions fleet, which we have impatiently awaited for so long, finally arrived.

The 28th - We have been assured that Admiral Byron, with eight ships-of-the-line, has arrived in American waters. Lord Howe again sailed to Rhode Island, where the French fleet has also gone again.

The 29th - Foggy with very cold wind. Nineteen thousand rebels have landed on Rhode Island and begun building strong points in order to place it under siege. The generals commanding are Sullivan, [the Marquis de] Lafayette, and Hancock. General Clinton has embarked 2,000 men who have departed today with a favorable wind.

The 30th - At seven o'clock, church. Two warships entered the harbor.

The 31st - Rather cool.

September 1778

The 1st - Admiral Byron has arrived. Three ships of 74 cannons, of his fleet, came in.

The 2nd - Another warship.

The 3rd - The entire fleet is lying just behind our camp. The sick, of whom there are a great many, were brought on land and placed in hospital tents behind our camp. On many ships, 300 men were sick. During the previous war, England lost 80,000 sailors and the present war will coast as many more.

The 4th - Cool weather.

The 5th - Now there is an impressive sea power in American waters. Lord Howe has 71 warships under his command, not counting the many armed merchant ships.

The 6th - Again we are conducting church services at ten o'clock after parade. Seventeen transport ships came in and just as we have had little hope of our recruits arriving previously, we now feel sure they are on these ships.

The 7th - Our yesterday's hopes concerning our recruits have been fulfilled.[2] Captain Sebisch sent a corporal to inform the colonel that he has arrived at New York.

The 8th of September 1778 - (Among the recruits landed on Staten Island) - They have had a long sea voyage, and most of them have had to be brought to our regimental hospital where they can be better cared for than in camp. I had the pleasure of receiving many letters, of which some had lain in a damp place on the ship and become so damaged that they were illegible. The ladies of Thalitter were so kind as to send me a tobacco pouch, which had partially rotted. Each one had sewn her precious name into the pouch.

The 9th - It rained all day today.

The 10th - Lord Howe returned and D'Estaing has entered the harbor at Boston. The admiral sailed in with his ship *Eagle* and was saluted with many cannon shots, which he returned with thirteen from the *Eagle*.

> To this point the notes were sent home with Major von Horn, but if they have arrived, we are still uncertain.[3]

The 12th - Was the anniversary of the King's coronation, and at one o'clock every ship of the fleet, of which fourteen lay behind our camp, not counting those at New York, fired a 21-gun salute, with the same number being fired by all the batteries at New York. This crashed as if heaven and earth were torn asunder.

> From this point on the notes were sent to Waldeck from Pensacola. They consisted of eleven sheets which contained the whole voyage to West Florida and a description of Jamaica. Captain Ferguson took this package with him as he was about to sail to England -- also in this package I wrote letters to the honorable court chaplain, the court secretary Frensdorf, to Bringhausen, a number to Thalitter, and four letters to the pastor at Enso.

The 23rd of September 1778 - General von Knyphausen is marching against White Plains.

The 24th - The British grenadiers and light infantry were ferried across the Hudson River.

The 25th - Those troops set up their camp at Hackensack in New Jersey and immediately began to fortify it.

The 26th - A small fleet of single-masted boats and galleys with eight cannons sailed past here and into Newark Bay, and from there, entered the Hackensack River.

The 27th - At ten o'clock, church. Everything was in confusion and the regiment was commanded to be ready to march at a moment's notice. Our beloved General Vaughan was now in command on the island. And this imminent march into the Jerseys was our most longed-for wish. The colonel told me after church that only a part of the regiment would depart, and that I should remain here until the second division marched.

The 28th - We were all still full of hope and expected to break camp at any time. An adjutant general officer came from Jersey in a rowboat manned by eight sailors and hurriedly passed by. Adjutant Stierlein asked him for news, but he did not bother to answer but at once mounted a horse and rode off to the general. At the moment, two English regiments are to march to Elizabethtown, and Admiral [Peter] Parker sent two boats from the warships, also, and all the preparations were made to transport the soldiers. We mounted our horses and rode there. We saw the enemy was advancing on the other side. We were at a distance of a cannon shot from them, and the pressure on their batteries at that point, where they were also sending reinforcements, continued well into the night. On our side, no effort was made to send the other troops across, and the regiments marched back. It appears the intention was to make a diversion before them, so that they would have had to pull troops away from Hackensack. On our return, we met a regiment and the light dragoons, who were saddled and massed as if there were still something in contemplation for tonight.

The 29th - During the previous night there was a heavy fire from the Jersey shore on our sloops which sailed in the Hackensack River.

The 30th - Two three-masted ships with cannons sailed past and lay in Newark Bay, in order to shell the Jersey shore, so that our sloops could retire unhindered from the Hackensack River.

October 1778

The 1st - The army withdrew from the English Neighborhood in New Jersey. This first affair was to our advantage. Several regiments, during the night, were ordered to attack 700 rebels who were in the region of Hackensack. Several deserters brought word, however, that the enemy had already retreated without waiting to be attacked. The 2nd Battalion of Light Infantry, the 72nd [Regiment], and the Queen's Rangers crossed the Hudson at Dobb's Ferry. That force met the 3rd Virginia Dragoon Regiment, which is known by the name of Washington's Guard and consists of men of good family with beautiful horses. Our troops attacked with bayonets and slaughtered all of them so that only three were able to save themselves by flight. The number of dead is unknown, but must be great, as our men gave no quarter and took only fifty prisoners, who were for the most part wounded.

Colonel [George] Baylor, who commanded, was severely wounded and captured. He wrote, among other comments, the following to Washington, "Nothing in the world hurts me more that the necessity to report to you, that your entire regiment has been slaughtered and taken prisoner." All the captured horses, 300 horned animals, and a great number of sheep were driven past here on their way to New York.

The 2nd of October 1778 - Our hopes of invading New Jersey now appear impossible.

The 3rd - Our army did not remain in New Jersey but was withdrawn to New York and assigned its previous positions.

The 4th - 10th - There is talk of all sorts of plans, and it will be difficult to keep us here.

The 11th - Because of stormy, rainy weather, church could not be held.

The 12th - We received orders to be ready to board ship.

The 13th - A detail was dispatched to bring all the regimental baggage from New York to the ships.

The 14th - Several Hessian regiments, which were known to be sailing to Halifax, were embarked.

The 15th - We were supposed to embark today but there were no ships available.

The 16th - Our baggage was put aboard ship today. The army received orders to go aboard ship.

The 17th - We finished preparations for our departure and sold our horses. I received five guineas for mine.

The 18th - It was another nice day. We held church in camp at seven o'clock and this is probably the last time for it to be held on Staten Island. During the service, we saw our ships approaching from New York. I dined with the colonel, during which time the captain of the ship *Springfield*, on which the colonel will embark, entered.

The 19th - Regimental baggage was put aboard ship.

The 20th - Today is the second anniversary of our arrival, and nearly on the same spot, we again board ship to leave this part of America. By eleven o'clock the entire regiment was aboard ship.[4] I knew that we would not sail today and therefore remained on land until toward evening.

The 21st - As we were hoping to depart, we took on provisions for another 25 days, as we had on board only enough for two months. Ensign Hohmann went for a walk on land.

The 23rd - Our destination remains uncertain, although it is reported to be Pensacola. We had the pleasure of receiving letters sent out in June and we know it will be a long time before we get any more.

The 25th - Held church aboard *Springfield*, where I remained all day.

The 26th - Several more transport ships arrived which are to sail with out fleet.

The 27th - Two warships also arrived.

The 28th - A beautiful, warm day. A regiment of Hessians occupied our camp. General Campbell requested a detail for his baggage, and it was sent from the *Springfield* by the colonel.

The 29th - As we still lay at anchor, we took another walk on shore. We will not set foot on land again for a long time.

The 30th - Now everything was ready for our departure and boats were no longer permitted to go ashore.

The 31st - The wind was favorable, the warships made the signal, and we set sail. One after another the entire fleet followed. Our negligent captain had not returned from New York. Nevertheless, we had to leave and immediately collided with another ship, so that we had to cut the ladder on the aftermast. While this was in progress, the captain arrived. The entire fleet dropped anchor near Sandy Hook.

The sea was so stormy and the movement of the ships so great that nearly everyone was seasick.[5]

November 1778

The 1st - Frightfully unpleasant, stormy weather. In the winter months when the storms and waves keep the sea in constant motion, a trip for me is unpleasant from the very beginning. The waves were as high as the ship and we feared we might break loose from our anchors, of which we had put three out. At night there was even less rest than during the day. No one could close his eyes because when he lay down in bed, he could hardly keep from falling out. Our bags, equipment, and everything that was breakable, broke during the night. There was such a clatter in the cupboards in the cabin that it seemed nothing could remain in one piece. Truly, I would rather participate in a land campaign in Germany during the winter, with all the resulting unpleasantness, than undertake a sea voyage in these winter months. No one can give a correct description of such an event. If I lie down under a tree, exhausted by wind and rain, the earth will at least remain steady under me and let me enjoy my rest, even though the wind howls and the rain beats down on me in torrents. But on the sea, the ship groans as if about to break in pieces. The waves throw it about from one side to the other, so that a man does not have enough hands with which to hang on. If a person, who has not learned patience, goes to sea, he will learn it, whether or not he wants to.

The 2nd - It was very cold. The wind eased somewhat, so that by evening a person could again go on deck. As an aid to our recovery, Captain Pentzel provided a warm punch.

The 3rd - At seven o'clock in the morning we raised anchor. The wind was favorable for our sailing toward the West Indies. It was not overly strong, and this great fleet, with its many warships, represented a wonderful sight. We hoped this wind would continue until we reached our destination. The captain, who understood the wind well, told us however, that by this afternoon the winds would be so strong that we would not be able to go on deck.

The 4th - A frightful night. The sea was very rough. The waves rolled crosswise over the ship. The ship lay nearly constantly on its side.

The 5th - We lay in our beds because no one could stay on his feet outside. Captain Pentzel was completely well and the young Mueller, also.[6]

The 6th - Everything upset me. I could not stand the smell of coffee and it was work just to pour it. It is easier to pour a cup of coffee and drink it while riding a horse at full gallop, than here. The ship's captain gave us a keg of the best port wine that can be found. I made my breakfast on a glass of this good wine and a piece of ship's bread. At noon, while the sea was stormy, I drank nothing else, and during the evening I would again drink two or three glasses. Young Mueller suggested this comforting practice to me. Above all the good man served me well in as much as he was in good health and I was sick. My man Volcke could not function because of the motion of the ship.

The 7th - During the previous night no one could sleep. I thought the ship would break apart. In the continual danger which surrounds us, we eventually become free of fear and so indifferent that we do not care if everything is lost. Heaven knows how one can endure it. A storm and one sees only mountains and valleys; great foamy waves build so high that it seems they will swamp the ship at any moment.

The 9th - The fleet separated and Commodore [William] Hotham went with General Grant and his troops toward Barbados.[7] Barbados is one of the most wonderful islands, and a miracle brought forth by English diligence. It is 25 miles long and fifteen wide. Products are sugar, molasses, cotton, indigo, pepper, pineapples, bananas, oranges, lemons .... the principal one is Bridgetown.[8] The number of white residents approaches 20,000 and the blacks about 100,000. The population is much too large for a little island, but it is well developed, and all foodstuffs, flour, meat, even clothing, they import, primarily from the English colonies in America. Terrible wind storms and earthquakes have frequently damaged this island. Barbados first came under English rule during the reign of King James I. Those who came here from England, first planted tobacco, then cotton and indigo, which have yielded great profits. In the year 1647 some English gentlemen, bored with their homeland, sold their possessions and sailed for Barbados. Among these were Drax, Madiford, and Walrond. They at once established large sugar plantations and made profits on top of profits. The number of inhabitants during those years climbed to 30,000 whites and 100,000 Negroes. In the year 1667 the Dutch Admiral Reuter captured the island of Barbados, but it was returned. In 1674 all the sugar works, and in particular the mills where the cane was crushed, were destroyed by a storm. Because of illness, the inhabitants die at an early age, as is common throughout the West Indies, and more die than are born. Further, the women in the West Indies are not fruitful. And if Europeans seeking quick profit did not migrate there, in 100 years, or even sooner, the population of the West Indies would die out. Seldom does anyone attain an age above forty years. The English do not come to the West Indies to die, but to make their fortune, and then to return as quickly as possible to Europe. This afternoon the waves diminished so that there was hope it would be a bearable night.

The 10th - During this night it was pitch black. The wind, although not strong, changed direction frequently. All ships had to work the sails. Only our sailors were inattentive to the course of the fleet, and continued on the old course when the rest of the fleet turned. The warship noticed *Crawford* was missing, went looking for us, ad found us at one o'clock, to our peace of mind and inner consolation. Captain [Thomas] Symonds of the warship immediately ordered the course for our crew to follow, and the crew now was stimulated to be more alert, because the authority of the captain of a warship, which leads a fleet, over the captain of a transport, compares to that of a major over a corporal. A "God damn" passed over from the warship set everything straight. Captain Symonds is a wonderful Englishman. -- This was during the night of the eleventh to the twelfth.

The 12th - We expected to find the fleet again today. However, we had not the least sight of it, not even a glimpse of the sails or masts. The warship called over to our captain to take pains to stay near the warship as many American privateers sailed in these waters, and one had to fear falling into the hands of a French frigate as well, as Count D'Estaing had left Boston and sailed for the West Indies.

The 13th - The wind was contrary and the frigate let go our tow. This afternoon we were in good spirits and the ship's crew only slightly less so. Suddenly we saw two strange ships. The frigate called for us to raise all possible sails and to do everything possible to follow it. Of course we could not follow it, because one must understand the difference in sailing between a warship and a merchant ship is comparable to an oxen wagon chasing a coach with six horses, around the world. Our *Solebay* was two miles ahead of us when we noticed that one of the two ships was a frigate of about the same class as ours. We thought if it is a French ship, the English will defeat it, fight as it might. Then we noticed the other was a privateer of eighteen cannons. Our warship had to take that into account. We sailed poorly and had no cannons on board. Our frigate raised the English flag and fired a cannon. The other ship did the same which indicated to us that it was also English. Both sailed so that the other ship was caught between them, lowered its sails, and surrendered. It was an American, which we kept with our fleet. The other was the frigate *Venus*, cruising in this latitude. An American frigate of eighteen cannons had been seen by the warship also, which without a doubt was to have accompanied the captured ship through these waters. This one used the opportunity to raise an English frigate sail and sail away. The guardian angel was surely looking over us -- if our warship in the same night, day before yesterday, when we followed the wrong course, had not set out at once in search of us, we would have been captured today. The American ship certainly would have captured us and taken us as prisoners to Charleston or Boston. And the regiment would have been unaware of our fate. But as it was, we had the protection, and all American privateers fled as soon as they saw our frigate.

The 15th - The weather cooled, without thunder being heard.

The 16th - Again we had surprisingly bad weather. The sea rolled the ship. The wind and waves howled so violently it was impossible to carry on a conversation in the cabin. One had to lie in bed, as it was not possible to stand or even to sit. Even the sailors said that this was such a stormy sea as is seldom made, and these sailors are for the most part tired of the war, and hope Spain gets into the game so they get additional opportunity to seize prizes on the ocean and in all waters, and get rich therefrom. The transports are nothing but merchant ships which otherwise, at this time of the year, would be engaged in sailing to the West Indies, or more likely, to America, and returning in the best possible time. Or they would be carrying trade to the Mediterranean Sea and their trips to Smyrna, Alexandria, Cairo, and all the parts of the world would not take longer than two months. During the stormy winter months they would be in a safe harbor and enjoy all the pleasures of a big city. On the present service, however, the seasons are ignored and wherever the demand for troops leads, that is where they are shipped, regardless of what season of the year it might be. All our altering the location of the army can only be conducted by water, and because of the great difficulty, I half wish the war would lead somewhere else, where a general could determine when his auxiliary troops should be at a certain place and position. But who will presume to determine when troops should be ordered to a certain place when instant help may be necessary. This is an advantage which the rebels have and will always keep. They march by land and always have enough to eat, and when we arrive, by water, we go on land emaciated, sick, weak, stiff, and without strength. The stoutest heart fails to accomplish its purpose when the body is too exhausted. I have almost come to believe it will be impossible to defeat them if they continue to use the advantage which they have over us. On the water we have the advantage, just as they do on land. Their trade is tied to the sea, and I hope England will give serious consideration to control of the sea, where she can survive the war, and eventually capture all the American ships.

The 17th - We sailed exceedingly well with a strong west wind.

The 18th - True, we did not sail as fast as yesterday, but were nevertheless, glad that the wind did not blow so strongly. We were again taken in tow.

The 19th - We saw two strange ships. The frigate cut us loose and chased after them. One was from Holland and the other was an American privateer. That one sailed away and the Hollander remained near us for 24 hours and then continued on its way. If the frigate had not protected us, here again we would have been taken.

The 20th - So hot that twice the ship had to be soaked down.

The 21st - Calm and unbearably hot, so that day and night one could wear only a shirt.

The 22nd - On the coasts of the West Indies, where we now are, the rainfall is very heavy. For several days the stormy weather and rough seas had kept us in our cabins. Today the skies cleared and the sea was no longer so frightful. We climbed up on deck like old women who leave their dank rooms after a snowy and fog-filled winter, and hobble on their canes into the new, shining spring sun, and there, in the fresh invigorating air, cough up all the stove smoke they have swallowed. In this manner we wobbled up on deck, and I again felt so strong that I sent my servant below to light a pipe of tobacco for me, something I had not tried for some time. The sky was bright without a cloud. Suddenly the wind sprang up, which immediately blew up a rain cloud, and in a moment poured down a torrent of rain. In ten minutes the sky was again as bright and clear as previously.[9]

The 23rd - Strong winds which were still contrary. We still knew nothing of our other ships, and because we had the warship with us we were worried about them.

The 24th - We were now in those helpful winds which please the seafarers. The English call them trade winds and they blow at certain times of the year, always in one direction. At this time we can keep these winds until we arrive in the West Indies, and they will soon carry us there. They are the best winds that can be wished for. They blow softly and make few waves, as if one were traveling on an even meadow.

The 25th - We saw two birds, one of which came to rest on top of the mast. We took this to be a happy omen that land was near. The warship sailed ahead to look for land.

The 26th - To this point, we still had extra provisions. Now that was all gone, however, and we had only ship's bread extra. So we also had to live like the sailors. We did, however, still enjoy a good glass of wine. And when it was calm, Captain Pentzel and I would sit at the table until evening, drinking a bottle of French wine, talking about Waldeck, and counting the young men, mainly those capable of supporting a wife, as compared to the number of marriageable women, and thus we sought to alleviate the boring days aboard ship.[10] We saw a whale. We held up because we were near the coast and the night was before us.

The 27th - For the first time we again saw land. It was the island of Tortuga.

The 28th - Again nothing but sky and water.

The 29th - A beautiful, clear day. We saw Hispaniola on our left. It could be seen so clearly that we could distinguish individual houses. If I had to live in the West Indies, I would choose Hispaniola. The land gives a mountainous appearance, but it pleases me.

The 30th - We were still near Hispaniola, but could not see it as clearly as yesterday. The warship was on alert here because Hispaniola belongs half to France and half to Spain, and from their harbors they had seen us come sailing past. During this afternoon, Cuba was to be seen on our right. Cuba shows itself from this side of the ocean more level and flatter than Hispaniola. In the previous war, England captured Havana, the best and most polished city and primary harbor of Cuba. Yes, one can almost say it is the master of the West Indies, but the French have taken all the sugar islands. Would to God that such great good fortune should bless this nation in this war, also.

Eighteenth Century America
Aboard the Ship *Crawford*
December 1778

The 1st - We hoped to see Jamaica, our assemble point, where we are to take aboard water and provisions, and where we are to join our other ships. We actually saw land again, but it was Cape Navasa, a small, uninhabited island, which because it has no spring water, has no buildings. We went to sleep with the hope of seeing Jamaica in the morning. One sleeps so well when the trade winds support hope, much as the weary traveler, who, near his goal, lies down to rest in the shade of a tree, his last provisions exhausted, and then once again takes up his staff and continues on to the waiting city.

The 2nd - Our hopes of yesterday did not deceive us. Filled with uncertainty contending with joy, we left our stale cabins before sunrise, hurried on deck, and saw Jamaica lying before our eyes. It was above all, the happiest moment; one which I can imagine but not describe, when a man after a long, miserable, stormy, and dangerous sea voyage sees land again for the first time. The view which Jamaica presents on this side from our ship was a large sugar plantation, where for the most part ships tie up to load the unpurified sugar. Next our eyes took in the lofty mountains which appear to be far higher than the Alps. On this side, the mountains are not covered with tall growth, but with the type of shrub which at this distance looked like juniper bushes. My grandmother had a saying when she was annoyed, "I wish you were where the pepper grows!" Now I am where the pepper grows. If a person does not know that Jamaica frequently suffers from earthquakes, when he sees the many shaped of the mountains, the heap of tumbled-down rock, and the many valleys which start wide and then suddenly narrow down or have been completely closed off by newly risen mountains whose over-hanging rocks and crags threaten to collapse at any moment, all this would at once bring to mind the idea, at least, that there had been a drastic change in nature at this place. Atop the peaks of these towering mountains, which rise above the clouds, a constant fog is to be seen. On these cliffs there is good soil where some savages and free Negroes have laid out plantations. The ship's carpenter, whose home is in Jamaica, told us that all the blacks and slaves who have run away from their masters, live on these high rocks and often disturb their former masters at night. This has caused

94

a black, King Jacob as he happens to be called at the moment, to be employed against them. He roams these high mountains with his black crew, and for every runaway slave which he returns to his master, he receives three pounds.

At eleven o'clock a flag was raised to request a pilot, who was all the more necessary as our captain had never been here, and a more dangerous coast had to be passed before we arrived at Port Royal. Now Port Royal was seen ahead, and a great fort. Opposite Port Royal lies another fort which must be passed before entering the harbor. This is called Fort Apostle because it has twelve large cannons. About one o'clock we dropped anchor near the mouth of the harbor. The entire construction was built over a swamp and must have cost a very great amount. There are eighty cannons and when these do not wish it, no French ship can enter. This fort has blown up twice in the last twenty years when lightning struck the powder magazine. This fort is named Muskite Fort and makes a beautiful view from the harbor.

We put off our lunch because we had planned to order it when we dropped anchor. This had only just happened when two boat-loads of black girls came on the ship with all sorts of fresh things to sell. We bought cucumbers, beans, carrots, oranges, lemons, and pineapples. When one thinks that in Germany it is now winter, and here it is the most wonderful summer with all its fresh produce, one can not believe his eyes. We ate, but we ate a very late afternoon meal. O, it is so delightful after being so long at sea, to enjoy again all sorts of refreshments which a person has done without for so long. After we ate, we made punch, which here in its native land can be thoroughly enjoyed. We took old Jamaica rum, said to be the best in the world, lemons which grow fresh here, oranges which really should not be used but were put in because they taste so good, and sugar grown here, but we did not stop with this, as the tower of pineapple had to improve the taste. Ananas, pineapple, raised on the island of Jamaica is a fruit unsurpassed in taste and smell, that nature attained perfection with in its beauty of color, the aroma, the taste, etc., and in short, the pineapple appeals to all five senses equally. All five are enjoyed in full, and fully satisfying. I will write more about it later, here, now.

Drinking this punch, which because of its contents we call royal punch, we again forgot all unpleasantness, all dangers, all that we had been through at sea. And how good and wise it is that the Creator put this ability in our souls, so that we so easily forget the unpleasantness of the past and enjoy the present good with a happy heart. O, if that were not the case, where could a poor soul find hope? And who is more lost than a man who has lost hope, who must remain forever on the ocean and never have the pleasure of being on land? God bless these dark-skinned beauties, who brought us these refreshments. They have done for us what the Good Samaritan did for the neglected, wounded man and this gives them favor in our eyes, although their intent was only to sell us something which would refresh us.

I was shocked however, by their attire. They wore a green or white summer hat of silk with many feathers such as would only be worn at court in Germany, but here have no more value than goose feathers by us. Their bare breasts and the most beautiful white skirts show off so well with their dark skin. That is their attire. They sat in a small boat, which was like a small child's crib, and in this traveled about the harbor from ship to ship. We were again as reborn and treated ourselves to the best. We took on another pilot who was black. He led us into the harbor as far as Kingston, where at twelve o'clock we anchored for the night. We heard the clock in Kingston strike twelve, which seemed strange to us as we had not heard a clock or a bell since the American War. We also heard that our other ships, fortunately, had arrived several days ago, but had sailed on to where they could more easily take aboard water.

The 3rd - Our ship had sprung a leak on the voyage and took so much water that it had to be pumped out every two hours. Additionally, we had the unfortunate situation, which could have had unpleasant results for us, that only one pump on this miserable Scottish ship functioned, and the other one was completely useless.

Because the one pump was in constant use, it developed such a leak that it lost all suction. The ship's carpenter, who most clearly understood the danger of the situation, told the captain the pump must be raised and repaired. This was accomplished with much effort. In order to overhaul the ship and restore it to better condition, it was taken to the dockyard. Captain Pentzel, Ensign Hohmann, and I immediately went into the city of Kingston. In Kingston everything was new and different to us. Therefore, I will describe step by step how it caught my eye. As we climbed on land from the boat and entered the first narrow street, a German gentleman greeted us with great respect. It is my belief Germans are to be found in every part of the world, and the German manages his affairs better than people of any other nation. This man, a Holsteiner by birth, took us to his home where we saw the most excellent cabinet work. He was a cabinet-maker by trade, who had done so well that he no longer had to work.

With great pride he showed us his workshop. Here nineteen blacks worked. They were all slaves. They work completely naked and finish the finest cabinet work, mostly from mahogany, which grows nowhere in the West Indies as well as here in Jamaica. They made cupboards, tables, chairs, and beautiful wardrobes. He had taught all nineteen. One worked at a lathe with the finest tools. Another black helped ease the task by turning a wheel which turned the lathe, and would have been operated by foot otherwise. I was surprised to see how competent the black slaves could be. All the wood lying about was mahogany or cedar. This, and especially the pile of wood chips, caused a most pleasant aroma in the workshop. What they consider scrap would have provided a nice profit for a man in England, and would have seemed like trees lying about his work place. The blocks look like wood from a chopped-down cherry tree, which has lain for some time and been bleached by the weather, but when polished becomes a light brown color and year by year darkens until it looks like chestnut.

Outside his door two coconut trees stand, such as stand before most houses in the city. The coconut grows rather high, sprouts limbs from the top, and is otherwise round and smooth. Instead of leaves, long fronds grow on these limbs. I can not think of a better description than to compare them with those reeds which grow on the slimy banks of our Eder. On these limbs grow the coconuts which are about as thick as a middle-size gourd. The nut does not hang on the tip of the branch as no limb could hold such weight. Also, it would not be safe for anyone to pass under the tree. The nut grows on the thick end of the limb near the stem. The fruit on the inside is completely white and contains a good teacup-full of milk, comparable as to taste and color with the milk from the almond.

This man lived on the island for thirteen years. He had started with nothing but a willingness to work and was now a wealthy man who owned seven houses in the city. Surprisingly few outsiders marry in

Jamaica, but live together with one or more black women. Even this German had such a housekeeper. I expressed my amazement about his life style. He answered that it certainly did not fit with my morality. But here, it was common practice, and he was not rich enough to marry a white woman whose support and maintenance require an expenditure of 500 pounds sterling, and further, they were very hard to find here. In this he was right and the women here are not only unfruitful, but die at a young age. And most English apparently do not come here with the intention of remaining very long, but with all haste to develop something, to leave an agent in charge, and then to return to Europe.

Most of the people on Jamaica are blacks and their attitude toward whites is as toward Jesus. The heart of the humanitarian bleeds when he sees the miserable life of the slaves. Except for their shape, a person sees no differences between these unfortunate beings and the animals. Completely naked, both men and women, they are driven to their work place, and between their legs they wear a folded linen cloth, tied on with a narrow band. Behind them goes a slave driver, a man compared with whom every other type of overseer seems to be a noble man. The women go about their work in the city, two by two, smoking their pipes. On the other hand, they enjoy a good fortune which their masters do not have. They have a naturally strong and healthy body as opposed to the whites, who are pale and appear to be half dead. The wealth of a man is measured by the number of slaves he has. The one who has ten has taken a long stride toward becoming a rich man, but there are rich people who have 300 or more. Originally they were treated badly here and fed poorly, which resulted in their deaths. Now the owners understand it is to their advantage to treat them better. During our discussion we arrived at Howard's Tavern which we had already accepted as our regimental club. Here I had the pleasure to meet many of the gentlemen of our regiment. The other gentlemen departed and Lieutenant Wiegand, the regimental surgeon, and I refreshed ourselves and drank a good punch with M. Howard. Our mutual enjoyment was very great. Everyone thought we had been captured and each assumed this to be the case as no one had met us in Jamaica. The fleet had taken a completely different course, and sailed in part among the Bahamian Islands because the agent, in the absence of the frigate commodore, decided that route was the safest course. And we sailed with the frigate, the straightest, although in the present circumstances, the least secure way, and arrived safely in port, also. We would not have been able to say this if the frigate had not provided protection for us. But then I would have written this in Charleston, Boston, or Philadelphia.

If a person fortunately survives a sea voyage and at the end is still in good health, the joy is so much greater than when he manages to survive another peaceful year-long period on land. O, what a stirring joy, even to shake the hand of the private soldiers and to see the unconcealed joy in their faces. We had so often discussed aboard ship the possibility of the other ships arriving here safely, and now we met one another and for the most part all were in good health. Our friends had worried even more for us, as they did not know if the warship had found us or not. Against all expectations and despite having given up all hope, we saw one another again for the first time today in Kingston. The entire officer corps of the regiment ate in one hall. Howard's Tavern is an attractive inn, three stories high, and around each level is a wide gallery on which six people can walk abreast, and from each room a door leads onto the gallery. The steps, the woodwork, the doors, and floors, all is made of the most expensive mahogany. In the entire building there is no stove or fireplace, and in Jamaica and all the West Indies such would be superfluous. Instead of windows, there are green Venetian blinds through which the sea breezes whisper and cool the room.

At two o'clock we sat down to eat, and all the items on the table were items seldom seen in our fatherland. The soup was made of all sorts of vegetables and hardly touched by the English. We found the beef not nearly as good as in England or America. Otherwise, everything was better. Before the war, many animals were shipped here for slaughter from America, and sugar and rum were sent in return. Because of the war this branch of trade has been destroyed. Therefore, the wealthy West Indians now find it necessary to slaughter their old breeding stock. The animals are slaughtered early in the morning and the meat market is already finished by seven o'clock, as otherwise the strong heat would cause the meat to spoil quickly. The price was affordable at one pound, one bit, which is about five guilder in German money.

Now the second course came, sea turtle, which would not be seen on every table in Waldeck. Still, I am not sure, although it has four types of meat, if for taste, I would not prefer to have ham. The carrots, fresh lettuce, and evenly broken French beans tasted very good to a person just arrived in port after a sea voyage. All these fresh vegetables tasted like they do at home, only here we had them fresh in December, January, and February. The carrots were not so good. It seems roast pork was the main dish. There was so much new and the island so large, so much to hear and tell, that I could no longer remember everything when I again sat down in my cabin on this day, and tried to recollect all the events of this happy day. We worked hard at the bar. At the beginning, before eating, we had a glass of cognac, passed about without formality. During the meal we drank port wine, English ale, cider, and punch. With desert there was Madeira wine, pineapple, oranges, melon. Next, a small bowl with water was set before each so that he could wash. Then came a small cooling fan and rolled tobacco, which is called a cigar, and with all this we were served punch. The service was exceptionally good, which can seldom be said about an English inn. Then came the day of reckoning. This amounted to no less than a half guinea each. Afterward we took a walk through the city and then returned aboard ship.

The 4th - The heat is exceptionally strong. However, it abated somewhat about ten o'clock when the sea breeze began to blow. This sea wind is called the doctor by the people in the West Indies. As unbearable as the heat might seem, the people have learned to build their houses so that the air can blow through from all sides. The streets of Kingston are not paved, with reason, because the sun on the stones would be so hot that no one, and especially the slaves who have no shoes, could walk on them. Nevertheless, it is a picturesque, and from the point of view of commerce, a very advantageously situated place on the sea. Beauty and richness are evident everywhere. The inhabitants dress in the most expensive silk materials. Their linen is regal. They wear white felt hats and coats of the finest English material, lined with silk. They change clothes several times a day and never wear a shirt more than one day. They are so pleased with their land that they immediately ask strangers how they like the land. No one ventures on the street without a silk sunshade. Their carriages are two-horse coaches or gigs and the streets are never empty of carriages. All these things come from England. Even the harnesses for the horses are not made here. The gentlemen live a good part of the time at their plantations outside the city. Early in the morning they ride into Kingston where they also have houses and where they conduct their business.

[Jamaica]

The 5th - We sailed from Kingston further up the harbor toward Rockford, where our other ships lay and where we could more easily take on water. The water springs out of a cliff about a quarter of an hour distance from the harbor. From there it flows through a narrow, paved, and white-washed ditch which leads to the harbor where the boats sail under a spout and fill their barrels with a minimum of effort. On the right and left side of this ditch was a paved footpath on which a person could walk with ease through the thick shrubbery all the way to the spring. The water bubbled out as clear as crystal and regardless of how hot the stones over which it flowed might be, it remained rather cool. Every weed, every leaf of every bush, which I saw on this walk, was unknown to me and completely different from anything at home. In winter -- everything green, and all the plants standing as they do by us in June. I did not go ashore, but went to the ship *Britannia* where I baptized a child, and then to the *Christian* where I baptized two others who were born at sea three weeks ago. I ate lunch on the *Christian*, where I remained until evening.

The 7th - Together with others, I went to Kingston early in the morning. It is about one and one-half hours distance. Generally people travel at night here, because during the day the heat is so strong that a person can only travel a short distance. If the fruitfulness were not in front of a person's eyes, he would believe nothing could be produced by this barren soil. We saw aloe, among other bushes, growing wild, like the thorn in Germany, and another class of aloe served as a hedge around gardens and fields. Of fruits which grow in Germany, I saw none. I did see Indian corn being planted. I saw some which had started to grow. I saw some which had sprouted and had ears starting to grow. I saw some completely matured. A person here can harvest crops as often as he wishes. The pastures for livestock are not good, being dry, parched grass. I saw sheep in their third year which had degenerated, and instead of wool, produced goat's hair. The number of lizards of all colors, which scurry about under foot, can not be described. However, they are shy. We drank tea at the coffee house, which cost about two and one-half bits, or about twelve guilder each. Then we went walking. By nine o'clock it is already so hot that a person can not tolerate to be on the street or walkways. We ate at Howard's Tavern. In a strange place, a person can never see nor hear enough, and to experience the most, a person must take advantage of every opportunity. Therefore, we visited the coffee house, where between seven and nine o'clock a very numerous social gathering takes place because the salespeople and other gentlemen, who for the most part live outside the city, travel to their warehouses in the morning and when business is over, travel back home at about eight or nine o'clock. They certainly would not pass up the opportunity of visiting the coffee house in hope of learning something new.

I was amazed at how curious the Americans were. This West Indian nation is even more curious than they were. This is also easy to understand as everything new must be brought from distant London by ship. When the ship can not sail, the news is less often received and each item becomes of more interest. A ship had just arrived from New York, and the news items which it brought were printed and posted on a bulletin board for everyone to read. It had left New York shortly after our departure, and as everyone was curious as to what Count D'Estaing planned to undertake in the American waters, there was a mob at the board and everyone wanted to get the news first. Finally it became known that Count D'Estaing had sailed out of Boston harbor. Admiral Byron missed him in a storm and thick fog, and now everyone was worried that in a short time he would be here in the West Indies. Therefore, it was assumed also, that we would not sail for our designated Florida, but would remain in Jamaica as a defense force against the French fleet. We had often discussed this possibility during our voyage. As we gradually neared the Tropic of Cancer, and as the candles melted, it became necessary in the West Indies to burn floating candles. Only where it is cold have people learned how to protect themselves against the cold, and so here in hot lands, from the heat. Here in Kingston the candles burn under the finest glass globes made of the whitest glass. Without these globes, the constant air currents would prevent the candles from staying lit, and if a person closed the doors and windows, no one could stay in the room because of the heat.

In this house there are thirty black waiters all dressed alike. Smoking is not permitted here. On the other hand, in Howard's Tavern no coffee can be poured, but if a gathering is there which wants coffee after dinner, the host is obliged to send out to a coffee house to have it delivered, and he is not permitted to make it in his own house.

Lieutenant Heldring and I decided not to make the long return to the ship, but to sleep one night on land. The colonel returned from a noon meeting with Admiral Parker and we ate our evening meal in company with the colonel at Howard's Tavern. We went to our night's lodgings, which were one block away. Our two rooms were side by side and a person could see from one into the other. They were nicely furnished and above each bed hung a mosquito net, which is also a necessary fixture in this region of earthquakes, as the mosquitoes allow a person less rest at night than during the day. Each of us went to bed in his room, but I could not go to sleep. We were accustomed aboard ship to being rocked to sleep. Therefore, we were not used to sleeping ashore. About one o'clock I fell asleep. Suddenly I was awakened by a noise at my window. I looked through my mosquito net and out the window and was aware of someone who was intent on climbing into my room. I thought someone who is alone certainly would not try to kill another who is alone. Therefore I was not overly frightened. I believed it to be one of the blacks who had been lying outside our door. Because I had not trusted them, I had put my purse, in which I had twenty guineas, and my watch, in a safe place before going to bed. It became quiet again at the window and I no longer could see anyone. As I lay in bed thinking about what had happened, I again heard someone trying to climb in, and suddenly saw a man lying half through my window. I decided it was at least prudent not to allow the man to enter my room in this manner. And thought myself strong enough to throw him out before he was able to get firm footing within the room. I spoke from my bed, and in English, *"Who is there?"* It was Lieutenant Heldring who identified himself even before I could get out of bed. During the day we had mixed all sorts of things together when eating, and drinking a goodly amount, also. Especially, we had eaten lots of fresh fruit, like pineapples and oranges. The lieutenant had felt unwell, had to go out, but could not get a door open. Therefore, he decided to climb out a window and because he did not want to wake me, climbed out quietly. That was the first movement I had noticed through the mosquito net, and the second was when he was climbing back into the room. The situation struck both of us as rather funny and we went back to bed fearing nothing. We had hardly laid down, when Lieutenant Heldring had to go out again. I thought I could open my door and so got up. As soon as I was out of bed, I felt sick and had to vomit. Lieutenant Heldring made his exit through the window as previously. And while we were both sick from the same cause, nature had chosen different ways to indicate it, which made us think we had eaten poisoned fruit or some other spoiled food, which in the West Indies, where so much was new to us, could have been the case. We could no longer sleep and I cursed all sea travel which makes a person so weak that when he comes on land, he, like a child's crib, must be treated with care.

Early that morning each of us had to pay one Spanish dollar for which we had received nothing but a night's lodging. That amounts to two guilder in hard cash and I would gladly have paid another guilder if I could have at least been able to sleep. I drank a bottle of London port and no punch, and with this wonderful strong beer fasted until two o'clock, by which time it had its affect and the food once again tasted good. However, I still did not eat everything, especially no fruit, drank the best Madeira wine, and was again cured.

It was a captured French ship with 550 blacks, slaves from the African coast of Guinea which came into port. This is also something which can touch the hardest heart. I will write down everything about the circumstances as I saw them. Those poor creatures are human beings like we are and we have no advantage over them except we are white and they are black. Have we privileges over them, and where do they stand in the general laws of nature that are spoken of so lightly concerning the inherent rights of all God's creatures? Who gives man the right to mistreat man? Certainly not God nor nature. That these tyrants are rich and can buy a black one for 100 dollars, that they therewith buy the right to treat him harshly and cruelly, where is that written? God, nature, reason, yes, every resort which man has throughout the world, nowhere is this given. In the morning a young boy with a bell goes through the entire city. He has the number of slaves to be sold written on a sheet of paper.

But to continue, I must say something of their way of life aboard ship. Anyone who has been to sea knows that he can not value too highly the enjoyment of fresh air on deck. When a captain brings a ship-load of blacks from the coast of Africa, he is responsible for their security, and to prevent their rioting, they are shut up in tight compartments beneath deck in the ship, and often he must chain them together, two by two. Because if 500 or 600 Negroes rise up against a captain with twenty seamen, the problem would soon be settled. Consequently, they are shipped as horses are shipped. They are not allowed out, but must make their excrement below them, from whence it is cleared away by an attendant. Their diet is such that they do not starve and they have only ship's water to drink, and I know quite well what ship's water is. Under these conditions they are transported on a ship for three or four months, without knowing where they are bound nor for what purpose.

To return to the previous comments. -- After the boy has rung his bell through all the streets, the buyers gather at the slave market at the specified time. Then the slaves are driven in like cattle, each with a number on a card about his neck. Men and women are presented completely naked, so they can be thoroughly checked for any shortcomings. The man who has bought a slave has his slave driver with him, and has the slave driven home. The slave is often fattened a bit, and if the buyer is kind-hearted, he may let the slave recover from the sea voyage before he is sent to the plantation. Here everything in their miserable existence really begins. On a diet of the cheapest food they must do the hardest work, and a man within whom all humanity has died is their supervisor, who beats them unmercifully for the least shortcoming in their work. In the dear, blessed America, they would be treated better, and better cared for. Wherever I went in that wonderful land, the slaves were treated no worse than the domestic servants by us, and they were not aware of their slavery. Certainly, in many houses they are treated as members of the family. And their masters had as an advantage, that they were good and faithful workers, who reproduced and allowed the master to work ever larger farms, because no one liked to sell members of their Negro family, which these people took as a form of cruelty. For this reason , also, I would like to return to America. I am set in my opinion and do not need to repeat myself, but if there is another land in which I would wish to live, it would be America. And who knows, but that I might have become the pastor if this separation to the detestable Florida had not occurred. Here in Jamaica they are held in contempt. They must go barefoot in the blistering sand and receive clothing which can be worn only on Sunday. They work naked and have only a cloth tied between their legs. They are driven to work in pairs, both men and women, smoking their pipes as they go through the streets, and if nature calls, they squat, unashamed, no matter where it might be, if they can escape the slave driver's whip. Parents are sold away from their children, and children are sold away from their parents, with no consideration given to human kindness. The wealth of a man is measured by the number of his slaves, and many here have 300 or more. It is surprising that the people do not see it is to their advantage to treat the slaves well, because without the slaves, they could not prosper, as only the slaves do hard work here.

This ship was a good prize for the English as each slave would sell for not less than 100 pounds sterling.

The ladies of the city who have Negroes as chambermaids, treat them better, and make a great display with them. They dress them in beautiful white dresses and beautiful hats, so that when a man does not see their faces, he thinks they must be ladies of high position.

The 9th - The ships had taken on their water by now, and we departed from Rockford and lay at anchor again at Kingston.

The 11th - Our entire company remained aboard ship today. The black maidens were kind enough to bring us all we desired of bread, fish, coffee, lemons, yams, bananas, and other vegetables. Yams keep as well as potatoes. They are larger and one is enough for six people. Some weigh as much as sixteen pounds. They look like tree roots to us, and when laid beside a beech tree, they look exactly like a root of the tree. Their skin is thick and rough. They grow in a variety of shapes; some look like a foot with toes. The islanders cook them like they boil potatoes and eat them instead of bread. They always replace bread for the slaves, as there are frequently times when even the rich people have no bread, because the necessary grains are not grown here, but only sugar cane. We have also eaten yams aboard ship, cooked in this manner, but I must say they are not to our taste.

Aboard ship a person eats what I would not consider edible on land, but I am thankful for the yams. We cut them in thin slices and fix them with onions, like a potato salad, and fixed in this manner, they are the most enjoyable. They are said to keep for a long time at sea and therefore we have taken on a good supply for our voyage. They grow like potatoes, but do not need a deep soil.

Bananas are a fruit which serve the slaves and the poor people as bread. They grow on a medium-size tree, which has the shape of a cabbage stalk. On the thick end of the branches the bananas hang in bunches like the large beans which hang on the stem by the handful. The trees are amazingly full of fruit and provide the cheapest nourishment which can be given the Negroes. They look like goat horns and have a yellow-green color. The skin is a thick as the skin of the large beans. They are cooked in the skin which makes the skin like parchment and very tough, but on the inside as soft as a half-baked apple, but overly sweet to the taste. These are not to my taste, either. Cassava, or manioc, is a bread. The juice of the root contains the strongest poison. The root is stomped in a tub. The juice is then pressed out very carefully. It is then dried in the sun and ground until it yields a fine flour, from which bread, starch, and powder are made. This is a discovery made by the Negroes and Indians.

There is another kind of fruit here which is commonly called Eve apple, prickle pear, or Jamaica potato, and for which the correct English name is mangineel apple. The tree is called the mangineel tree. This is a fruit which looks wonderful and beautiful, but is deadly when eaten. It contains a poison which is a purgative, which can not be controlled, and death results. It is singular that this apple does not harm a pregnant woman. Mrs. Malone, the wife of a captain of the Pennsylvanians,[11] who lived a long time in Jamaica, told us that she was pregnant and went walking with her husband. She saw the mangineel tree loaded with the most beautiful fruit. She was like all expectant mothers. She knew that this fruit was poisonous to eat, but because she had heard that it was harmless for pregnant women, appetite overcame reason. She broke loose from her husband's arm, with a begging of his pardon, went to the tree, and ate to her heart's content. She did not notice the least bad consequence. She is still in such good health that she is sailing with us to Pensacola.

In addition, cocoa grows here which is used to make chocolate.

Cocoa trees, coconuts, I have already covered.

Cotton plants from which cotton cloth is made. This branch was neglected by Hamburg, and I have been assured it is forbidden to export cotton from Jamaica and thus disrupt the East India Company, and the beaver trade in Canada. Otherwise, the cotton is said to be very good. The plants themselves grow very high. A wonderful plant. -- How rich nature is in its variety.

Everyone has great profit from this trade. Here there is no secret to becoming rich. Everyone has his own mine with rich holdings, and if it is not a sugar plantation, it is some other branch of trade.

China tamarind, sarsaparilla, pepper, and other items of value to the medical profession are also grown here.

I also saw a wonderful tree. The leaves were green on one side, as green as silk, and on the other side, a dark yellow. When the wind rustled through the branches, one saw such a quick change, now green, now dark yellow, as the leaves turned. The leaves were so soft that had a blind man felt them, he would have thought them to be taffeta or silk. The remaining growth is the wonderful pineapple. No fruit in the world compares to it. Lemons are of almost no value because there is such an over-abundance of them.

Oranges we ate every morning, and took a good supply to sea with us. They are considered very healthy if eaten in the morning, but not in the afternoon. Therefore, there is a saying in Jamaica, that in the morning they are gold and in the afternoon they are lead.

Limes are best used in punch. They are as common here as plums by us, yet in other places they are so expensive. On all the fruits, the only profit made is that of transporting them from the plantations to the city. Very little value is put on limes, certainly less than where they are not grown. Melons are of two types, musk melons and water melons. The first is of an uncommonly pleasant taste.

Coconuts have a milk similar to the almond. I find the coconut to be nothing special.

These are all wonderful fruits and in a land where they are not grown, one values them more and tries to force nature to produce such fruit again. It is true that a forest of oranges and lemons, whose fruit is a fine golden yellow, or apples on a green tree, look very pretty. Man wants them and wonders at what he does not have, and fails to value what he does have, even though it is ever so beautiful. That is the folly of mankind.

Tobacco, sugar cane, coffee, and many sorts of European vegetables also are grown here, which, however, are not as good as in Europe.

I was in Kingston again. I saw sheep which had changed, as here they no longer have need of such a heavy coat. The goats, of which there are many here, are very small. The horses are neither beautiful nor large, but spirited and swift. They are not fed oats nor any other grain, but fed throughout the year with a sort of grass similar to that which grows on some swamps by us. Oats would be too expensive here because here neither oats, nor barley, nor corn, nor wheat is grown. The horses are kept in open stalls because they could not live in closed stalls due to the heat. They are only used for riding and as coach horses because there is not a man who does not have a coach. No land in the world surpasses the West Indies in luxurious living. Grass and other things are transported with oxen which are of an unbelievable large size and work in yokes.

The 12th - We saw two forests burning today. The ship's carpenter informed us that new plantations were being laid out and that the forests on the side of the island were always burned down at night because at night the wind blows from the land side and in this way the fires are kept from spreading. During the day however, the wind blows from the sea, and truly if this wind did not come up by about ten o'clock, no one could live in the West Indies. That is why it is called the doctor. It is worth noting, and the inhabitants recommend this precaution to all strangers, that a person must be careful and take precautions during the night, and even during the evening, against the land wind, and when it begins to change in the evening, not be in the free air. This is what the islanders do, when the wind comes they hurry to their houses so as not to catch cold. This is no joking matter. A man came through the fog one evening with a little fever, the next day he was sick, and on the third day he died.

We have had the same experience with our soldiers, who have gone ashore with their wives to do laundry and stayed too late, became sick, and died, there being no cure, and their wives died also. There is nothing we can do to insure our health, because if we are in the city, we must return aboard ship in the evening, and therefore, we are exposed both on land and on sea. We can not change it, even though a sudden death may follow. Even disregarding this, Europeans do not live long in the West Indies.[12]

There is no ebb or flood tide here, or at least, very little, and this advantage is replaced for the seamen with the sea and land breezes. Just as ships in other places generally enter port on the flood tide, here they enter on the sea breeze, which is as certain as the flood tide, and depart with the land breeze.

[Jamaican Life]

The 13th - I attended church in Kingston, which began at ten o'clock. I was already there at nine and as all the gates were open, I spent an hour reading the inscriptions on the gravestones with which the churchyard was almost completely covered. The churchyard was surrounded by a high wall made of brick and had three gates. The gravestones were mostly of alabaster or marble, and beautifully decorated. Many were from seven to eight feet long and of one piece. Anyone who doubts that Kingston in particular, and Jamaica in general, is an unhealthy island, need only go to the cemetery, look and read, and he will encounter proof enough. In general it is said a European seldom lives to the age of forty here, and if he arrives as an adult, lives only another twenty years. Jamaica is the cemetery for thousands of English sailors, who, when they arrived here from the sea, expected to be well-cared for, but instead paid with their lives.

The first gravestone that met my eyes covered the remains of an entire family which had died out in five years. The name of the father, who died in 1735 at age 35, was on top. Next followed his eldest son who died in 1736 at age seventeen; in 1737 both of his daughters; in 1738 an eleven year old son; and in 1739 his wife, at age 37. I stepped to another stone which covered a lawyer. It was in Latin and indicated his age at 25. Beside this was the grave marker of a merchant who died at age 27. Beside this a beautiful alabaster stone of a woman who died at age 33. Another was over a merchant who died at age 36. God, I thought, here our life lasts only thirty years, or at most, forty. In this hour I read the inscriptions on fifty or more gravestones, but among these, I found only a single one here was over fifty at his death. No, in North America it was completely different. I read a gravemarker in Amboy which covered the remains of a Mrs. Faehnrichin, who died in the 83rd year of her life.

This churchyard was rather large, but so full of graves, that it would be difficult to find a site for another body. While I was occupied with these gravestones, it struck ten and at the same time, a bell rang. Now coaches and gigs began to arrive, and I believe I was the only one who came to church on foot.

The church is built in a very simple style, and yet more beautiful than is usually seen. The windows and doors were open during the service and the air drafts made it pleasantly cool. By us it would not be necessary to have ventilation on the Third Advent. Here, however, it was necessary to create a draft to break the heat, at least partially. The stalls are all on the floor level, and the pulpit and the organ are the only places built at a higher level. The pulpit and all the stalls are made of the rare mahogany, and the lectern and handrails on the steps of cedar. When most of the congregation had assembled, the organ played a song. When the song was ended, the congregation stood without bidding and a preacher read a number of prayers and some Pslams. Then the organ played again, and the preacher went before the altar where he read the Articles of Faith and the litany. The congregation repeated the Articles of Faith and the Ten Commandments, as well as a short declaration of faith aloud after the preacher and did likewise with the litany. *We beseech thee to hear us good Lord. Grant us thy peace, have mercy upon us.*[13] The altar was of mahogany, as was the canopy above it; with silk fringes without gold. Above the altar was a wainscoating of glistening brown mahogany on which was written with golden letters the Ten Commandments and the Articles of Faith. Now the lead singer indicated the Psalms which were to be sung. The preacher left the altar and went to a closed closet where he changed his clothing. Before the altar he had the Eucharist vestments. When the Psalms ended, another preacher entered the pulpit and several more verses were sung. The first preacher came from his closet in white stockings, white vest and pants, and set himself in the pastor's chair and listened to the sermon. The sermon was on Acts 1:30, *What must I do to be heard?* which lasted not more than a quarter-hour.[14] The blessing was given from the pulpit. Immediately the congregation dispersed.

I did not see a single person of either sex who appeared fresh or healthy, but their faces were pale and the entire body appeared to be half like a corpse. All women mature earlier here than in Europe, and one errs very greatly when he estimates their age according to their size. On the other hand, they also die earlier, and a woman of thirty years already has the appearance of a grandmother. Dress and fashion is greatly exaggerated by the women. Feathers of many colors and beauty are used in dressing their hair. Silk and linen is the daily costume. The men wear a tasteful white costume, a white felt hat, the hair as it is generally worn in England, short and lightly powdered.

Their coats are beautifully made without pleats, and lined with silk. They wear vests and trousers of fine linen and silk. They change their clothes three times a day. That is not display here, but a means of remaining clean. In the whole world it would be difficult to find a place where finer linen is worn. Clothing is expensive here and I believe a gentleman can not get by on 24 guilder a month. I did not see a single coat worked with gold, but only the more beautiful silk. The English do not like gold on their coats. Men and women have an indescribable adherence to fashion throughout the West Indies.

I remained standing for a short while before the church where the street and the road into the country crossed. Many gentlemen came, riding or in coaches, along this way from the country into the city. Most of them were in a sort of light gig. Behind the seat stood a black holding a sunshade over the gentleman's head. The black is dressed all in white. Another runs, or rides, ahead, dressed in the same manner, and I must say that this is not a bad sight. It is especially funny when they are dressed all in white. The knee-bands fastened with silver buckles, beautiful shoes, and in between the naked black legs, which appear as if they were wearing the finest black stockings. The harnesses on the horses are beautiful and all of them come from England, as do the gigs, as nothing of this nature is made here. Everything is dependent on the fruitfulness of the land. They ship sugar, rum, and indigo to England and bring all sorts of manufactured goods back.

On Sundays the free blacks and other slaves hold a market, and bring all possible products from their farms into the city. Coffee sells very cheaply, and compared with other prices, has very little value, as is the case by us with peas or beans.

They sell tobacco, potatoes, which by weight are expensive, yams, bananas, pineapples, oranges, cocoa, etc.

Ten thousand blacks are to be seen at these markets, all with something to sell, as the majority of people here are Negroes and they are in a ratio of ten blacks to one white. I tried to push my way through the throng in order to see everything. The terrible smell of the sweat of the blacks was enough to make one sick. And anyone who had not become accustomed to all the various smells aboard ship would not have been able to stand it. They bring their products to market from the high mountains on mules. The men then turn over the marketing business to their wives, and use the time to their pleasure and advantage, but bring their wives, who sit at the market all day, something to drink, also. One would expect them to drink only the best punch, since they have all the ingredients at hand, but that is not the case. Everyone prefers to drink rum and water. They bring a great number of children and their entire families with them.

I ate lunch at Howard's Tavern. Toward evening I saw a Negro funeral procession. This is as comical a parade as there is to be seen. One sees sketches in travel descriptions of wild men who in their joy continuously dance about a tree or some other object. This gives a clear idea of the scene made by a black funeral. I will tell it just as I saw it. From a distance one could hear a wild roar, and because the streets of Kingston are not paved but filled with sand, their dance made a cloud of dust which could be seen from a distance. Two black men led the procession, beating on two drums which looked like leather buckets, and which were beaten with balled fists. Close behind came two others, one of whom shook a chain, and the other had a coconut covered with pearls. Both danced, and all the black natives accompanying the corpse hopped and leaped about. Next came the coffin which four women, who were all similarly clad in fine linen, carried by hand. Each had a burning pipe of tobacco in her mouth. The coffin itself was covered with white satin, which was draped over it. Behind the coffin was a woman carrying on her head a bowl, in which there was a pipe and tobacco. Each black female who followed the casket was smoking a pipe, and most were dressed in beautiful linen, which was surely their Sunday best.

The entire following hopped, danced, and sang a single monotonous tone. At the end of the street a circle was formed, the coffin placed in the middle, and a strange place for a ball developed, where one played on the jawbone of a horse's head by hitting the teeth of the horse's head with a bone in such a manner as to produce a sort of music to which the others danced. Funerals are their greatest enjoyment. With great eagerness the coffin was placed in the middle, and often 300 persons at a time danced around it, until the sun was about to set. Then with a friendly shout, the deceased was committed to the ground. At such a time, the strictest master is generous to his slaves and allows them not only their enjoyment, but provides food and drink enough to satisfy all of them.

Their belief provides the greatest expectation to be happier at their friends' funerals than at their births. They believe that when they die here in the West Indies and are buried with great ceremony, they will be reborn in their native land on the Guinea coast and need never fear that they will be sold as slaves again. And it follows, if they give up the ghost quickly, they can make arrangements of various kinds in Africa for their friends who are left behind. If their master punishes them by whipping, it is of less consequence to them than if he threatens not to give them a proper burial after their death, but to leave them lie like cattle, in which case they certainly do all that he desires of them. I did not see the burial, itself, because the coffin was taken across the harbor to Port Royal.

The 14th - Our ship *Crawford*, which was still taking a lot of water, was repaired. Each black who worked on it earned, for his master, one Spanish dollar, or two pounds, and the master's cost for each black was only one or two bits, that is five and one-half guilder. Therefore, each earned eight bits of clear profit for his master, daily. They worked naked so that clothing cost nothing; except on Christmas Day it is customary that the master give to each a jacket and a pair of pants, and the lady of the house gives her Negress a dress. Here each lady tries to out-do the others, and this vanity enables their maids to get pretty dresses which, however, they can only wear when celebrating, or mainly on Sunday when they are not working. It is easy therefore to understand why a gentleman who owns 100 black slaves becomes rich, and how quickly he regains his cash outlay when he can buy a slave at the slave market for 200 pounds. That is over 1,000 dollars in our money, and therefore the master lets them learn all sorts of trades. Sunday is for these oppressed a free and rest day, and no master would expect them to work on Sunday. An Englishman, no matter how impious, holds Sunday as especially sacred and he will not gamble, sing, or whistle. All of these things are scandalous to him. The slaves are assigned no work on Sundays, and when they have the opportunity to earn something, the money is their own. Some worked on our ship on Sunday, so hard that since they took no rest periods, they earned two Spanish dollars, four guilder in hard money. The wealth of a man is measured by the number of slaves he owns. An individual has taken the first step to being well-off when he initially has five to ten slaves. Then the owner himself has no need to work, which is the custom in the West Indies anyway, that the whites do no manual labor, while on the other hand, the blacks are strong enough to earn their keep by the sweat of their brow.

The 15th - The German is fortunate throughout the world and successful wherever he goes. Also, here in Jamaica several of them have greatly improved their fortunes. The colonel rode into the mountains with a cabinet-maker to see the plantation of such a man. The road to this plantation led over steep mountains, over rocks and cliffs, where it was only possible to go on a mule. Above, in the mountains, the rocky ground breaks off and the most beautiful, fertile land appears. The house of this man hung over a cliff where he had to cut a place for the house out of rock. Behind the rock is a level place where he could not build, however, because of the strong storms to which the spot is exposed, and which would have blown his house into the valley below. This was a sugar plantation which is the most common kind of all. The sugar cane grows about twelve feet high, like the reeds along an undisturbed pond by us. The colonel also brought back several ripe and unripe coffee bushes with him.

The coffee grows on small trees, like the common wild cherry by us, and looks similar in the shell, also. Those which are completely ripe are dark brown. In each cherry there are two beans, side by side, and a brown skin covers them, which looks to us like an unripe cherry. The leaves look like cherry leaves, but are rather thicker and smoother to the touch.

If the coffee gets too ripe, it falls off the bush, which the grower does not desire. Instead, he spreads a cloth under the tree and shakes the fruit down. Then, as it is done by us with a plow to level the ground, the coffee is spread on a cloth so that the outer shell will get the heat of the sun and pop open. After this happens, it is put through a sieve and all impurities blown away by a windmill.

The sugar cane requires considerably more preparation. It must have a rich, damp soil. To this end this planter laid out a waterway, over mountains and rocks, which cost him nearly 100,000 pounds sterling. This nearly bankrupted him, but one of his neighbors, who lived below him and used the water which flowed down on his plantation, was good enough to pay half the initial cost. A man with a fortune of 50,000 dollars is far from a rich man here. A sugar plantation provides an amazingly large income. Just the plain sugar is pure profit. All expenses are paid for by the rum, which is made from the refuse which can not be used for sugar.

The 16th - 20th - On the sixteenth we were still completely at ease in the harbor at Kingston.

The 21st - The time dragged for us, so Captain Pentzel suggested a visit aboard the ship *Britannia*. After dinner we went there and again met Captain Alberti who had just arrived from a beautiful sugar plantation the previous evening. The captain entertained us with a glass of wine and told us of what he had seen and noticed. This plantation was also owned by a German who was a cabinet-maker by trade and who had lived in Jamaica for some time. His German countryman had hosted him with the greatest politeness. He had been born in Halberstadt and had named his plantation Halberstadt, also. Another, who lived on a mountain still higher up and who had married his sister, named his plantation Blackberry. This man had a mill near his house, from which the mules carried the sugar cane down the mountain. Then eight blacks were employed to push the stalks between two rollers, which were turned by mules. When the cane has been passed through the rollers twice, all the juice has been extracted and is then led off through a channel to a distillery to be cooked. The planter, if he desires, can sweeten his afternoon tea with sugar from cane cut in the morning. All of the cane is usable and nothing remains unused.

The pulp stalks are used as fuel in the sugar cookers or fed to the donkeys, which like to eat them. The foam, and the remaining sediment from fermenting the sugar is the base of the world-famous rum which is shipped all over the world, and which here in the West Indies, and in all of South and North America, is the most common drink. Here, however, the sugar is not processed to its end product, but sent to England where it is refined for use in the home. Spain has gold mines in Peru, but England has the produce of the West Indies for which everyone must pay with gold and silver. Sugar plantations give a greater profit than mines, and this is a trade which Jamaica exploits. The cattle of these planters run wild and fend for themselves without care. The other animals, horses, cattle, and pigs are always in the wilderness, and it is necessary to shoot them when a person wants to get hold of them. Where do they stay during the winter? Here in the West Indies there is no winter. The Negroes live in a circle around the plantation. The captain had met Robinson's satire. O, dear blessed author, how you would have laughed if someone had told you that your book, which makes fools wise, on this side of the world was once again being read for morals. The Blackberry is a coffee plantation where also lemons, limes, and oranges lie in great heaps under the trees, and have almost no value. Lemons are so little valued on the plantations that for a small tip, a black will let you have all that you can carry. Here there is such a fruitful climate that every product can be turned to profit. No wonder that everyone here becomes rich in a short time.

The 22nd - In exceptional and nearly unbearable heat, we remained aboard ship and continue to hope for our departure.

The 24th A pilot came aboard and we raised sail, and shortly dropped anchor again at Greenwich. On such a hot Christmas Saturday, when every European is snuggled comfortably behind his stove, we gave our lives over to the stormy sea.

The 25th - Truly, I have never experienced such a hot Christmas Day. Instead of like our countrymen, who can hardly protect themselves from the cold, we find ourselves in a part of the world where on Christmas it is warmer than in Europe during the dog days. I write this with open doors and windows and wearing only a shirt, which still makes me too warm. What a change -- and how many reasons to think kindly of us in the West Indies, to drink our health in Rhine wine and we drink theirs in Madeira and glasses full of punch, which we here in this island source of its creation, enjoy. I will always remember this Christmas Day sealed deep in my soul.

We raised anchor but could go no further than Muskite Fort.

The 26th - We again set sail, but the lack of wind prevented our passing through both sandbanks and we had to drop anchor again. In the evening twilight, the packet boat from Pensacola came past. Our pilot asked about news of that place but only learned that sixteen merchant ships had been lost there during a storm.

The 27th - We departed early and came to anchor at nine o'clock at Port Royal, where our other ships already lay.

The 28th - Everything was now ready for our departure for West Florida, but we remained at anchor. During the evening a strong storm arose which blew throughout the night.

The 29th - Still at anchor. Port Royal is a small place destroyed by many disasters.

In the year 1692, Port Royal was originally destroyed by a frightful earthquake. It lies on a tongue of land which extends twelve miles into the sea, but on which no trees or grass grow. For shipping it is well-situated, as ships can anchor safely or load and unload directly at the city. At that time it had 1,500 houses, and commerce and trade were greater here than in any city in the West Indies. The earthquake of 17 June 1692 destroyed the greatest part of the city. During a frightful storm, the earth opened, and the water gushed out of the opening, swallowing up many hundreds of houses and people. Just at that time, the frigate *Swan* lay at anchor in the harbor. It sailed over the sunken houses and saved hundreds of people in boats and hanging onto pieces of wood. Earlier we sailed over the sunken houses where now the sea is and where formerly a large part of the city stood. The sailors still pull many beams and pieces of wood from the bottom on their anchors.

Before the quake the air was bright and clear. And in a moment everything became red as fire and the air so close as the heat from a stove. Then a terrible roar was heard under the earth and at once mountains and rocks crashed down upon one another. Next the earth opened; the streets sank, together with houses, into the abyss. A part of the city remained standing, but the houses were severely damaged.

The entire island of Jamaica received an indeterminate amount of damage during that earthquake. At Savanna, another city on the other side of the island, 1,000 acres of land, at that time, together with houses, people, and livestock sank and became a sea, which later dried up and the land once again appeared, but no house was ever seen again. That earthquake leveled a mountain which destroyed many plantations and people. No house, especially no sugar mill, was left undamaged.

In the city of Port Royal the flooding is still visible. It lies so close to the sea that one must assume every storm would drive waves over the city. But, as it is so well-situated for shipping, it was rebuilt, and then on 19 January 1702 the new city was entirely destroyed by fire, so that only the royal magazine remained standing. Then people regarded this place as the site of misfortune, and built on the other side of the harbor the present city of Kingston, which then received all the privileges previously accorded Port Royal.

At the same time, many who refused to leave Port Royal rebuilt the city. However, in the year 1722, on 20 August, it was again destroyed as if the powers that be would not allow a city to stand at this place.

Suddenly the sea became very stormy and the wind drove the waves over the breakwaters and shores, tearing houses and people away, and few houses were left standing. Just at that time a richly laden merchant fleet was in the harbor, about to sail for Europe. All of the ships were driven ahead of the storm, destroying all but one. The warships rode out the storm, but had to cut down their masts and throw everything overboard.

Who would not say that Port Royal has an unlucky star, although it is presently far rebuilt so that it resembles a small city? Primarily however, the seamen live here. This was a short history of Port Royal which had the same customs and the same fate as Sodom.

General Remarks

Jamaica is divided into fourteen parishes and the main cities of the island are : 1) St. Iago de la Vega 2) Kingston 3) Port Passage 4) Port Royal 5) Savanna. St. Iago, or as it is presently called, Spanish Town, lies on a pleasant plain on the River Cobre, which enters the sea at Port Royal. It has about 1,000 houses and the governor resides there. The general assembly and the court of justice sit there, also. Kingston lies close to the harbor, ten miles from Spanish Town. It is a densely populated city of seamen. The residents are of English ancestry, next, blacks live here to the number of 100,000, also mulattoes, who are the offspring of a black and a European. Children born of a mulatto and a white are called mestizo, and with time, they will all blend. I wrote more about this in my report which Captain Ferguson took on land on the eleventh.

The 30th - We still remain at anchor at Port Royal.

The 31st - We headed out to sea with a fresh wind, and the same day the land was lost from view.

Eighteenth Century America
January 1779

The 1st - Again a year is past and truly the first on the stormy, unfriendly sea. Captain Pentzel treated with good Madeira wine, which enabled us to toast the New Year properly. On this New Year's Day we were as comfortable as one can be on the ocean. We conversed and discussed our distant homeland.

The 2nd - Strong but favorable wind.

The 3rd - Frightfully unsettled, stormy weather. The best however, was that the strong wind favored our trip.

The 4th - The ship continued to roll, and made such unpleasant movements that one would have preferred to be shaken.

The 5th - We must be near the Bay of Honduras. We saw a large part of the island of Cuba and saw Cape Corinthos especially clearly. The heat has not let up.

The 6th - We have already entered the great Gulf of Mexico.

The 7th - Our ship took a frightful amount of water. The captain blamed the strong sun under which the ship had to sit for an entire month in the West Indies. The heat eased considerably, and a blanket was again needed at night.

The 8th - No favorable wind.

The 9th - The frigate made a prize of a ship.

The 10th - In the morning, pleasant weather with which we were completely satisfied. About ten o'clock a stormy wind arose which forced us to retreat to the bunks in our cabin.

The 11th - The waves crashed and the sea howled so that it was nearly impossible to converse with another person. During the day the wind eased somewhat, but the sea remained rough and the waves would not calm down.

The 12th - Today a man could once again control his legs. The sea was still. The weather cool as it tends to be by us in October.

The 13th - On the previous Sunday and Monday the storm drove us fifty miles backward, which we recovered with today's favorable wind. And in order to get the most use from the good wind, our ship was taken in tow because it could not sail as well as the other ships of our fleet.

The 14th - The wind was still favorable, the weather foggy and not as pleasant as yesterday. At ten o'clock the frigate turned us loose and sailed in search of land. At that time it made a signal with a red and white flag on the mast for the fleet to check the ocean floor. We cast the lead and found bottom at 55 fathoms, that is still 330 feet of water. The lead was coated on the end and we were all curious to learn the composition of the bottom. It came up with nothing but white sand and some pieces of mussel shell. Now our only wish is for land, which we will surely see tomorrow.

The 15th - A thick fog hid everything from our eyes. Bad, dangerous day, which might have been even more dangerous if there were not a complete calm. The sea was as placid as a pond and therefore one had no need to fear that our ship, which the others could not see, would be in a collision. The attentive frigate fired a cannon shot every half hour, and then every quarter hour, so that the ships would know the course being steered. Here, where no one could see the pathway, one learns how to value the use of a compass. We cast the lead and found 43, then twenty, and at one o'clock, thirteen fathoms under us, which was the surest sign that we were close to the land which the fog prevented us from seeing. It is worth noting that in the Gulf of Mexico the depth can be measured long before land can be seen. The fog continued to thicken and it was necessary, for safety for all the ships, to drop anchor. While I was writing this on my bunk, and was complaining about the miserable finish, I heard one of our soldiers call from the mast, "There is land and the whole fleet!" Full of joy, I ran up on deck and saw through the thinning fog, but as in a dark distance, the peaks of the sand dunes of West Florida. God be eternally thanked! The blood again raced through the arteries, and joy was to be seen on everyone's face. In the evening we raised our anchor.

The 16th - It was foggy and the wind blew against us so strongly that we were driven so far away from the land that the flag on the lighthouse could no longer be seen.

The 17th - The weather and the wind changed so that we were able to steer directly toward the harbor of Pensacola.

At eleven o'clock the pilot came aboard. We met an outbound fleet here, part of which was bound for Jamaica, and part for England. And this fleet would inform the English newspapers that the reinforcements for Florida had arrived. And I hope that through this channel the people in our fatherland will also get the news.

The wind died down and we could not proceed further into the bay. It was a beautiful day, cold in the morning and warm during the day.

The 18th - We raised the anchor early but could not sail far as the wind and waves were against us. At noon the wind improved and we were fortunate enough to enter the harbor at three o'clock. Anywhere else that one might enter a port, he would be curious to see the city. Here, however, one could already see from the ship that this must be a miserable place.

The 19th - After we had, according to the reckoning of the ship's captain, sailed 3,463 English miles between 20 October 1778 and 18 January 1779, we saw the end of our prolonged and stormy sea voyage. But instead of the hourly anticipated debarkation, the order came that we were to remain aboard ship, and then later transfer to smaller ships on which we would sail to the Mississippi River. This was certainly a sorry damned situation. Here there were no ships that could take us there, and there nothing to eat or drink.

The 20th - The order that we were to go to the Mississippi has been lifted. We are to debark. But that too is cancelled because first, houses have to be built in which the troops will be quartered. Truly the English are not employers worthy of hiring Germans into their service.

- - - - - - -

That portion of the diary covering the period up to our arrival in Pensacola, I have sent to Waldeck.[1]

- - - - - - -

The 21st - 29th - We remained aboard ship, although we have already been bored with this for a long time. In the city absolutely no preparations have been made for quartering the troops. Also, no kitchens set up where the troops can prepare their food, and only now the soldiers have been ordered to begin work on the cooking excavations.

The 30th - Troops debarked from the *Springfield*, *Crawford*, and *Christiana* [sic]. The day was as hot as in Germany in mid-summer. Our entire officer corps was assigned six rooms. The parole today was Waldeck and the countersign was Hanxleden. Our cooking facilities are still not set up. Therefore, we had to eat our meals at the coffee house or wherever we could get something, and all of it was bad and expensive.

123

February 1779

The 1st - We went ashore in the city to see what a sorry sight it made. Pensacola is built rather widely scattered, and taking all buildings into account, one can say there are about 200 houses. These have all been built since the last war when this pitiful land was surrendered to the English crown. They are all made of light wood, and as dictated by the hot climate, built so that air can circulate through them. There are still three old Spanish buildings here, an old, dilapidated house where the governor had lived, another equally dilapidated, in which the Indian agent, [Colonel John] Stuart lived, and a powder magazine, the stones of which came from I know not where, because there are no stones to be seen here, even if man were willing to pay hard cash for them.

The streets, if they can be called that, are full of sand in which one walks with the sand, like snow in Germany, over the shoes, and in summer, so hot that the shoe soles and feet are burned. Initially, the English must have been very industrious here in an effort to improve this miserable place, as otherwise when they knew the land better, they would not have built it up so well. The garrison is still the primary reason for the city, and both the barracks, for officers and men, are as fine as could be wished, although only half-finished at this time. Both barracks are on the water's edge and well-ventilated by the sea breezes. The rooms are airy and large, and on each level there is a wide gallery around the entire barracks, on which three people can walk abreast. The lodgings are as good as could be desired, and I fear that this is the only thing that I can say that is good or of note about Pensacola. The harbor is a great, wide bay, about forty miles long. No ship, not even small sloops, can sail directly up to the city because the water is too shallow. Therefore, there are piers built far out into the water, which are destroyed every few years by the storms, and then must be rebuilt at great expense. From this it is clear that loading and unloading ships is very difficult here and this is a major drawback of the harbor. It is a safe harbor because the island of Santa Rosa lies like a bulwark on the sea side of the harbor and protects if from the wind. Nevertheless, the storm in the previous October had driven nineteen ships on land, all of which were lost, and those not entirely destroyed, were thrown so far inland that there is no hope of returning them to the water.

If the land surrounding the entire gulf, which is what one can almost call this harbor, had some worth, and if only a small part of Pensacola was so situated as to more easily handle trade and serve the plantations, then all foodstuffs and necessities could be brought to market. Such, unfortunately, is not the case, because this was never foreseen, and also can never happen. The harbor also has another fault, in that worms eat into the bottom of the ships, and if a ship remains a half year in the bay, it had better be moved to a point where fresh water enters the bay; otherwise in a year it has rotted and is unusable. The bottom is sandy and good for anchoring. Because of the worms, seamen do not like to remain here but prefer to sail away as quickly as possible. At the present time there is neither church nor pastor. The ground for the church has been designated for several years, but has not yet been built, so that they must express shame to strangers that no house of God has yet been built. A salary of 100 pounds sterling has been suggested as pay for a preacher. However, I have heard from many that this is not enough, and a man with so little income can not live in this land where all necessities are so very expensive. Therefore, the council wishes that the preacher assigned to the garrison will also serve as the preacher for the city.

Beside the garrison, in the middle of the city is a great level courtyard where people stroll in the evening. And that is the only place where a person can go without getting his shoes full of sand.

The garrison is surrounded by a palisade of stakes about ten feet high. The defense works on the sea side are of sand and held in place by high stakes. Since our arrival, the stormy waters have washed out all these sandhills and carried off all the defense works. Our soldiers, like the Israelites in Egypt, must work unceasingly to rebuild them. The business people, at great cost, have planted gardens about their houses, in which, however, things only grow in the winter, and all the vegetables produced, cabbages, pumpkins, and beans, are not nearly as good as that which in Germany are used to feed cattle. Also, in those gardens despite all efforts to improve them, the ground and soil remain nothing more than sterile, white sand.

The 24th-30th - We had to remain aboard ship because the two barracks designated for use by the regiment had not been refurbished and cleaned.

The 30th - The troops were put ashore from the *Springfield, Christian,* and *Crawford.* The three companies were moved into the barracks and the officers moved into the very nice rooms of the large barracks which lay not far away. The parole today was Waldeck and the countersign Hanxleden.

February 1779

The 2nd - The two companies on the *Britannia* landed today. We began to take our meals with a German native, to whom we give two Spanish dollars in addition to our regular ration money, that is, four pounds per week, and we are fed quite well. A packet boat came from Jamaica and brought the news that Russia and Holland had joined England, and that both powers will declare war on France, if it does not cease supporting the rebels.

The 4th - We wished to hold church services but a sudden downpour forced a postponement.

The 9th - I went walking with Mr. Montgomery. We saw all kinds of bushes, and among others, a bush on which black berries, similar to juniper berries, hung. He told me that a very good wax can be drawn out of this fruit. The berries are squashed and then cooked with water in a large, clean tub. A scum forms on the top of the mixture, which appears gray in color.

The 10th - I rode with Lieutenant Wiegand into the woods. Along the way we met two women on horseback. We rode with them through an Indian camp until we came to a miserable hut, where a company of rangers lay.

The 14th - We held our first church services.

The 15th - Communion.

The 23rd - The entrance of the savages [into the city ?].

The 24th - 25th - Rather cool.

- - - - - - -

March, April, May, June, and **July** - Nothing special.

- - - - - - -

August 1779

The 17th - The entrance of the savages [into the city ?]. We listened closely to their discussion. A chief,[2] who saw us enter the room, said he would interrupt his speech because he saw many strangers enter, who perhaps had business with the commissioner of Indian affairs. The interpreters must be able to speak the language very well. He had to please everyone present and continued. We had only come in with the desire to listen to his speech. We were the warriors which had been sent by their big-brother-across-the-water, and the gentleman, indicating Colonel von Hanxleden, who sat next to the chief, was their leader. Their discussion covered several requests. The chief ended his speech saying that they had come a long way and had many old people and women with them, so that it was necessary that they be furnished with fresh meat instead of salted and spoiled meat. He was told in reply: The cattle ran loose in the wilderness; it was not necessary to ask for meat. The chief was quick with his answer. They had seen a large number of cattle close to the city. He asked that they be furnished to the weakened, older persons. Further, he said at that moment, they were very poor. They could not go hunting because they were fighting for the King, and the English commissioners who lived among them, would not extend credit to them. He asked that the commissioners take all this into account and he would return tomorrow at twelve o'clock for an explanation. Hearing this, the entire assembly said Ha!

The 18th - Today they came with their wives and the entire families. We gathered again in the house where the English commissioners and we sat around the table. The chief sat on a bench and as many, especially the older members of the tribe, as possible squeezed into the room, sitting on the bench and on the floor. Each smoked from his tomahawk. The chief, a serious, mature man of about forty years, had the wing of a wild fowl, which was painted red, in his hand. Deep in thought and searching inwardly, he resumed his speech. As long as he spoke, he looked at no one but the interpreter, so that this one would be sure to get the correct meaning, and he never said more than one sentence to him.

They were about to undertake their march as warriors and friends of their big-brother-across-the-water to Savannah and Georgia, but he could not take his young people there until he had led them against a certain fort, where some of his people had been killed, and revenge against the enemy not yet taken. For this purpose he requested good weapons, such as the guards had who stood before the house. And he needed good axes so that once the fort was captured, it could be completely destroyed. Now he said, he had nothing more to say, except to request foodstuffs for his people who were hungry and thirsty. Finally, he requested permission for his subordinate chiefs to speak. Thereupon, he arose from his place and one of the leaders of his warriors assumed the seat.

After this one made a short introduction, he said that he was one of those who led his people into fire. Their weapons were for the most part unserviceable, and he requested better ones to replace the bad ones. Their powder and balls were used up, and he wished them replaced. All this was promised, at which all the Indians present expressed their pleasure with Ha! Another leader assumed the seat and said that he agreed with what had been said previously, was satisfied therewith, and had nothing more to say.

As they left, each gave his hand as a sign of friendship to as many of those as were sitting about in the room. During this afternoon, I watched how they divided all this in a very orderly fashion. The chief and his lieutenants worked for more than an hour before they had divided all the balls and powder evenly. Then they received the provisions, which they likewise divided.

I have seen many troops of Indians here, but none by whom everything went so smoothly and with such complete satisfaction for all. They had painted themselves as is general in the Creek tribe. Among others, there were some more than seventy years old, who had not painted their faces. Their faces were of a copper color but without a beard. Among them were young people who were most wonderfully developed, large and strong. From the soles of their feet to the top of their heads, they were amazingly beautiful. All were mounted on horseback and it was a pleasure to see them ride. Surely, no horse is too wild for them. The wives, who had been busy tying up the provisions, then mounted their horses and followed after the men at a full gallop.

The weapons which they received were very light and all were poorly painted. Their conduct toward one another was friendly and the relationship with their wives and children, according to their ways, was tender. Their camp is four miles from the city. I saw no drunkeness among them and that is something out of the ordinary. The chief rode away last. Their departure was so pleasant, they were so self-contented, as if they now had everything one could wish.

The 19th - Tea at Mr. [Arthur] Niel's, and then dinner, also.

The 23rd - We saw a group of wild Indians from the Choctaw tribe. They were not as tall nor as well-built as the Creeks, but are braver in war and can run exceptionally fast. A very good horse is needed to outrun them. The Creeks and Choctaws are not good friends, but when they come together, there is much trading. They come from west of the Mississippi. I had the pleasure to attend their reception. They were not very numerous. There were fourteen chiefs who sat themselves on a bench in the room and then began their speeches. This is something of the situation. There was no interpreter in Pensacola who could speak the language of the Choctaws, although there are interpreters here of whom one is for the Creek tribe, another for the Chickasaws, the third for the Choctaws, the fourth for the Cherokees, and so forth.

These chiefs had been so careful, however, as to bring along an Indian from the Creeks who spoke the language of the Choctaws as well as his own. The language of the Creeks, because much trading is conducted with them, is spoken by many people here. The principal chief spoke to his Indian interpreter, who then spoke to the English in the Creek language. The Indian was attentive and took his time so that the sense was fully understood. While all this is sort of rambling, the Choctaw chiefs made it very short. They requested weapons, powder, lead, and rum, which was promised to them. Next, one of the chiefs said that he wanted winter clothing for his old people, but was refused because nothing of that sort was stored here. Another chief began and said that since they were as good fighters as the other friends of their big-brother-across-the-water, he therefore wished to be supplied with flags and drums. They will be given the flags. There were no drums available, however. Then the chiefs were told in rather rough fashion that they must control their people so that they cause no damage. They did not answer this and seemed to consider these remarks uncalled for. Another chief said if things which they desired were not stored here, they would go to the Indian commissioner at

Mobile, to which remark they were told bluntly, they should not go to Mobile. A new commissioner has been installed here and this gentleman does not yet seem to have the knack of handling these Indian chiefs. The deceased Colonel [John] Stuart, whom these people still love and honor in memory, knew better how to do business with them. He could get them to do whatever he wished.

The chiefs did not appear satisfied with the answer, but broke off the meeting and left without shaking hands all around.

One, a man of about thirty years, assumed the place on the bench where the other had been and said his father was dead and that he was chief in his place. One could rest assured that he would follow his father's footsteps and would conduct himself as a friend and warrior of the big-brother-across-the-water. He jumped down from the bench then, and shook hands with everyone.

The appearance of the Choctaws is quite different from the Creeks. They do not cut their hair like the Creeks, but part it along the top. They smear bear fat on their hair which makes it a shiny black. The chiefs wear a band or other decoration around their head. They do not cut the ears as the Creeks, but hang a small ring from the earlobe and none from the nose. Each chief painted himself in a singular manner. Some of the eyebrows and the ears red, some of the forehead. Others had painted the entire face with white, red, and black spots so as to look frightening, but all had decorated the entire uncovered portion of their bodies with circles of all sorts of figures. These they made by putting powder under the skin and igniting it. About the arms they wear two or three silver bands. About their necks they wear all sorts of decorations made of coral. Their legs are completely bare and on their feet are shoes of deerskin, which are tied on with strings across the arch. The chiefs, although not especially old, had a serious, rather dour appearance, which may have been caused, however, because all their wishes had not been fulfilled. It struck all of us, as many as were in the room, that their faces had the appearance of the old Roman heads. Each found among the Choctaw chiefs one whom he had previously seen in pictures of a Roman. There was one in particular who looked exactly like the head of Julius Caesar.

Almost all wore a mirror hung around their neck, but with the glass covered. And truly, children with a watch in their pocket for the first time, do not look at the watch as often as these look at their mirrors each moment, and they always find something to tend to. First they pluck an eyebrow with their knife and then they find where their paint is missing and must be retouched. at once,

The color of their face is more black-brown and not as copper-colored as by the Creeks; their forehead is smooth and not sloped. They, like the Creeks, carry a scalping knife and tomahawk, from which they also smoke. Their tobacco pouches are made from various materials. Some have skinned the entire hide from a young bear, as one would skin a rabbit, and that is the tobacco pouch. Others have used a martin skin, otter, or fox. On occasion they bring, as do other Indians, bear fat to sell. Wax candles melt from the heat and olive oil is very expensive.

September 1779

The 1st - The days are quite pleasant and the nights cool so it is necessary to use a blanket. We are constantly making preparations for a trip to the Mississippi.

The 2nd - A ship came from England. We are all anxious to hear the news, and even more so than normal, as we seldom get any news here, and the sea around us is full of warships. This ship had a long trip via the West Indies and had run out of fresh water. They had to distill sea water for the past three months.

The 3rd - The heat began to increase again; the nights are still bearable, however.

The 5th - At five o'clock, church.

The 8th - As we were dining Commissary Marc wrote a note that a three-masted ship was just outside the harbor. We were full of curiosity and anticipation. Late in the evening it entered the harbor. It was a packet boat of eighteen cannons, which could sail indescribably swift. How we were deceived. It brought no good news, but just the opposite. Spain had declared war, and the battle between the fleets had not been to our hoped-for advantage. Byron and [Samuel] Barrington had fought like lions and their ninety gun ship had captured seven French ships. Barrington had dueled with the French flagship *Languedoc*, but been seriously wounded. Immediately after the engagement, Barrington sailed for England in a frigate, and took seven French ship's captains as prisoners with him. Because they had not done their duty, the troubled situation in the West Indies will be put before the Admiralty. The French fleet is stronger than ours by twelve ships-of-the-line.

The 9th - The colonel received some letters from Waldeck, from which we learned that Major von Horn is on his return trip to us with 21 recruits.

The 10th - I wrote a letter home which the packet boat took. It goes by way of New York where it will deliver the bad news.

The 11th - We received orders to be prepared to march at a moment's notice.

The 12th - We did not hold church because the entire garrison is busy with preparations for battle and the light infantry has been chosen for a special assignment. There is nothing but war to be seen here and we are in such a fix, that I can not see how we will work our way out of it. If only a warship would come to strengthen the harbor.

- - - - - - -

P.S. -- Our grenadiers left here on 20 June and the reports from them which we occasionally received were worse than one can imagine. Many troops have died and the rest are sick.

The 2nd of August - The major's company left for the Mississippi. On 29 August Captain Alberti, Sr., departed with a part of his company.

- - - - - - -

The 13th of September - The packet boat which brought the Spanish declaration of war will not depart, but will remain here for some time as a protective force for the harbor.

The 14th - As anticipated, we are to make an attack on New Orleans. With this in view, four Indian chiefs from the Choctaw tribe met with the general this morning, and 200 from that tribe will take part in the attack.

The 15th - One hears that 700 rebel light dragoons attacked the Creeks and handled them very roughly. The Spaniards have reportedly landed in Apalachee Bay and tried to seduce the Indians to their side with rich presents. That is bad news from both the east and the west. An express came through the wilderness from the Mississippi with letters for the general. The commandant, Colonel [Alexander] Dickson, who was not aware of the Spanish declaration of war, saw activity on the other side of the river, however. He sent an officer across to ask the Spanish governor what that meant. The governor only answered that he was too busy to answer at that time, but hoped that would not be taken in any wrong way.

The 16th - Colonel Dickson today sent another express by land, who rode through the wilderness in thirteen days. The Spanish have taken the field with 1,500 men. Captain von Haacke has already gone to Baton Rouge with our two companies, and most of the troops are sick. Colonel Dickson has pulled back from Manchac and burned everything that he could not take with him. Two ships which had taken our troops there have already been captured by the Spaniards and Colonel Dickson sank another himself. Captain Alberti's command had to pass the Spanish batteries. As was expected, the good man, his command, and even his ship, were captured. *O what the Mississippi has cost us in good men. It has ruined our regiment. O Mississippi, spare our noble legions!*[3]

The colonel paid past due allowances today, which amounted to fifteen pounds, ten shillings for me.

The 17th - I wonder if more bad news will arrive today. Now winter has set in with its constant rain. Occasionally it freezes, but not until October, and even then, there will be days when it is warm enough to cause one to sweat, and during the night it will freeze. This we know from experience. When we arrived here and I went into the city for the first time, it was as cold as at home in the month of March, when a sharp wind blows. Some days later, on 30 January, we landed when it was as hot as it gets in Europe in the month of July. Last night it was very stormy, foggy, and it rained all night. I thanked God that I was not at sea on such a night, but rather in a good room and a comfortable bed while listening to the wind outside. Currently there is considerable sickness among us, which is common at this time of year.

The 18th - Terrible weather. The air is thick and foggy, and it rained all day.

The 19th - Church was again postponed because of the rain and the large work commands which are taking the cannons to the ships. Now an expedition is to go against New Orleans. It is surely not an opportune time of year because during this month there are frequent storms. During war this can not be avoided, however.

The 20th - Still one more day survived without Spaniards. As soon as a person awakens, he looks out to sea to check if a Spanish fleet has arrived. What will become of us? Certainly nothing good. This is no land for human beings, and no war can be waged here. If the Spaniards do not get us, we will nevertheless die out in time. That is certain. Germany seems like such a good land where there are all sorts of good fruits to be had. If only wild plums and crab apples grew here. No, even these are too fine for this cursed land. Truly, we ask now for nothing better than wild plums and crab apples. But it is our burden, of all those which life holds, to be robbed of all pleasure. Spain held Pensacola as a penal colony, but even for criminals this is a hard punishment, if endured for very long.

The 22nd - The Maryland Light Infantry returned from the Cliffs.

The 23rd - The packet boat which arrived recently, sailed out in order to cruise at the mouth of the Mississippi, and to gather intelligence on the condition of the Spanish batteries, and if armed ships are present there. I rode out with several good friends to a so-called plantation which is eight miles from here. It is a bit strange to ride eight miles through the wild forest, where not a living creature, not even a bird, is to be seen. Several savages, whose camp is close to the city, met us on our return, but we did not see anyone else. The land is more despised by all of us each day. Who would not prefer being a common laborer in Germany rather than a gentleman in West Florida. Anyone who does not agree, needs only to spend a year here to get his thinking straight.

The 26th - 28th - Nothing especially new. Many warlike preparations, a new battery placed near the storehouse and a floating battery built. News arrived that the Spanish have cut communications between Baton Rouge and Natchez. Lots of bad news and poor prospects for our unfortunate troops on the Mississippi.

The 30th - More Indians than usual, and from all tribes, have been gathering here to ask for presents. They clearly see that in the present situation, it is more necessary to flatter them so as to keep them friendly. And if it is not to our advantage, still we must give them presents so that they will not take up arms against us. On the other hand, the Spaniards do all they can to draw these savages away from us.

Well, another month in this miserable land has passed. Hopefully it will be the last September that we must spend here.

October 1779

The 1st - Cool, rainy weather. October has always been a month during our time in America which held something special for us. In 1776, during this month, we were still aboard ship and arrived at the beloved New York. In the year 1777, we went aboard ship again during this month and sailed up the Hudson, or North River. A miserable and very difficult passage. In the year 1778, we again went aboard ship on the twentieth of the month and traveled via the West Indies to this cursed West Florida. And in this year, we will undoubtedly undertake a sea voyage which is certain to be the most unpleasant of all.

The 11th - Again bad news. An express came from Georgia, and reported that 26 French ships-of-the-line had arrived at Savannah. Everything is going amiss and this affair will end as it did for Burgoyne's army. Now we must worry whether the major and the recruits will arrive, and our situation becomes more dangerous every day.

The 13th - Drill every day.

The 17th, Sunday - It was rather cool, but again no divine services could be held as most of the men were on duty and the others were loading baggage aboard ship. It is a miserable ship on which all the crew is sick. They had a long voyage from England and were without water.

The 18th - We firmly believe the embarkation of troops is about to occur, because the baggage is already on board. But it remains undone.

The 19th - Still full of expectation but everything remains as before.

The 20th - This day has always held something special for us, and we anticipate, from all signs, that we will go aboard ship today. The day was very stormy and the sand blew about in clouds. Yes, the day held something special for us. -- A courier came from Mobile. Colonel Dickson with his entire command have been taken prisoners - and that includes most of our regiment. Mississippi, a loss for our regiment, which will be irreparable as long as the war lasts. Now the general's proposal to go to the Mississippi to rescue that corps will be even more difficult. The English, who are proud of their military strength, refuse to believe all of this, but it must be true. If there had been another bed in the cabin of the ship when Captain Alberti last left, then I too would have been captured. God knows how long or how short the time may be, how long we will remain free. Any night our fate may be determined, and it is strange that no fleet has arrived from Havana.

The 21st - The express, about which one spoke yesterday, did not arrive, and the English are willing to believe it all to be lies and that the newly arrived reports were fiction. I kept the discussions which I overheard to myself as I heard so many foolish things, such unjustifiable pronouncements, such discrediting of Colonel Dickson, so many accounts of his activities, that I could not avoid similar thoughts. O you fools, who understand nothing of the situation, but would force your advice on others. ---

The 22nd - Still no express, although he should have come already yesterday. It is really surprising, even though we know that the present strong winds have swollen the rivers which he must cross. Also, he does not have the best horse. And who knows what problems can arise for a courier who must travel through savage tribes before he finds the best way?

The 23rd - The English continue to believe it to be only lies and a trick which the governor of New Orleans, [Don Bernardo de Galvez], has circulated to the effect that the English troops and positions on the Mississippi were in Spanish hands. Otherwise our general would carry out his plan of going to the Mississippi with the designated troops, and if the wind did not blow too strongly, the order to board ship would be given. Adjutant Stierlein came into our room at nine o'clock and brought the news which we had dreaded for two days, that the express from the Mississippi had arrived at headquarters. The news and letters which he brought in no way contradicted what one had surmised already yesterday, but placed the unfortunate, and until now doubtful, situation in a clear light which as near as we can determine this evening, puts us in the following position.

Colonel Dickson, who could no longer hold out at Manchac, and whose full situation and unfortunate circumstances the general, already a week previously, had hindered by refusing reinforcements and cannons, saw himself forced to abandon Manchac. He sent the troops from our regiment, under the command of Captain von Haacke, to

Baton Rouge and placed himself with the English troops between Baton Rouge and Manchac, and hoped there to await reinforcements from Pensacola. And that heaven still had so much patience -- here ships are built, armed with cannons, armored with stinking cowhides instead of leather siding -- and that all proceeded so slowly, so lazily, as if there were no war. O that everything should be lost. No wonder that a person who sees it all curses the establishment.

The Spaniards had sought to bring the savage Indian tribe which is called the Choctaws to their assistance through all kinds of gifts and especially with pearls and jewelry for their wives, and 200 of those set themselves between our troops and Colonel Dickson, and prevented the retreat of the latter and the consolidation at Baton Rouge. The next day the Spanish Governor Don Galvez came with a vastly superior force and launched an attack from all sides. Colonel Dickson saw no alternative but an honorable capitulation, which the clever and deceptive Don Galvez offered. All the troops at Baton Rogue and Natchez were included in the capitulation. Although the rashness of some Englishmen passed judgment on him concerning this point, at least we know his carefulness was prudent. At least we have such a good opinion of Colonel Dickson's character, that it would be impossible for us to form a premature judgment about him until we know all the details. According to the capitulation, all troops departed the Mississippi, were sent back to an English port, and on their word of honor, were not to serve again for eighteen months. The inhabitants have eight months in which they have the freedom, either to become Spanish citizens or to dispose of their belongings. Their stock and other produce will be purchased at a generous price by the Spanish governor. The corps at Natchez had been cut off by the Spaniards, and even if that had not occurred, Natchez would have been captured by the Americans who were already on their way down the Ohio. We will learn more exact details through a flag of truce which is expected every hour from New Orleans.

The 24th, Sunday - The wind was very strong and quite sharp. We held church at seven o'clock. When the weather is so windy, I always wish for at least a shed in which to hold services. It is now nearly four years during which we have held church services in the open air, and this during winter and summer. In other wars, there are winter quarters and in such, churches are also to be found. Here in this lousy war, there is only a wilderness, 500 miles long, and nothing more, to give one pleasure. On all sides here, one has to put up with a lot of unpleasantness, and everything joins together to make this war even more so.

The 25th - Is it possible to think of something more stupid than that one would again doubt everything that was heard yesterday from the courier as well as from others? The general, who is still disturbed by the whole annoying situation wherein he finds himself with all this troops, and the whole province of West Florida, does not now know how to determine if he should go aboard ship, or how he should strive alone to defend Pensacola. Is that not a cursed land in which to conduct war, where most of the corps are captive for five weeks, and a 1,200 mile stretch of land can be captured without the commanding general being sure it has happened? Yesterday the general unloaded his baggage from the ship. Today at seven o'clock the order was given to remove the provisions from the ship *Thomas* again. At eight o'clock another order to cease the operation and the general ordered that his baggage be loaded as quickly as possible. This afternoon, the troops are to embark. Nothing here is firmly decided, first one thing and then another. In this fashion the whole thing is finally accomplished in the most likely manner. To tear the general out of his vacillation and get a firm decision, the governor and his entire council sat down, studied the incoming reports and querried the couriers who had recently come in. They found, after all this searching, that a 1,200 mile stretch along the Mississippi had been captured by the Spaniards and all our troops had been taken captive. As a result, it was too late to send support and too far and too difficult a sea voyage to undertake. It seemed best to secure only this place. This was the decision of the Governor, His Excellence, Peter Chester, with his councilors. The general was satisfied with that and gave orders for the baggage to be brought ashore again.

It was our prince's birthday and we drank his health in port wine at Commissary Marc's, and ate today at Mr. Bachstaedter's.

The 26th - Today the express returned, which the general had sent to Colonel Dickson. Because the savage tribes during the present war adhere more to Spain than to England, he had been unable to penetrate their territory, but had seen it as necessary to return with his letters. The Indians, in general, complain that they can not carry on further trade with the English traders because the prices are too high. Therefore, the express brought his letters back unopened. However, he told us many special circumstances concerning the incident on the Mississippi. Initially our troops forced the Spaniards back with severe losses, which on the Spanish side amounted to 400 dead to our 23. The following day the Spaniards set up a battery, against which our troops made a sally, and after the Spaniards lost 150 men, they were dislodged. Finally, Colonel Dickson saw no other choice except surrender, as he could not save himself in any other way. Our situation is still unknown. The general gave the order that the baggage should be brought ashore again, and the contemplated expedition to the Mississippi has been canceled.

The 27th - From the lighthouse this morning a signal for unidentified ships was made. Already at daybreak one could see smoke at the side of the lighttower which signified that ships were visible to the west. It was a sloop and a schooner, but as soon as a cannon was fired from the lighttower, they turned toward the sea. Here in the city everything was in an uproar and several companies were put aboard ship and six armed ships lifted anchor and sailed against the enemy. The enemy ships were no longer in sight as ours moved out. This evening pickets were posted, who at the first alarm are to assemble at their designated places. Several gentlemen have already fled from the city to the garrison with their prize possessions, and everyone believed the Spanish fleet was at hand. It is strange, that it is not already here.

The 28th - There is a great urgency to get the batteries ready for use and to provide them with heavy cannons.

The 29th - Very cool and stormy weather. One bit of bad news follows close on another just now. Today intelligence from Georgia that our army is completely surrounded, and the French fleet was close on the coast to assist in cutting off relief from New York. At the time when this express left Savannah, the capital of Georgia was already under siege so there was no hope that the troops could be saved in any way. The naval hero, who has captured so many ships and thereby created such an impressive fortune, Sir James Wallace, was reportedly captured with his ship *Experiment* during that incident. He surely sold his capture at a high price.

The 30th - The constant drumming and the drill of the many corps awakens one from sleep at an early hour. I get up early, go out on the gallery, and look toward the sea, but still neither Spanish nor French fleets are to be seen, and this provides one with the knowledge that one more day can be lived in peace, but that can be changed in the morning. And considering the dangerous situation in which Pensacola finds itself, the words of the song are appropriate:

> By nightfall the situation can easily change
> From that which it was at break of day.

Work on the battery on Gage Hill was pushed, but it was feared the Spanish would arrive before the battery was finished.

The 31st, Sunday - There was no church because our regiment provided the watch and the picket. Further, it rained all this week so that no services could be conducted previously. Toward twelve o'clock the weather cleared, and suddenly an armed warship could be seen beyond Rosa Island. Now, suddenly there was alarm everywhere. The gentlemen gathered on the roofs with their telescopes and generally agreed, yes, yes, it is a Spanish ship which is reconnoitering. A strong fleet will follow it. Captain [William] Johnstone of the Artillery had all the batteries heavily loaded. The watch was reinforced and all preparations were made as if we were already under attack from the sea, and now awaited an attack from the land side. A thick fog moved in accompanied by a heavy storm, clouds, and rain, wherefrom the sky grew very dark and the ship was again hidden from our view. This interlude gave time to discuss what kind of ship it really was. The belief, as the English are so individualistic, was divided on this issue, also. One wanted to wager that it was an English ship from New York, another that it was from Jamaica, the third, that it was a Spanish ship from Havana. During this discussion, the sky brightened and the ship could be seen nearing the coast, and on a mast a flag requesting a pilot, who was sent out at once. Now it could be ascertained that it was not an enemy ship. The wind changed and prevented the ship sailing further than into the mouth of the harbor, where it had to anchor overnight. Once again everything quieted down in the city.

November 1779

The 1st - The ship which came in yesterday is a privateer of sixteen cannons and a ninety man crew, which has been cruising in the Gulf of Mexico near Jamaica. It had captured a Spanish sloop but encountered a Spanish frigate not far from the island of Cuba. After a two-hour engagement, the Spanish frigate sailed away, but because this ship had been hit between wind and water, and was taking much water, it felt compelled to enter here to keep from sinking. The news which it brought us is not much. Admiral Byron has sailed for England and the closest available help is from Jamaica. Further, two frigates from Jamaica sailed toward Honduras with the intent of making prizes of two Spanish ships from Peru which are loaded with silver.

The 15th - I went walking with Captain Pentzel and other good friends. In the evening Captain Jones of the Marylanders invited me to the main watch where there was a big party. The news came, while there, which suddenly raised the spirits of all the English. The French had landed 10,000 men from their fleet in Georgia, and an equal number of Americans came from the side toward the Carolinas, in order to capture the capital city of Savannah, and all of Georgia, as quickly as possible. Relying on their superior numbers, they planned to capture our troops who numbered only 4,000. As earlier at Rossbach, however, they also came to such a sad end as did the men there. The French as well as the Americans suffered heavy losses, and during the retreat, a serious breach developed between the Americans and the French, when the former accused the other of not fulfilling their responsibility. From our side, 300 cannons, taken from the ships run aground by the English upon the approach of the French fleet, were turned on the enemy. This victory instilled in the people of Georgia a great confidence in our troops, and they now believe that Charleston will soon be captured.

The 16th - 18th - A thick fog, common here at this time of year and which often lasts for several weeks. Following this will come the months of rainy weather, which also last for several weeks at a time, and thereafter, the weather clears and becomes cold. And that constitutes an entire winter. It never gets so cold here that the garden produce freezes.

The capitulation articles concerning our captives on the Mississippi arrived here. The officers as well as the enlisted men have retained all their personal belongings, and marched out with flags flying and music playing. Along with this came another report. Our wives, during the siege, together with the children, left the fort and in order to find a place of refuge, apparently went into the forest, and there both women and children were slain by the savage Indians.[4]

The 19th - An Indian prince of the Delaware tribe is in the city. I have not yet seen him. Last summer there was one here whom I frequently saw with his wife.

The 26th - Nothing but a flag of truce from New Orleans, under which the grenadier company of the 16th Regiment returned.[5] We also had the pleasure of receiving a few letters from our friends in captivity. In these letters we were informed, unfortunately, that our people are dying off like flies and many more have been struck down sick. Lieutenant Leonhardi died 26 September on the Mississippi on the journey from Baton Rouge to New Orleans, and Ensign Noelting was killed in the fighting aboard whip on the 22nd.

The 27th - Several ships were to be seen through the fog beyond St. Rosa Island. Already during the previous night several cannon shots had been heard, and this morning a signal was displayed at the lighthouse. By afternoon the ships could be seen more clearly, and it is assumed that they were our fleet from Mobile. We had gone for a walk and upon returning to the green place, we were told that the *Earl of Bathurst* ship was entering port with Major von Horn and the recruits. This raised our spirits, especially as there was so much other good news, including: four frigates were en route to protect the Pensacola harbor, the French fleet in the West Indies was not preparing the disaster which we had feared, but had left the West Indies and sailed toward Boston. The passage between the West Indies and us was again open. As a rule , news which arrives in a land such as this, where one is cut off from the rest of the world, is accepted without any thought of confirmation as to whether or not it is true. It is about time, also, that an occasional ship from Jamaica calls here as prices for all articles which normally come from there have risen to unbelievable heights, for example, a pound of sugar costs a dollar.

The 28th - All our hopes of yesterday are gone and all our expectations shattered. Major von Horn was not on board. It is now a year and one-half since we received mail from Germany and in all probability, the letters we have sent have been lost.

December

The 3rd - We had a rather sleepless night. About three o'clock the cry of fire was raised as the general's house was burning. There could have been serious consequences if the fire had spread. The storehouse stands close behind the general's house, and if it had caught fire, we would have had no choice but to starve to death or to surrender to the Spaniards, as this land does not produce any means of nourishing people. The same situation applies to the nearby laboratory in which much powder was stored. Only today I received my letter from Lieutenant Strubberg. He wrote that his life as a prisoner was quite satisfactory. He praised the hospitality of Governor Don Galvez. Privates as well as officers are given friendly treatment by the local inhabitants, and the captives are allowed complete freedom of movement. And anyone who has been to Pensacola will never again in his lifetime be hard to please. The captured officers are frequently invited to dine with the governor.

The 6th - We saw three three-masted ships, but at evening still did not know what they were. Concerning the cause of this problem, one certainly had to right to wonder. Yes, during a war with Spain when any day we could be visited by warships from Havana, a ship could still enter our harbor without our knowing whether it was a friend or a foe. They had the appearance of transports, even the English merchant flag flying aft as well as on the mast.

The 7th - The ships we had seen yesterday were from Europe, and had left England in the month of March. They made a voyage of not less than nine months. They were loaded with provisions for the garrison. One of them had 3,600 casks on board. Another fleet is still awaited which sailed from England in September. The next day another ship came in which belonged to the previous three.

The 12th - Now the work on the fort on Gage Hill is being pushed twice as hard as before. The most stupid preparations which can be taken in wartime are undertaken here. Since the outbreak of the

Spanish war, we have begun hastily to construct batteries. Previously, kitchens, bake ovens, and latrines were laid-out and then built with the greatest care. The news arrived today that the Spaniards are marching on Mobile and that they will visit us, by land, from there. Now everything is in turmoil. The general ordered work on Gage Hill to be speeded-up, but the carpenters from the city pay no heed to the general's orders, do not show up for work, and neither the governor nor the general can force them to work as it is against English independence. These carpenters consider themselves to be gentlemen equal to the governor and general. A room which cost two dollars is now four bits; a pound of bread, twenty guilders; one pound of sugar, one dollar; one egg, six guilders; one pound of tobacco, two dollars. Is it reasonable to assume that somehow one can get out of this situation, and above all, get away from this cursed and uninhabitable Florida? The Mississippi has always been praised. We too have praised it. Now none of our people return from the Mississippi. They die there like flies, currently as many as three a day. The grenadier company of the 16th British Regiment, which served near Natchez, has returned and the troops are so sickly, that they will never regain their health. They look like death and die daily. It is certainly no place for human beings, otherwise nature would have provided for them by allowing foodstuffs to be grown here. But there is nothing but two, three, even four hundred miles of white sand, and those who build here are called fools, as there are better regions to develop.

The 10th - Again a sudden change in weather. Yesterday was as cold as it can be and today, on the other hand, as warm as it is in Germany in the month of May.

The 25th, Saturday - Once again it is Christmas. We held our religious services out-of-doors as usual, at nine o'clock. At noon I went with several other regimental officers to eat with the general.

The 27th - I wrote a letter home. Because I know many are lost, I sometimes wonder if it is worth the bother. I spent the evening with the colonel talking about home.

The 28th - There are 800 Americans not far from Mobile and reportedly, together with the Spaniards from New Orleans, they have plans for Pensacola.

Eighteenth Century America
January 1780

The 1st - Thank God, another year has passed and life takes a new direction. This is the fourth year which we have spent in an area of the world so far from our homeland. The first in America was celebrated in Elizabethtown and it was the most pleasant. The second was on Staten Island and still good, still filled with joy. The third was spent in the West Indies during our sea voyage here. Now the year 1780 here in Pensacola. When I write that word, I need write nothing more to refresh my mind, as it encompasses everything which fills my heart with sorrow. The entire officer corps gathered at Captain Pentzel's at seven-thirty and went to congratulate the colonel. At eleven o'clock everyone paraded over to the general's and from there to Governor Chester's.

The 3rd - 7th - Our soldiers must work like the Israelites in Egypt, going from watch duty to fatigue duty, and this continues day after day. The soldier's life here is really one of slavery.

The 8th - 10th - Very cold, colder than we would have believed it could get here. Water froze in a bucket, but now it has become quite pleasant during the day. Things are so quiet now that nothing is seen or heard from any corner of the English possessions.

The 17th - An Indian came with the news that a Spanish ship had run aground at the mouth of the Perdido River and the crew was lying on the bank drunk. It supposedly has a good cargo and if the ship stays as it now is, it would make a good prize for the governor.

The 18th - The Queen's birthday was celebrated. At eleven-thirty the general was feted and then we went to the governor's. The fort on Gage Hill was designated Fort George today and the cannons from the fort fired for the first time. At one o'clock the two warships each fired a 21-gun salute.

The 24th - Everything is so quiet now, so free of all activity and information. We will not learn anything new until our packet boat returns from Jamaica, or an express comes from Georgia with a dispatch pouch full of wind. As far as mail from Waldeck is concerned, we have given up all hope.

February 1780

The 3rd - The general has assigned Captain Pentzel the task of escorting the officers, here on parole, back to New Orleans. They left today with a flag of truce on the sloop *Christiana*. Commissary Marc was sent by the general, when this opportunity arose, to arrange the financial accounts of our prisoners.

The 5th - Early this morning news came from the Cliffs that two ships had been seen and the lighthouse hung out a signal, but in the end it turned out to be nothing more than a small sloop, loaded with corn, from Mobile.

The 6th - Storm, thunder and lightning, and an earthquake. Everything in the room shook, and clothing, hung on the wall, fell to the floor. This quake lasted about one minute, and truly, it could not have lasted much longer nor come again without causing the barracks to collapse. As soon as our door burst open, sparks from the neighboring room were blown over the gallery and into our room, so that the outbreak of fire as well as an earthquake was to be feared. Several chimneys were blown down by the wind. The quake itself, the crashing of collapsing houses, and the shrieks of a family caught under the debris, the lightning flashes which followed quickly one after another, and the night made darker by the black thunderclouds, the roar of the stormy sea throwing its billowing waves upon the shore, and the rolling crash of thunderclaps, were startling. All this contributed to make the night so frightful that I could hardly believe such a storm could be survived on land. It is only in Pensacola that nature exerts all her fearfulness through the strength of the elements to destroy as she pleases. Thank heaven that despite all this no lives were lost. The wind eased about one o'clock in the night, but we did not lie down to sleep until morning.

The 7th - A certain Mr. Holmes came by land from Augustina and brought various items of news with him, which in part were quite good. Among other things, we have abandoned Rhode Island and the main theater of the war will be moved to the Carolinas, and that Admiral Parker had captured a Spanish fleet of seven ships-of-the-line, 25 frigates, and twenty transports. These circumstances may be to our advantage, and result in our prisoners, held at New Orleans, being exchanged before the end of the war. This news must be true and the shoe must be squeezing the Spaniards somewhere, otherwise we would not be left here in peace for such a long time as we have been.

The 8th - After dinner we saw various signs from the lighthouse indicating the approach of a fleet, but as the wind was not blowing from the sea, no sail could yet be discovered on the coast.

The 10th - The signals displayed yesterday and the day before supposedly were meant to indicate that two Spanish ships were cruising in the Gulf of Mexico.

The 12th - Late yesterday evening an express came from Mobile with letters for the general.

The 13th - The express which arrived yesterday from Mobile brought a report to the general that thirteen Spanish ships had arrived at Mobile Bay and men had already landed. These ships are waiting for Governor Don Galvez to arrive from New Orleans with his land forces, will then attack Mobile, and then visit us in Pensacola. Many preparations are being made here for a brave defense, and a picket was posted at Fort George which will be withdrawn at sunrise tomorrow.

The 14th - The number of workers at Fort George was doubled, artillery and cannonballs delivered there, and everything is astir as the Spanish are expected here, by land and by water, at any time. If our Fort George were finished, if it were in fighting condition, I would hope we could win laurels here. It is a shame that no ships from Jamaica have been sent to lend support. It will cost many heads on both sides, but where can a soldier die with greater glory than on the bed of honor?

The 15th - Last night we had a thunderstorm, an exceptional storm, which churned up the sea and continued until midnight. We hope this storm will have held back the Spaniards and given us time to make our fort more defensible. An express came from Mobile. The Spanish ships have departed from Mobile Bay and are no longer to be seen. The only idea which presents itself is that the fleet came from Havana, and is waiting near the islands off Mobile Bay for Governor Don Galvez from New Orleans. Then the combined force will place Pensacola under siege. Whoever amongst us survives, will see what occurs. The most that can be hoped for is that at this critical point, a frigate will arrive from Jamaica to support us, and one is expected this month. Certainly one must not lose courage, but here the power of angels is needed to fight, to defend this place, and still, -- still hope.

147

The 16th - We had a social get together this evening, and were speaking of the Spanish war when Lieutenant Keppel, who was in charge of the guard, entered and with excitement and elation said two Spanish deserters had just come in. They each had a weapon taken from our captive soldiers. The news, which they brought, was good news for us. It was definitely the plan of Governor Don Galvez to besiege and capture Mobile and Pensacola. All the armed ships and troops which he had been able to muster were with him. He even had 1,000 Negroes with him. His victory apparently certain, he was approaching the coast on the night of the fourteenth to fifteenth when a terrible storm arose which battered and scattered most of his fleet. Don Galvez was on board a brig of sixteen cannons which was driven so far this way that it had been seen here. Those who saved themselves from shipwreck, assembled at Mobile Point and off Dauphin Island, and fortified themselves as they anticipated we would take advantage of their misfortune and launch an attack. A single frigate and 200 men could have carried out that action. The deserters also told us that they suffered greatly from lack of provisions because the provision ships had been scattered and for each man the ration was half a biscuit and for four men, four pounds of salted meat.

Don Galvez had reportedly sent an open boat to New Orleans with the order that all ships there should be sent to him with provisions and to take his men on board again. Six hundred men drowned in the storm, and seven ships were wrecked, so that Don Galvez is no longer in a condition to undertake any action against us. That is how God alone has fought for us, and none of our strength has been used to help. He caused the storm to strike, which scattered our powerful enemy who was so near to us. That could have taken its toll from us, also, as we had outfitted ships to attack New Orleans, and chosen a stormy and inopportune time of the year for an attack. And this all-powerful rescue by God could have come at no more opportune time, as it is during this month that we now await not only the packet boat, but also a frigate from Jamaica. And if our harbor is thus protected, I am of the belief, that we can withstand a number of attempts against Fort George. How fortunate we are, to win time by the Spaniards' misfortune, so that our fort can be placed in a defensible condition.

In addition, however, I am glad that Don Galvez has come out of all this safe, as everyone must respect him for his intelligence and humanity. He chose the best time of year for his undertaking, he had no heavy defenses to fear in our harbor, our fort was not finished, and still he was not successful, because it was not God's will.

The 18th - Captain Baumbach and I attended a conference of savages. It was a meeting of Choctaw warriors, but as there was no interpreter, except a young Creek Indian who understood very little of the Choctaw language, there was very little said. The Choctaw king could not express the number of his people, who were with him, so he took a stone and broke it into as many pieces as he had followers. The king was a strong, young, well-developed man. His body, as well as his face, was painted and, except for a red apron pulled between his legs, he was naked. He received his own provisions in his blanket. The others had bags of deerskin or marten skins, which only had openings at the head, and when filled with Indian corn, the shape of the animal could clearly be distinguished. Captain [Alexander] Cameron, the Indian commissioner, filled his tomahawk with tobacco, took several puffs, and passed it on to one after another as a sign of friendship. And this is the custom among all the Indian tribes, and when the peace pipe is smoked one can be sure that they consider it as binding as any treaty.

The 20th, Sunday - On every side signs were to be seen that a strange ship was approaching the coast. The *Earl of Bathurst*, which lay at the mouth of the harbor, hung out three flags and fired three cannon shots. If it is Spaniards from Havana or English from Jamaica, we will learn today. I wrote this at nine in the morning and by twelve o'clock all signals had been taken down. The fleet sailed past, either to support Don Galvez at Mobile or directly to New Orleans. This much is certain, they were Spanish ships. And if our harbor is not occupied soon from Jamaica, we will be lost beyond hope.

The 23rd - An express arrived, which brought news that the Spanish fleet had left Mobile Bay and sailed toward Pensacola. This was contradicted by another report that there are thirteen ships to be seen in the bay.[1]

The 24th - Today a camp was laid-out and Colonel von Hanxleden pointed out each regiment's position. Fifteen Indians were also sent to gather exact intelligence at Mobile as to whether the enemy was really on the march to this place.

The 25th - The colonel took all our servants to work on the defensive position near our camp at Gage Hill. The colonel himself indicated the work to be done. Service in the regiment is so pressing now that no soldier could be spared for this detail. And this good example of the colonel has been adopted by the English. When the soldiers finish guard duty, they go on work detail, and from that to picket duty, and this goes on day after day. And as the days become warmer, the troops will not be able to continue at this pace on such poor rations. They will become worn-out by the work and the fatigue will kill them.

The 27th - Everyone with healthy arms must work today, Sunday.

The 28th - Everything is scarce and that which is available is so expensive that no one can afford to pay for it. For a supper which consists of nothing more than four eggs, a glass of beer, bread, and cheese, one must pay two bits. Half a twist of tobacco costs five bits, and one pound of fish costs one and one-half bits.

The 29th - The light infantry company of the 60th Regiment left the camp and assumed duty at Gage Hill. The light infantry company moved into camp yesterday. An express came overland from Georgia with the most pleasant news that we had not been forgotten, and that our post was not to be left unsupported. On 25 December of the past year, three regiments were embarked on twelve transport ships, the 57th, 42nd, and Lord Rathers, plus three frigates and two sloops-of-war, for Pensacola. Those ships are to be expected here soon and it is just in time as everything is now in disorder. The general at once sent a courier to Mobile, where this news will have a good effect and cause great joy, as Don Galvez and his fleet are already at the city, and have cut communications between here and Mobile. If those frigates come in the next few days, Don Galvez can be trapped in Mobile Bay. That is the way of events during wartime. Changes occur making a situation look so dark that no way out can be seen, until suddenly there is hope where one thought no hope could have been expected. We had only hoped for help from Jamaica, from whence none came, but instead we will be strongly supported from New York. And if the Spaniards hear of this, it can only make us more peaceful and secure.

March 1780

The 1st - A restless night, caused by a thunderstorm which lasted all night. The news from yesterday, which I so happily recorded, is doubted today by everyone, and I assume it is a fantasy meant to frighten Don Galvez. And if that intent is obtained, it will have served its purpose. Above all, every bit of news which arrives tends to make us more mistrustful, as we have been deceived so often. The light infantry from the 60th Regiment moved out of the camp again and into the city. [Lieutenant] Governor [Captain Elias] Durnford reported to the general that the Spanish Governor Don Galvez has called upon the fort at Mobile to surrender, to which he returned the answer that because of his duty to king and country, he could not surrender until forced to do so by the most strenuous onslaught. Therefore, Don Galvez sent a galley further into the bay and close up to the fort, but cannon fire from the fort forced it to retire. The Spaniards then took position on a height opposite the fort and set up a battery to fire on the fort. Therefore, the general began to prepare to march on Mobile with every soldier who was in any condition to undertake such a march.

The 5th - Early today the 60th Regiment marched out, although it rained the entire day. Our regiment is to follow tomorrow.

The 6th - Our regiment, or more correctly, the greatest part and most useful part thereof, marched toward Mobile at six o'clock. Every soldier received a five-day supply of rum and bread which he had to carry. Officers and men took only that which could be carried. The officers had their own rolled blankets fastened on their backs. This is a march which would be unheard of in German wars, and if described by a participant, many would consider it impossible that troops and light artillery could travel 120 English miles through an area consisting only of wilderness. Immediately behind Fort George the wilderness begins and extends more than fifty miles before any developed place is encountered. The troops must spend every night under the open sky.[2]

The 7th - Continuous, heavy rain. What have we had to put up with in the way of changes in this barren Pensacola? The pitiful transports continue to depart, one after the other, leaving us with fewer people, until now only five are here (Lieutenant Heldring, Lieutenant Wiegand, Ensign Knipschild, Colonel von Hanxleden, and the chaplain). The general rode out with his retinue at eleven o'clock.

The 11th - A string of pack horses which are to pick up provisions for the troops came into camp.

The 13th - Another thirteen pack horses for the provisions for the troops came in today. The troops have enough fresh meat but are short on bread. In addition, they must roast it on the fire as the Indians do, as they have no cooking utensils with them. Four men of the 60th Regiment drowned.

The 16th - A man came from The Village which lies opposite Mobile.[3] He had heard a heavy cannonade the previous Sunday and seen the Spanish flag flying on Tuesday. It seems Mobile fell before our relief troops arrived.

The 18th - It rained hard and the 16th and 60th Regiments returned this evening, and there are reports that our troops have recrossed the Perdido River. The general arrived earlier and all the inhabitants are displeased with him, as they are of the belief that he could have saved Mobile, which his vacillation lost. They wish that he had remained here and given the field command to Colonel von Hanxleden, which they believe would have made the expedition more successful.

The 19th - Toward four o'clock the artillery and our regiment, plus the Pennsylvanians arrived. All our men and officers returned here healthy and in good spirits. It is hard to imagine, after hearing the stories of the difficulties our troops encountered, that not a single one from our regiment was lost. They waded water to their knees, and during the entire fourteen days, have not once had dry clothing. They had to cross deep rivers on fallen trees, where a single misstep meant drowning without hope of rescue. Except for the rivers and a few plantations, here is nothing but wilderness as far as can be imagined. They heard wolves howling in the distance and close by. They had more than enough fresh meat, of which there is available all that one might wish, if he shoots it. The ground and soil is so good thirty miles from here, that they passed through grass higher than their heads. The livestock graze in herds in those pastures, and many owners do not know how many head of stock they own, although there are few who own less than 1,000 head. The stock generally becomes wild in time, and like other wild game, must be shot. In place of bread, which was in short supply, the troops received Indian corn which they roasted over the fire like Indians. During the march, the Indians were always on the sides as flankers, and during the evening held their war dances. At those times all the officers had to share their black war drink. Two Indians sang as long as the others held the cup to their lips.

The 22nd - Both this morning and this evening cannon fire was heard out to sea. If it is our long awaited fleet from Jamaica, it could not be arriving at a better time, as the Spanish fleet is expected at any hour. And the guard force at Fort George has been strengthened this evening for that reason. Just now fourteen days could make a difference in our fate, either to conquer, to triumph, to withstand a siege, become exhausted, or --- or ---. *Teach that which may be beautiful, brave, great, and virile. The remaining may willingly rest in conquering the enemy and pursuing the fugitives. That which is contrary to our lives, is unknown to us.*[4]

The 27th - The *Earl of Bathurst* made a signal at nine o'clock to indicate a fleet approaching from the east, and at eleven o'clock fired twelve cannon shots. No one knew if the fleet were friend or foe, but we assume it to be our fleet from Jamaica. Toward three o'clock we were able to see from here that there were a great many Spanish ships, and the entire fleet consisted of 21 ships. They are at anchor now on the other side of Rosa Island and will undoubtedly take control of the harbor tomorrow. This I write in comfort in my own peaceful room, but what the day will bring is already written in the book of omniscience, in which is recorded the fate of all provinces and all nations. We have had it in Pensacola, which has never had a lucky star shining on us.

The 28th - The Spanish fleet still lay at anchor this morning, but everything is stirring here. We have packed and at ten o'clock are to move into our camp at Fort George. Just after ten o'clock the regiment marched off with flags flying. The cannons of the battery in the garrison were tipped-over and everyone moved to Gage Hill. The *Earl of Bathurst*, which lay at the mouth of the harbor, raised her sails and sailed in, because the Spanish were too strong.

The 29th - Once again we have moved to a new field camp and spent the night sleeping in tents. Very early this morning we heard heavy cannon fire from the sea and believed it to be signaling by the Spanish fleet, which was again under sail yesterday evening. It has been reported that the Spaniards have landed twelve miles from here. Work on the defenses is being pushed strenuously so that the soldiers are almost never idle, and as a consequence, the general has ordered an extra half pound of bread be issued to each man. Our campaign can not last long; it must be decided in a short time.

The 30th - Today the Spanish fleet could no longer be seen and we can not understand that, as they have the best wind today for entering the harbor, or at least to move closer to the Cliffs, and take anchorage there. Work on our camp continues to be pushed. Everyone is waiting in anticipation and no one understands why the Spaniards have not launched an attack. The English flatter themselves with the hope that this means an English fleet from Jamaica has followed the Spaniards. However, we believe that the admiral is not concerned about our harbor, and since the greatest and best part of West Florida has been lost, retention of this post has insufficient value to justify sending reinforcements here. In a few days we will learn what the Don's intentions are.

The 31st - It was very warm. The Spanish fleet appeared again from the west, and the wind is so favorable that they can enter the harbor this evening, and then, if it is the Don's desire, they can hit us with a strong bombardment from their ships early in the morning. Two more companies of Pennsylvanians moved into the camp.

April 1780

The 1st - An officer who came from Mobile on parole solved the puzzle as to why the Spanish fleet had disappeared from view. The entire Spanish fleet, with 1,500 men, was at Mobile Point and was to join Don Galvez and then come here. We have received reinforcements, also, but on whose assistance little is to be relied, namely 300 Choctaw Indians, who are divided within their own nation, and 300 Creeks, of whom a great many are already here, and whole families pass our camp daily. We can trust the Creeks a bit more than the Choctaws, as the Creeks have had a more constant friendship with the English, while the Choctaws tend to favor the Spanish.

Today two companies of Marylanders joined us in camp. Colonel von Hanxleden has the overall command in the camp on Gage Hill. Lieutenant Heldring was presented his captaincy in the regiment. The governor announced that in our present dangerous situation the inhabitants were not to sell or trade rum to the Indians as the problems of dealing with drunken Indians is well known. Colonel von Hanxleden, in appreciation for the hard work, gave the regiment an oxen and decided to continue this practice every Sunday in the future in order to bolster the spirits of the soldiers from the depressing workload, and to encourage their eagerness to continue working for the King.

A sloop was seen cruising before the harbor, apparently sent by the Spaniards to observe whether or not help for this province was awaited from Jamaica, and if a fleet was being sent to provided relief. The neglect of the admiral at that place will surely serve to our downfall.

The 2nd - I was sitting peacefully in my tent when I suddenly heard small weapons fire close to the camp, very much as if an outpost were under attack. We ran from our tents and saw a party of Choctaw Indians, who had been thirty days traveling from their land, here. They were all dressed according to their own way. They camped, spread out in an almost oriental fashion, and smoked from their tomahawks. If one enters among them, he does not have enough hands to greet them all, and they shake hands so vigorously that after shaking hands with thirty of them, it can be felt in the arms. The Choctaws do not cut their hair like the Creeks, but smear bear fat on their heads and powder themselves with fine white feathers. Their limbs, as well as their entire bodies, are naturally stronger than those of the Europeans. Their wives sit separate from their husbands, and generally speaking, are not as well-built as the men. And the women do all the work. They carry their children, their food supplies, and even the blankets of the men, while these march unencumbered with only their gun or bow. These women carry heavy loads, and nevertheless, walk as swiftly as the men. I saw no small individuals among them, and even less to be seen were cripples or deformed persons.

The 3rd - Another corps of Indian warriors arrived, who upon entering fired their weapons as those who entered yesterday. It is truly worth noting, and I should like to see, such a troop of Indians, acting in this manner, marching through Germany. Their old chief, a sworn enemy of the Spaniards, led them, and the interpreter assured the old warrior that he would be treated correctly. There are many especially handsome young men, few of whom were under six feet tall, who through their life style are accustomed to long marches. What a wonderful regiment could be made of them. But would they accept discipline? Discipline is something about which they know nothing. Even the chief does not control them, but each one does as he believes necessary from an inborn sense of honor of being a good warrior. To hear the singing of their feats prior to an engagement, instills a greater desire for further accomplishment than any reward of honor in other armies.

The 4th - Several of the Indians came with the very welcome news that Charleston is in our control, and that the wished-for peace between England and America has been established. How happy we will be and how universal the joy which shall reign if this report is entirely true. We wait for confirmation by express from Georgia. Many have arrived here who tell us the same story, and even mention some of the peace articles. God grant that we will learn more of this today. Truly there is no news which I would more joyfully record in my book than that England had concluded peace. There is no need to take revenge on France. It is reported here also, that the fleet of two 74-gun ships, seven frigates, and 21 other ships, which recently sailed past here, was not a reinforcement for Don Galvez, but were destined for Vera Cruz. If this is true, we will be able to speak with Don Galvez through the muzzles of our cannons.

The 5th - Our Indians held their parade in the city. When they marched past the fort an eleven-gun salute was fired in their honor, as the chief had not been happy with the greeting they received when they initially entered the city and had fired all their weapons, but had not been answered. After they had gathered at the large green place, the king, Peka,[5] sat down on the ground with all his chiefs and other minor leaders about him. The king was a strong, serious, old man. Behind the king and his chiefs, sat the younger chiefs, and behind them, the warriors. There was a rather long delay before the speeches began, and during this time, the king sat still and somber. Finally, Captain Cameron arrived with his interpreter. That one turned to the king and said: The general was sick and could not shake his had. He had sent his most senior warrior to shake hands with the king. They answered with their usual Ha! which is forced out rather strongly when something pleases them. Thereupon Colonel von Hanxleden extended his hand to the king and then to every chief along the row, and the

156

other officers did the same. The king and his chiefs remained sitting on the ground until the ceremony was finished.

When the hand-shaking was done, the interpreter turned to the entire group and said: All the warriors of their big-brother-across-the-sea could not shake hands with each one of them because they were too numerous and scattered, but in their hearts they felt the same as if they had been able to shake hands, to which there was a common answer of Ha! Then the interpreter again addressed the king: The general and all his warriors were happy that the king and his warriors were so quick to respond to the call to support their big-brother-across-the-big-water against his enemies. The Indian king answered: He was not called to Savannah in Georgia, otherwise he would have assembled his warriors and gone there. But as soon as he did receive a call to come here, he had assembled his warriors and had hurried here. His people had been hunting all winter and had just come home, but had, nevertheless, all joined him. He was answered: That the general would be sure to convey these good intentions to his big-brother-across-the-big-water. In turn, he will send ships with presents for the Indians. The war however, which their big-brother-across-the-big-water is presently waging, was the cause of a limited supply of gifts now. King Peka answered: His young people had been hunting all winter, and their ball ammunition had all been shot up, and their powder horns were empty. Therefore he requested powder and lead instead of provisions. These were promised him. Then he was told: That we have enemies all around us and we would like his help in holding them back. After this conference ended, Colonel von Hanxleden, as the host for our warriors, shook hands with King Peka, then the chief sitting in front of him, and continued as at the beginning. As long as someone was speaking, he was never interrupted, but everyone listened attentively. Peka, as the leading general, wore a red coat worked with gold and on his head, a cap made like a helmet, but wore no paint.

Many ships were seen drawing near the coast, but no one knew if they were from the enemy or English. The admiral in Jamaica had given the general a signal which enabled us to determine that they were friendly. If the Jamaican fleet arrived at our coast, the King's ship which convoyed it was to fly a white flag on the foremast, and the *Earl of Bathurst* was to answer in the same way. This was the signal that Pensacola was still in our possession. If the *Earl of Bathurst* did not answer, the fleet was to return to Jamaica, because that would be the signal that the Spaniards held the city and the harbor.

The 6th - Now we are certain that it is an English fleet, and what pleases us more, is the certainty that our Major von Horn and everything which belongs to the regiment is also there. The wind is contrary however, so that the fleet can not enter today. There has also been hung out a signal that a fleet is coming from the west. I can not believe that it is Don Galvez with his old fleet, but neither can I hold back the fear that it really is. That would be something, if our recruits and everything which they have with them were to be captured when so near their destination, after having sailed for so long across such an expanse of water. Then heaven would have given us only a hint of joy. We have received no mail from Germany for nearly two years, but now we will receive bundles enough. Only an hour more of good wind, then we will have nothing more to fear. At one o'clock the Choctaws marched in, firing all their weapons near the camp. They marched to the green place and formed in a half circle. They did not sit down as the Creeks had, but remained standing, leaning on their weapons. Colonel von Hanxleden, as the host, after the general, welcomed them and shook hands with each one. Then through the interpreter, the colonel said: They had made the warriors of their big-brother-across-the-big-water very happy by their eagerness to stand by us in the war against the common enemy, and even if we are now surrounded by enemies who are stronger, we will nevertheless, not only push them back, but completely defeat them when the Creeks [sic] remain steadfast and help us. This speech by the colonel pleased them greatly as indicated by their mutual Ha! The chief who could well have had the rank of major general, as he stood third in the row, said: That if the whites would be as good warriors as the reds, he was certain that they would defeat the enemy. The oldest chief then said: He had come a long way with his people in order to visit their old father, Stuart. That was not the only or most important reason, but he had heard in his tribe that their brothers, the English, were at war with their common enemy. Therefore, he had asked all his warriors to travel here to support their friends. He had only a few of his warriors with him as the others were off hunting, but would join him upon their return. Thereafter he was told that we were delighted they were so willing to join us and to help us, and that it was unfortunate that we could give them so few presents at this time.

However, when the ships of their big brother arrived, and could not be far away, they would receive the finest presents. The gifts meant for them, had, from prudence, been sent away aboard ship so that the Spaniards would not capture them. To this, one of the chiefs, in an even tone, answered: Why have they been retreating from the Spaniards? One should not be frightened by his enemies. Then a few questions and answers followed, which for a savage people were intelligent enough. Colonel von Hanxleden and all the officers who were present made the rounds as at the start of the meeting, shaking hands all around. The caps of the various Indians caught our attention, as they were made out of many beautifully colored duck feathers. They had been plucked in such a way that the duck's bill stood directly over the forehead. The chiefs wore a silver medallion with the bust of the King on their chest, others had mirrors hanging, which is much in style with them. Their wives were not in the line with them, but sat quietly behind the circle. In general, the Choctaws are not nearly as tall nor as well-built as the Creeks, but are said to be very brave in war. The Chickasaws are preferred over both.

The 8th - This afternoon all the ships but two came in and we had the pleasure, toward evening, of welcoming Lieutenant Colonel von Horn and his sons.[6]

The 9th, Sunday - Our recruits landed today, all in good health, after having been a full year aboard ship. They were wonderful, young Waldeckers who are always more reliable than the weak outsiders.

The 10th - The businessmen are working very hard to unload their ships. Previously the city has been dead as everyone had fled. Now open doors are to be seen again.

The 11th - Since Saturday I have no longer thought about the Spanish war, because I had other European news to hear and read about. This morning however, Don Galvez reminded us, through a flag of truce, that we still had a war with Spain. All that I know so far concerning the flag of truce is that Don Galvez requested that our Indians stop scalping or he would be forced to resort to the same practice. He has 5,000 men with him, two 74-gun ships, and seven frigates. We can take the measure of his 5,000 men, but with the ships? --- The admiral at Jamaica has much to answer for. Great losses are now occurring in Pensacola, since the richly-laden ships have now come in. I wish the Spaniards had waited just eight days more before visiting us, so that we could have opened the newly arrived cases in which the letters and other possessions were packed that were sent to us from Waldeck. But now we must leave everything just as it is.

The 12th - The businessmen are hurrying to unload their cargoes because all the armed ships are ordered to the harbor entrance. The Spanish fleet is stronger than ours in every respect and our ships only sloops, while theirs are 74-gun ships and frigates, but we believe that ours can close the harbor to them. The reasons, which an experienced naval officer provided, are these. The Spaniards can not enter the harbor with 24 [74 ?] gun ships which must remove their cannons in order to lighten the ship. We know how much effort that requires, especially in the presence of the enemy. Their seven frigates are certainly stronger than our pair of ships, but they can not force their way into the harbor without being fired upon all day by our ships, and unable to return the fire because of where our ships lie, If they wish to lie at anchor under the protection of the Cliffs and drive our ships off with the weight of their cannons, they must consider that the flood tide will turn their ships so that the stern of the ships will be exposed to our cannons. When the tide ebbs, the bow of their ships will turn toward our ships, so that they will receive the greatest damage without being able to fully utilize their cannons. If things go as we hope, the defense will reflect to the glory of our sailors, although their reputation needs no added glory, and our seaward side will be protected. The defense of Gage Hill will contribute to our honor and reputation, and it will not fade from the pages of history in future years. True, it will be a difficult task, but who expects to win laurels in an easy chair?

There was a big get-together at Cameron's today, including the leading generals of the Creek tribe. General Campbell sat beside Reko, the supreme Creek general. After everyone had shaken hands with us and we with them, a tomahawk was filled with Indian tobacco. King Reko lit the pipe and gave it to General Campbell, and so on to all the leaders, and as many more as were in the room. The tomahawk had to be refilled three times, because when the Indians mean it seriously, they smoke the peacepipe so strongly that the smoke comes out of both nostrils. Reko had his tobacco in a beautiful wildcat's skin.

When this ceremony was finished, the general addressed Reko through the interpreter. He, the general, was very pleased, as were all the warriors of their big-brother-across-the-big-water, that the Indians, as old brothers and true children of their common father-across-the-big-water, had hurried here in order to fight against their common enemy. Therefore, the general expressed his true thanks. They listened attentively while the interpreter said this and then expressed their approval with the usual Ha! They did not reply until the interpreter said that his speech was finished. The general continued through the interpreter, that their big-brother-across-the big-water would be pleased to learn that they were such true brothers and children, and as proof of his good feelings toward them, who always had been as brothers to the English, had sent a shipload of the finest presents. They answered with the usual Ha! The general said that the presents could not be unloaded quickly at this time, but there was no reason to worry. The most necessary items would be delivered tomorrow. Ha! Ha! Further, there had been reports of the young Indians injuring livestock, and of shooting many head. As the supreme chief, Reko should control these excesses, as what the Indians would receive, would prevent any shortage of foodstuff. --- Ha! --- Further, the enemy was expected here any day and everyone must be alert to receive the Spaniards. Therefore, Reko was always to keep his people together so that they could resist the enemy at a moment's notice.

Next King Reko asked the general for permission to begin his speech. He was told that everyone was most desirous of hearing him speak, as he had the reputation of an old and intelligent warrior. He began in his distinct voice: He was pleased to have the opportunity to see and shake hands with the greatest warrior of the big-brother-across-the big-water. He did not come here to get presents, but had heard rumors in his tribe of a war with their common enemy, Spain, and at once had sent his warriors, and accompanied them, here. True, he was sorry that he could no longer meet with his old brother, Stuart. (He meant the deceased Colonel Stuart, who had taken every opportunity to represent the interests of the Indians.) But he was pleased to see Stuart's replacement and especially to get to know him, whereupon Captain Cameron was pointed out to him. He continued, that he could not prevent the excesses of his young warriors who had shot the cattle. They were widely scattered and their camps far apart.

They had not committed their acts due to a shortage of provisions, but in youthful exuberance. Other than that, he had nothing more to say. He had accomplished his purpose of getting acquainted with the warriors of his brothers, and shaking hands with them. Then he shook hands with the general and the other officers and the meeting broke up. The subordinates had listened to his speech with close attention.

The 13th - Today there was a meeting with the Choctaws and Chickasaws. The ceremony with the hand shaking and peacepipe as yesterday, and the general gave the same talk to the Indian generals as the interpreter said to the Creeks yesterday. I will, therefore, only record their conversation here. An old, dignified chief of the Choctaws began. They presented themselves as old friends and children of the English. They had shaken hands with them earlier than the Chickasaws had, therefore they felt that these younger children of the big-brother-across-the-big-water should have the advantage of speaking first and then he would give his speech. Everyone's attention was drawn to this old chief. His decorum and tone were suited to his conviction and the friendly moderation and peaceful, undisturbed expression with which he spoke, had to be seen to be felt in its entirety.

I would have wished for a talented painter to paint this man just as he was at that moment. Even the young chief of the Chickasaws was so moved by the eloquence of this old man, that he was struck dumb. I must present some little information about this youngster. He was, to the eye, about six feet tall and not more than twenty years old, from head to toe well-built, all of his limbs strong and muscular, a very attractive person. His face was one of those which pleases everyone. He had narrow, black eyes. His expression was too serious for a young man, who is carefree and lightly slides away from considerations of danger and the unfamiliar, but one could also read many youthful but spirited thoughts therein. He wore a cap of marten fur on his head, decorated with all kinds of pretty feathers and beside both ears, but standing erect, were two horns which had been fastened securely on the cap. His face was not painted; he had only a ring in his nose and several in his ears. His dress was a fine white shirt around which he had tied an apron decorated with numerous pearls. His other companions were all fine looking young people who had decorated themselves as is customary among the Indians.

The general now offered the handsome young Chickasaw chief the chance to speak. I wanted to hear him if he spoke. Then it became obvious that he had never spoken in an open meeting. He was just like a schoolboy who must give his first speech during a ceremony. And he had not expected the Choctaw chief to give him the opportunity to speak. So he began, at first very shyly. They had come, not to hear a speech, but to earn the name of good warriors. All the old chiefs, who had the talent and experience speaking, had gone off to the Ohio region because they heard that the enemies of their big brother were going there in order to attack their good brothers. While the interpreter translated this, the young chief glanced at his comrades, who sat beside him smiling, as if to say, well I have started it and now must finish it, and he did. Previously he had hung his head, but now he sat completely at ease and continued without embarrassment. They were all young people, without wives or children. The older warriors had not wanted to make this long journey, but they, the young men, still had to earn their good names in war. He was well aware, he continued, that taking scalps was not customary among the white folks, but one should not deny them the right to retain this custom, because they would earn the praise and especially the name of warrior in the tribe only when they brought the scalps of their enemies back home in triumph. This speech ended with several witty interruptions, over which the Chickasaws had a good laugh, but which were not translated.

The general said to an Englishman who lives among them, and who came here with them, that he should repeat to the Chickasaws what was told yesterday and today to the Creeks and Choctaws, since each tribe has its own language and none understands the other. Then the man, who is respected and honored in this tribe, turned to the young Chickasaws and by the strength of the speaking eloquence which he had in that Indian language, created such pleasure, that although they normally answer Hikae! when something pleases them, now they shouted it three times. When that was finished, one of the favorite Chickasaw chiefs filled his tomahawk with tobacco and smoked. Next it was the turn of the old, honorable chief of the Choctaws. As old and good friends and brothers of the white people (meaning he English), they found it impossible to look on in patience when their common enemy attacked those white people. They should be assured, just as they reached out their hand in friendship, so they have extended their hearts at the same time, and as they have held their hands together, so their friendship shall hold together. It would be the greatest and most shameful ingratitude, he continued, if we would not stand by our big brother at this time, as he has watched over us with so much love. Yes, I must not be silent, this big brother has made no distinction between his white children and his red ones, and in all circumstances has treated them as equals. And the opportunity does not always arise, but it has now, where we can support our brother and prove that we are true to him.

The big-brother-across-the-water has recently helped us and clearly demonstrated that his affection remains as strong and his friendship as constant as ever. We had heard, and many have told us, that this big brother has sent many ships with presents for his red children, and one may well believe it is for that reason that they have come here. But they do not wish to accept the presents until they have proven themselves worthy of such by their bravery in this war. However, they ask these goods for themselves because they know that they would not be thought less of for that reason, and they want to defend the presents as if they were already their own.

The 14th - Another tribe of Indians, the Cowites, paraded into the city and were greeted with all the artillery at Fort George, which they answered with a constant discharge of their weapons from here all the way into the city.

The 15th - Almost all of our armed ships are now lying in the harbor entrance and with every good wind, await the arrival of the Spanish fleet. And we work increasingly hard to strengthen our camp.

The 17th - The defensive position right behind our camp was named Waldeck as it had been constructed entirely by our regiment.

The 18th - We hear that Don Galvez embarks and then debarks his troops so that no one can fathom his intentions. His fleet still lies quietly in Mobile Bay. I can not understand however, why he has not had a frigate cruising in our area. If he had done that, he would have captured our recruits and the merchant ships which were kept out of the harbor for three days by contrary winds.

The 19th - Today 200 Indians marched past our outermost fort and were greeted by all the cannons. This was the first time this had occurred at the just-completed, new fort.

The 20th - The Spaniards have now fired on our outposts for the first time. Don Galvez sent a small patrol across the Perdido, which is the border between us and the Spaniards, to round up all our horses. Therefore, this afternoon, 200 Indians of the Choctaws and Chickasaws marched out to show them the way back across the river. At least it is a good thing that these gentlemen have something to do, as they seem to us to begin to be too boisterous in camp. They are our good friends and if one offers them a glass of rum, they become daily visitors.

The 21st - It is getting very warm. The news, which we have awaited for three weeks, arrived. Don Galvez has embarked his army and sailed down Mobile Bay. The wind is very favorable for him. We should be able to see his fleet here on the coast by tomorrow evening, or it will mean he wants nothing to do with us. Had he come three weeks earlier, his task would have been easier, but now our defenses are filled with cannons, and will be defended to the utmost.

The 23rd - Don Galvez used every trick to win to his side the Indians recently sent to the Perdido. He had won several of them over from the Alabama tribe, who remained because of the fine presents received when they joined him, and he hoped thus to bring the whole province under his jurisdiction. However, reportedly, the Indians are turning away from him again.

The 25th - Our flag of truce to New Orleans returned. Major Pentzel returned in good health and we received letters from our acquaintances there. The major and Commissary Marc had to put up with a great deal as they were not allowed to enter New Orleans.

The 27th - Today the hams and sausages, which had been sent to our men now dead, were auctioned off. A ham sold for seven dollars.

The 30th - A Spanish ship from Havana mistakenly entered the harbor believing Don Galvez had already captured Pensacola.

May 1780

The 1st - Our Indians commit all sorts of excesses. They get drunk and then are unmanageable. Today they even attacked our own outpost.

The 2nd - More work on our defenses has been accomplished in two months than could have been done by twice as many Negroes in six months, but the increasing heat will again impose great difficulties in our path.

The 8th - I ate today at MacDonald's. The Choctaw Indian king came with his wife. He was a clever, handsome man. He sat at the table with dignity, and his two principal chiefs sat on the floor. He toasted the King of England, which he indicated using the medal hanging on his chest. The queen seemed to be a sprightly woman. She had combed her hair down over her forehead to the eyes, wore a string of pearls around her neck, eleven large rings on her right arm and five on her left arm, a red dress which came down to the calf of her leg, and the usual deerskin shoes. She carried her husband's tomahawk or pipe.

The 17th - We get little news of the Spaniards, and Don Galvez proves his intelligence by preventing our learning his intentions except as he gives them the light of day. The latest that we know about him is that he landed 2,000 men this side of Mobile Bay. They will cross the Perdido in three columns and march on Pensacola.

The 18th - Our Indians received their presents and will return home. Their reason is that the life style and diet which they have here is unfamiliar and makes them sick. They must go home where their usual diet will enable them to recover.

The 19th - This morning two large Spanish ships appeared on the coast, apparently coming from Havana, and of the belief that Pensacola had already been captured. However, when they saw the English ships and heard a shot from the *Mentor*, which also hung out an English flag, they turned about and quickly departed.

The 21st - The Spanish officers, who are stationed aboard the Spanish ships near the Cliffs, came into the city.[7] The Indians were so stirred up against them that they were in danger of being scalped. The Indians forced their way into the house where the officers were, and to insure their safety, they were returned aboard ship this evening.

From these officers we learned that Don Galvez had positive orders to attack Pensacola and that he could count on further reinforcements from Havana.

The 27th - As we now know Don Galvez has definitely returned to New Orleans, our merchant ships can reenter the port and finish unloading their cargoes.

June 1780

The 14th - The captured Spanish officers returned to New Orleans on parole.

The 22nd - The Indians and several Spaniards attacked our outposts on the Perdido and plundered several plantations. Therefore a patrol was sent out this evening.

The 26th - The patrol sent out on the 22nd returned this evening having seen nothing of the enemy and only heard that the Indians sympathetic to the Spaniards had stolen our riding horses. When these Indians were found, our Indians fired upon them, but without effect.

July 1780

The 1st - Another patrol left Pensacola for the Perdido to occupy Morris Ferry. Today there was another crossing in an attempt to seize our posts on the Perdido.

The 3rd - The report of the capture of Charleston: It was captured on 12 May; 7,780 men and four generals were made prisoners, 480 artillery pieces and unimaginable quantities of supplies.

The 19th - Lieutenant von Horn died, buried the 20th.

The 21st - Captain Alberti [died] in New Orleans.

- - - - - - -

The transcript to the end of July from January 1780 was sent to Waldeck, via Georgia, in the little packet boat.

- - - - - - -

August 1780

The soldiers' rum was reduced. There is a shortage of everything; a pound of tobacco costs four bits and a pound of cheese, one bit.

The 13th - The frigate *Mentor*, which had sailed out on a cruise, sent in a Spanish sloop loaded with cannonballs destined for New Orleans.

The 14th - Aboard the captured Spanish ship were many letters from Mobile, some to friends in New Orleans, some sent to Havana, which held the most bitter complaints about the miserable conditions in Mobile. We have no complaints of this nature, yet. We suffer shortages of several things here. However, the Spaniards have a surplus of all miseries at Mobile. We are healthy and they are sick and have no medicine. And most of all, the complaints are about the Indians who take scalps so close to their sentries that no one dares to go a half mile into the woods.

The 15th - The regimental surgeon and I decided to close our campaign today and return to the city because life in the tent was unbearable. The other gentlemen built huts and covered the roofs with bark as the Indians do. Previously we have always had good winter quarters in America.

The 21st - Things are looking bad if no ships arrive this month. We are especially short of rum.

The 26th - Last week there were Indians here from the Choctaw tribe who had been with Don Galvez. They had received presents there but were dissatisfied with them. They were made to understand that since they had been on the Spanish side and wanting to use their scalping knifes against us, therefore, we would give them nothing. They answered that they were unworthy of presents and deserved to be dressed in tree bark rather than with wool blankets. They promised to be true, however, and to remain so in the future. They received some presents and left. On the other side of the Perdido, where they set up their camp, they encountered a Spanish patrol of a sergeant and seven men with whom they spent the day. When night came however, they murdered and scalped three of them and two escaped to Mobile. They brought these scalps here in triumph in order to ingratiate themselves again, but received no reward, and for their cruelty, which no one desired of them, were treated with contempt. It was rather startling to see these savages, howling and screaming, approaching with the still fresh scalps.

The French are held responsible for inventing the scalping knife and supplying the savages with it, to be used against the English, which as long as the French were in Canada and on the Great Lakes, they did. Now all these Indians are on the side of the English and hold a great hatred against the French and especially against the Spaniards.

The 28th - A flag of truce came from Mobile to the Perdido and delivered a letter at that outpost for the general. The Spanish commandant strenuously complained against the conduct of the Indians. He said that the way of waging war did not allow such barbarities to be used by his side, and if a general did allow it, he must be held accountable for the acts which were committed. One could expect the same from the Spaniards' side, and several tribes of savages would be employed by them to insure payment in kind. This had been caused by the Indians who had recently attacked the Spanish outposts. The general need not reply, other than in conference with the Indians. After being presented to them (made as a suggestion), they answered: The Spaniards are our enemies, have always been such, shall always remain such, and we will scalp them wherever we find them. Now that they are at war against you, they are even more our enemies, but they would be our enemies if they were at war with England as an ally, against another enemy. They have taken Mobile, the place where each year we are welcomed and entertained and receive our presents. Therefore, we wish to punish them wherever we can.

The 29th - Our usual way of life is quite remarkable. In the morning we drink water and eat a piece of dry bread. At noon we likewise have nothing to drink but water. Our evening meal consists of a pipe of tobacco and a glass of water.

September 1780

The 8th - Here nothing from the entire world is to be seen or heard. It is like a prison. The most exciting events can transpire by the army or navy and we will hear nothing about them. In addition, our general seems to have a poor correspondence or few good friends in the army. When an express comes from Carolina, he learns of the news from the so-called merchants in such a roundabout way as to make one wonder why he had not known it long before.

The 16th - Don Galvez made his presence known again. He had called the New Orleans militia together and given them the order to be ready to go to Mobile, and from there to Pensacola, but the French as well as the German planters on the other side of the Mississippi refused to obey. If he receives no reinforcements from Havana, he can come here with his army whenever he wishes. We also hear that our prisoners at New Orleans are to be brought to Jamaica in order to be exchanged.

The 30th - Now we are suffering a serious outbreak of sickness caused by weakness and shortages.

October 1780

The 3rd - There is nothing more to drink here except water. The colonel, who has a special ability to hold out somewhat longer, had a small supply of German cognac, of which he made each a present of two bottles. No, there is no worse place in the world. Satan and all his angels should be banished to this place.

The 6th - Choctaw Indians came in. They had attacked The Village near Mobile and plundered everything they saw. They brought a family of prisoners with them. It is a frightening experience to fall into the hands of these savage people, and for an inhabitant from across the Perdido, doubly unfortunate, because they are all considered Spanish citizens. The family brought here was French. The members had been stripped nearly naked and even the children were not left with even a shirt. The Indians dragged them through the wilderness for three days. What a society this must have been for these people who are from the first families. They were released in exchange for some presents. These unfortunate souls were taken in by the people here and given a house and clothing, as they have many acquaintances and friends in the city.

The 8th - I fear we will lose many men. All the regiments which come here die out in a few years and we will not be an exception. We have already experienced it.

The 16th - A glass of cognac costs eight bits hard cash.

November 1780

The 1st - Many families which at one time or another had built on the river, now flee here, because they are considered Spanish subjects by the Indians.

The 6th - The Indians returned with three Spanish scalps. They had attacked the posts at The Village and routed the defenders. Three of the Spaniards were shot to death when cut off from their barracks. Only one of the Indians was wounded.

The 7th - A captured Spanish ship, the *Potaee* (by *Mentor*), arrived at the Cliffs loaded with flour, coffee, sugar, taffeta, all articles needed at Pensacola.

The 15th - With much exertion, our 32-pounders were brought back down from Fort George and are to be shipped to the Cliffs. How fickle our general is! Since Fort George was finished, we thought we could resist a superior Spanish force, but now for the first time, we see that it will be dangerous for us to neglect the Cliffs at the entrance of the harbor, and therefore they must be strengthened as quickly as possible.

Some of our ships sailed to the harbor entrance today and lay at anchor there. By the first favorable wind we expect to see the Spanish fleet, which we fear will come from Havana, and I still hope that an English fleet from Jamaica will follow it. In our dangerous situation we have had more luck than we have earned with our preparations, and if that luck deserts us, we have no other hope for assistance. *All this does not have a good aspect, this is the notice. Don Galvez has proposed our destruction.*[8]

The 16th - A sloop loaded with rum came in during the night. It had captured a Spanish prize loaded with powder.

The 18th - Yesterday we only knew of one sloop. Today two more arrived, loaded with all the things most needed here and for which we have long had a taste. One was loaded with 150 casks of rum, the other with sugar and coffee. For the last three months we have had only water to drink, but in this climate that is not entirely healthy.

The 19th - Major Pentzel went to the Cliffs yesterday with a command of fifty men to whom we have given the sentry duty.[9]

We hear that Don Galvez had actually sailed with a fleet from Havana to conquer Pensacola and West Florida, but a severe storm near La Tortuga scattered his fleet, and nothing was known of his whereabouts.

The 27th -We hear that Don Galvez with most of his fleet has arrived at Mobile and will soon make his visit to us.

December 1780

(The Indians, who have now become our enemies, planned to attack the camp and massacre everyone.)

The 3rd, Sunday - At nine-thirty we held church in our mess house, where Fifer [Christian] Klee and Drummer [Jacob] Peter, whom I have been instructing during the last ten weeks, were confirmed.

The 5th - Lieutenant Stierlein, Ensign Schmidt, and I visited the major at the Cliffs. We rode out about eight o'clock and were there by ten. We passed the lagoons, of which the first is especially deep and dangerous, because it is necessary to ride over a narrow sandbar, and on both sides the water is very deep. The second is very broad and not so deep. It required nearly one-half hour to cross through. We left at three-thirty on our return, but could not find our way through the woods. After we had ridden around in the brush for an hour we decided it to be the best policy to make our way back to Mr. Moore's house, and to get one of his slaves to serve as a guide. Fortunately, we met a soldier of the 60th Regiment who waded ahead of us, even though the water came up to the saddle. It is certainly a gigantic, unpleasant region, where every moment another swamp is encountered.

The 31st - Another year is at an end and if it will be the last one in Florida, we need not know. It is all immaterial. All is in vain.

Ph. Waldeck

Addendum

Although no additional diary entries seem to have survived, Chaplain Waldeck probably continued his diary during the remaining period of the war and the return of the regiment to Germany in 1783. Carl Philipp Steuernagel, a member of the Waldeck Regiment, noted in his memoir that his account of the closing years of service in America had been lost when the ship carrying it back to Europe sank. Waldeck's final diary entries may have met the same fate.

After his return to Germany, Chaplain Waldeck began publishing a "revised" version of his diary in the *Waldeckisches Intelligenz-Blatt* (newspaper) published at Mengeringhausen. However, his early death on 20 March 1784, while visiting his former regiment at Mengeringhausen, precluded future generations from the pleasure of reading his comments on the final events leading up to England's recognition of independence for the American colonies.

A brief summary of the closing years of the Revolution, as experienced by the 3rd Waldeck Regiment, is included here to complete Chaplain Waldeck's story.

On 31 December 1780 Colonel von Hanxleden was sent against The Village, also known as Frenchtown, a Spanish strongpoint near Mobile. His command of 100 infantry, 11 mounted provincials, and 300 Indians, included Captain von Baumbach, Lieutenants von Wilmowsky and Stierlein, Ensign Ursall, 3 non-commissioned officers, 1 fifer, 1 drummer, and 7 privates from the Waldeck Regiment. The unsuccessful attack on 7 January 1781 resulted in heavy losses. The Waldeck Regiment lost Colonel von Hanxleden, Lieutenant Stierlein, and three soldiers killed, and Captain von Baumbach and 7 men wounded.[1] Ensign Ursall was killed in the defenses at Pensacola by a cannonball on 4 May 1781.

During the siege of Pensacola, beginning in March 1781, The combined Spanish-French force out-numbered the garrison with 7,000 Spaniards and 3,000 French, plus some Americans and Indians, a large artillery train, and many warships against 800 regulars of whom about 250 were Waldeckers, 200 sailors, and 1,000 Indians.[2] A Spanish shell which exploded a powder magazine in an outer redoubt killed 81 persons and necessitated the surrender of the entire garrison.

According to the terms of the capitulation the garrison was returned to New York on Spanish ships, arriving on 12 July 1783. The *San Pedro and San Pablo* provided transportation for 6 officers, 82 men, 5 women, and 7 children, a total of 100 persons. The *Santa Rosalia* transported 113 persons, including dependents and one free Negress. Lieutenant Colonel von Horn also listed himself and five other staff officers by name.[3] As three of the staff positions were filled by civilians, it seems likely that part, if not all, of the staff personnel were on board the ship and not included in the summary total.

The Waldeck Regiment served as part of the garrison in the New York area for the remainder of the war. Men of the 1782 recruit shipment landed at Halifax and may have been part of a reinforcement sent to Penobscot, Maine to prevent a French expedition against that place.[4] In 1783 the recruits returned to Germany from Halifax.

Finally, following the Treaty of Paris Chaplain Waldeck and the Waldeck Regiment returned to Germany with 418 men and women and 13 children, departing from New York on 15 July 1783.[5]

Notes to Organization and Brief History

1) The German word in the manuscript translates as servant, or, in the military, batman. The men who served as batmen for the chaplain and surgeon were privates from the ranks. As the war progressed, former Negro slaves were used as batmen and listed on the regimental rolls.

2) The German word translates as surgeon, but because of the level of command, it would appear to compare with the present day medical aid personnel, or surgeon's mate..

3) The solicitor was apparently a non-existent supernumerary with the position providing pay and allowance money to be used by the company commander as a unit, or personal, fund.

4) Albert W. Haarmann, "The Spanish Conquest of British West Florida, 1779-1781", *The Florida Historical Quarterly*, 39, 2 (1960-61), 133.

5) Max von Eelking, *The German Allied Troops in the North American War of Independence, 1776-1783*, Joseph G. Rosengarten (trans.), (1969), 133.

Notes to 1776

1) "At night, between eleven and twelve o'clock, no one can grind at this mill nor remain therein, because in that hour Satan has his time and wants to operate the mill for himself. It is already more than three hundred years since this mill was built." Johann Conrad Doehla, *A Hessian Diary of the American Revolution*, Bruce E. Burgoyne (trans.) (1990), 249. The Devil's Mill is still in existence and visible from the excursion boats which sail on the Weser.

2) The Grot is an old Bremen coin.

3) Eighty men of the 2nd Company and 35 men of the 4th Company, plus the 2nd Company officers and Chaplain Waldeck were transferred to the transport *Adamant*, master Josias Walker, on 26 June 1776 at Spithead, so the Waldeckers had four transports for the ocean crossing. Library of Congress photo copy of a Staatsarchiv Marburg, Germany, manuscript from the *Fuerstlich Waldeckisches Kabinett*. 1003, vol. II, 155v-156, hereafter referred to as L.C. and appropriate number.

4) The convoy was escorted by the English frigates *Diamond*, 32 guns, Captain Fielding; *Ambuscade*, 32 guns, John Macartney, commander; and *Unicorn*, 20 guns, John Ford, commander. William B. Clark et al (eds.), *Naval Documents of the American Revolution*, 8 vols., (1969), 6, 419-420.

5) The name is given as Hille in the Learned version of the Waldeck diary translated by Dr. William E. Dornemann.

6) Chaplain Waldeck's adventures in New York, from this date through 27 October, are, understandably, not mentioned in the more polished Learned version. The reader will notice in the text the chaplain's remarks about witches, hard boiled eggs, and other similar signs of immaturity. Not shown in the text, but related in the Learned version, is his recitation of a series of incidents which make it seem as if he were with the regiment during its first few days in America. As translated by

Dr. Dornemann, the Learned version covers the events of those days as follows; "The 22nd - All troops were brought down the East River in small boats. From this side New York could again be seen in its previous flourishing condition. A countless host of ships lay in the harbor, where they are both loaded and unloaded from houses. This river, which we traversed for thirty miles, forms many fine islands. It is even navigable for frigates. The regiment spent the night under the open heavens in the area of Neu Roschelle. The 23rd - Today we remained where we arrived yesterday and almost nothing in terms of food stuffs was available. General Howe came to our quarters. The 24th - We pitched our tents; however, received orders to break camp at dawn the following morning. The 25th - We marched quite early in the morning. However we halted quite often, in order to allow the Jaeger and English light cavalry to pass through to the front. We saw the large army on our right and left breaking camp and attached themselves to our column at the rear. After we had marched for approximately two hours and had come to a rise, from which we could see the camp of the rebels in front of us, the cavalry and light infantry moved out. The enemy took flight and the march continued. We had to march alongside of several English regiments to another rise. Four cannon had been placed in front of us. After we stood here awhile we marched back a short bit, and occupied the camp next to the English regiments. This area is called West-Chester. Thirty men from our regiment stood picket duty. The 26th - We remained in our previous position. In front of us we saw the enemy camp. In the evening a picket once more moved behind our front. 27th - We held our first church service in camp. We received orders to break camp as early as possible this morning. Quite good fresh meat was brought into camp and vegetables were available at quite a low price. We heard cannon fire all day long." William E. Dornemann (trans.), "A Diary Kept by Chaplain Waldeck During the Last American War", *Journal of the Johannes Schwalm Historical Association, Inc.*, 2, 3, (Millville, PA, 1983), 35.

7) Waldeck makes no mention of the men from the regiment who were wounded or captured at this time, in either version of the diary. However, Corporal Carl Philipp Steuernagel noted that in late October some men of the regiment wandered too far from camp in order to buy some things at a farm. They were attacked by a party of Americans, resulting in Waldeckers being wounded and some taken prisoner. The Waldeck soldiers included Corporal Johann Friedrich Christian Nelle and a number of privates. Several of the wounded men ransomed themselves and returned a few days later. Privates Zoellner and Philipp Stein Meyer were seriously wounded and left on the field. Zoellner returned to Germany as an invalid in early 1777; Steinmeyer died of his wounds on 7 November 1776. Of those who were taken prisoner and taken inland, some offered to join the American army, and probably did so, while others were allowed to return to their unit shortly after being captured. Carl Philipp Steuernagel, "A Brief Description and about the expedition of the Prince of Waldeck's Third Regiment in America from 20 May 1776 until the return from America in the year of 1783", Bruce E. Burgoyne (trans.), a German language manuscript in the Bancroft Collection of the

New York Public Library; Bruce E. Burgoyne (comp.), *Waldeck Soldiers of the American Revolutionary War*, (1991).

8) Apparently a copying error in the German manuscript as it should be 22 weeks.

9) The view today from the castle at Waldeck has been changed due to the construction of a hydroelectric plant on the Eder River, and the creation of the resulting Eder Lake. During World War II the dam was bombed by the English Royal Air Force using a skip-bombing technique and a large area of Waldeck was flooded causing many deaths and doing considerable property damage. The dam has been rebuilt and the view is still beautiful.

10) The Learned version mentions a sharp engagement on this date and that 124 Waldeckers participated. If, as I believe, the Learned version is a rewriting of the original, it would seem that Chaplain Waldeck tried to enliven his account for publication.

11) Again, the Learned version has no reference to horses and forage money, but mentions Captain Pentzel having been in a sharp encounter with the enemy and having talked, under a flag of truce, with an American officer who was a native of Hannover.

12) As to the comment "I'll show you the big city", the direct translation is "I'll show you Kassel." I am not sure just what this implies. The comment is not included in the Learned version.

13) Most accounts list Waldeck casualties at six dead and sixteen wounded. My count of men wounded in November is seventeen, but may include an individual wounded at some other place and time. Four of the wounded Waldeckers later died of their wounds. Those killed were Georg Backhaus, Wilhelm Brand, Johann Philipp Roll, Bernhard Bueddecker, Johann Henrich Knocke, and Paul Fleck. The wounded were Johannes Werle who died 17 November, Daniel Scheideler who died 23 November, Henrich Giesing who died 5 December, and Konrad Lock who died 7 December. Others wounded were Christoph Andre, Johannes Kesthans, Dietrich Frede, Corporal Otto Wiedlaake, Adam Schmidt, Adam Weirauch, Ludwig Berger, Johann Henrich Keitel, Henrich Mueller, Adolf Siebel, Henrich Pieper, David Schuettler, and Johannes Weidenhagen. Total losses for the English, Loyalists, and German forces was 77 killed, 374 wounded, and 7 missing, a total of 458 officers and men. American casualties at Fort Washington were 59 killed, 96 wounded, and 2,818 captured. L.C. 978; Frederick Mackenzie, *Mackenzie Diaries, Diary of Frederick Mackenzie, Giving a Daily Narrative of His Military Service as an Officer in the Regiment of Royal Welsch Fusiliers During the Years 1775-1781 in Massachusetts, Rhode Island, and New York*, 2 vols., (1930), I, 110; Willard M. Wallace, *Appeal to Arms, A Military History of the American Revolution*, (1951), 122; Burgoyne, Waldeck Soldiers.

Notes to 1777

1) The Learned version has the Waldeckers outnumbered ten to one.

2) The Learned version has no reference to the frequent alerts. It does mention in a 10 January entry that one church was used for English quarters and the other for hay storage. On 11 January, Waldeck then wrote that General Charles Lee, while eating breakfast, had been captured by the English light dragoons, and was then led through here on his way to New York. General Vaughan had Lee to dinner and addressed him as lieutenant colonel rather than as general. Also, in a 16 January entry, the Learned version mentions 42 captured rebels being brought through the town. In neither version did Waldeck comment on the thirty Waldeck soldiers captured on 9 January 1777.

3) The Ansbach-Bayreuth contingent had arrived at New York on 3 June 1777 and landed on Staten Island two days later. Johann Conrad Doehla, *A Hessian Diary of the American Revolution, Translated and edited by Bruce E. Burgoyne, (1990).*

4) This is a reference to General Howe embarking the troops for the Philadelphia campaign.

5) Although von Dalwigk returned home due to illness, he was later promoted to colonel. He died during he night of 14/15 October 1788 in Helsen, Waldeck. As a Waldeck ensign in Dutch service during the Seven Years' War he was captured by the Prussians and held as a prisoner of war in Magdeburg for a long time. The estate where he was born, Gut Campf, is still owned by his descendants in Waldeck. Conversation with Linda, Baroness von Dalwigk, in Dalwigksthal, Waldeck, 4 November 1985.

6) Although Waldeck referred to Wagner as being a catholic chaplain, he may have been referring to his philosophy rather than to his religion as Ansbach-Bayreuth was a Protestant territory. Waldeck also referred to the Ansbach-Bayreuth regiment on Staten Island as the Ansbach Regiment. The regiment from Ansbach-Bayreuth which was serving on Staten Island at that time was actually the 2nd or Bayreuth Regiment.

7) This was apparently meant to represent cannon fire from the ships and may have been some sort of signaling or the exchanging of honors.

8) Numerous Germans were recruited in Germany for service in the English army units. Two members of the Waldeck Regiment exchanged regiments with two German soldiers serving in the English 55th Regiment. L.C. 978; Burgoyne, *Waldeck Soldiers.*

9) David Grimm is mentioned in several "Hessian" diaries, and a David Grimm was a correspondent of the Muhlenberg family of preachers. A David Grimm is also listed in the 1790 census as living in a household of four adult males, two females, and one slave in the East Ward of New York City. An entry in an Ansbach-Bayreuth church book mentions a baptism in New York of a Maria Carolina daughter of 1st Lieutenant Johann Andreas Carl von Stein zu Altenstein and Maria Elisabeth, nee Grimm, daughter of the New York merchant David Grimm in 1782. Paul A.W. Wallace, *The Muhlenbergs of Pennsylvania*, (1950); *Heads of Families at the First Census of the United States Taken in the Year 1790 - New York*, (1976); Chaplain Georgius Michael Stroelein (comp.). "Ansbach-

Bayreuth Military Church Book", Translated by Bruce E. Burgoyne from the Landeskirchliches Archiv, Zentrale Kirchenbuchstelle, Regensburg, Germany.

10) When the Ansbach-Bayreuth prisoners held in Maryland were exchanged after the war, Wagner remained behind in order to marry. He then went to Nova Scotia in 1783 with his four children (?), where he was to have been the Lutheran pastor in the Old St. Edward's Church in Clementsport. However, he returned to Europe, possibly believing the position would not provide an adequate living. Doehla, *A Hessian Diary*, entry for 15 June 1783; Maxwell Sutherland, "Case History of a Settlement", *The Dalhousie Review*, 41 (Spring, 1961); Virginia DeMarce, *The Settlement of Former German Auxiliary Troops in Canada after the American Revolution*, (1984), 256.

11) He lived and was promoted to 1st lieutenant in November 1`777. Erhard Staedtler, *Die Ansbach-Bayreuth Truppen in Amerikanischen Unabhaengigkeitskrieg, 1777-1783*, (1956), 102.

12) Members of the Waldeck Regiment who died of heat exhaustion on the march on 23 August 1777, were Jakob Butterweck, Stefan Dietz, and Jakob Muus. L.C. 978, 3v-4.

13) The mention of the King's birthday is in error as it was celebrated on 4 June in other years. It seems likely that the celebration may have been to recognize the date of the King's coronation. See the entry for 12 September 1778.

14) The Learned version mentions that the children's only books were the Old and New Testament.

15) One of the ships which grounded was the *Stag* carrying members of the Bayreuth Regiment. Doehla, *A Hessian Diary*, entry for 15 October 1777.

16) Doehla recorded in his diary that the Waldeck Regiment was near mutiny at this time and "wanted to desert to the rebels because of the intense cold and wet weather. This situation was resolved and they were quartered in houses." I have found no confirmation to this information, except that the Learned version mentions that the regiment moved into houses on 29 October. Upon his return to command General Campbell ordered the Waldeckers back into the field, so that they could more quickly respond to any attack upon Staten Island. *Ibid.*

17) A portion of the diary was apparently omitted when making the Bancroft copy and I have accepted that the camp was called Waldeck town as shown in the Learned version.

Notes to 1778
(Through 31 July)

1) The copyist obviously skipped words as the sentence changes so abruptly.

2) The Learned version has the eclipse occurring on 25 June. As the Bancroft version has two entries for 21 June, so the Learned version has two entries for 25 June. Apparently Waldeck made an error in the original diary dates and did not know how to correct it.

3) This is a reference to a height north of the Eder Lake.

4) In the Learned version Waldeck referred to these Germans as men recruited by an individual named Scheiter who recruited in Germany for the English army. I am of the opinion that the reference to tailor's draft in the Bancroft Collection meant German apprentices forced into English service in New York.

5) Written as New York instead of Newark in the Bancroft version of the diary.

Notes to 1778
(Continuation from August)

1) This was Johannes Knueppel of the 4th Company. L.C. 978.

2) The 1778 recruit shipment, consisting of 142 men, including Major Sebisch and Lieutenant Becker as escort officers, was mustered at Bremerlehe on 5 April 1778 by Colonel William Faucitt. They sailed to America on the transport *Two Brothers*, master Joseph Patton, and arrived at New York on 13 September 1778. Eight wives and three children accompanied the recruits. Three men died en route and 39 were sick upon arrival. L.C. 1003, II, 125, 125v, 135, 155v, and 156.

3) Major von Horn and some invalids were the eleven Waldeckers victualled aboard the *Echo*, master J. Menenir, from New York on 8 October 1778 to Portsmouth, England, on 1 January 1779. *Ibid*, II, 155v-156.

4) Ships assigned for the Waldeckers were *Britannia, Christian, Crawford*, and *Springfield*. When mustered to go aboard ship, the regiment consisted of 21 officers, 39 non-commissioned officers, 20 musicians, 629 corporals and privates, 15 batmen, 35 wives, and 15 children, a total of 774 persons. Five other ships were assigned for General Campbell and some Loyalist troops. The escort for the nine ships which sailed to West Florida was the frigate *Solebay*, Captain Thomas Symonds. *Ibid*, II, 153; Clark, *Naval Documents*, IV, 740.

5) The Learned version lists the escorts by name and that they were commanded by Commodore William Hotham. It also has an entry that Waldeck's ship's captain was "a right good man". It does not say "our negligent captain" had not returned from New York.

6) In the Learned version Waldeck wrote that the ship's company, meaning Waldeckers on the ship, numbered 153 persons, including four women and four children. A 16 October Embarkation List of members of the Waldeck Regiment embarked at Staten Island gives the following breakdown of personnel of Captain Pentzel's Company: 3 officers, 7 non-commissioned officers, 4 musicians, 121 corporals and privates, 2 batmen, 4 wives, and 4 children, for a total of 145 persons. This company obviously sailed on the *Crawford* and the other eight persons were apparently Chaplain Waldeck and some other staff personnel. L.C. 1003, II, 153.

7) The Learned version states that "General Campbell on the agency ship, the *Solebay*, and 10 transports, including our 4, set off to the right."

8) It appears that the copyist omitted part of the entry in the Bancroft version at the point where I inserted the ellipsis

9) The Learned version is completely different for this date. Instead of discussing the arrival of pleasant weather, it relates that the ship crossed the Tropic

of Cancer and to avoid suffering the crew's pranks, Waldeck bought his release from such treatment for one guinea, which made the crew hopeful of crossing the Equator and the Tropic of Capricorn.

10) At this point the Learned version gives a breakdown of ship's rations, but omits the rest of the entry concerning Captain Pentzel, wine, and the discussion about women. As might be expected, the Learned version contains very few references to Waldeck's use of intoxicants.

11) The other units which sailed to West Florida with the Waldeck Regiment were William Allen's Pennsylvania and John Chalmer's Maryland Provincials. Strength for the Waldeck Regiment was 551 fit for duty and 660 effectives; for Allen's, 146 fit for duty and 165 effectives; for Chalmer's, 244 fit for duty and 277 effectives. Mackenzie, *Diaries*, II, 412; John Mollo and Malcolm McGregor, *Uniforms of the American Revolution in Color*, (1975), 35.

12) While it is doubtful that any men died due to the effects of this wind, five men did die aboard ship during the stay in Jamaica. L.C. 978, 5v.

13) The portion in italics was written in English and repeated in German.

14) The portion in italics was written in English.

Notes to 1779

1) While the Bancroft version continues in chronological order into February 1779, it suddenly returns to the period 24 to 30 January, and then once again into February 1779. The reader will notice this when the debarkation of troops is again mentioned on 30 January. The Learned version does not record this duplication of entries, which are written in different hand styles and may have resulted from more than one person making the copy for Mr. Bancroft.

2) One of the Indian chiefs encountered by the Waldeckers was a former comrade, Johann Konrad Brandenstein, born 25 June 1730 in Koenigshagen, who had deserted in Germany and gone to America. He married an Indian chiefs daughter and eventually became a chief himself. His story was the inspiration for Hans Lehr's book, *Der Herr der Wildnis* (The Lord of the Wilderness), published in Germany many years ago.

3) The last sentence is written in Latin. Captain Alberti's command had been captured on the Amite river on 4 September 1779 and Baton Rouge surrendered on 21 September 1779. Haarmann, "The Spanish Conquest", 112-113.

4) The Learned version omits this report of the massacre of Waldeck women and children and I have never found any other reference to such an occurrence. Possibly Waldeck originally included it as a rumor and then removed it from the later version after he learned that it was unfounded.

5) Waldeck prisoners captured on the Amite River and at Baton Rouge were held in New Orleans until late July 1780. They were then sent to Vera Cruz, Mexico, then to Havana, Cuba, and finally to New York. The movement of these prisoners can be followed by noting the deaths reported along the way. At least three of the Waldeckers who were prisoners of Spain, escaped, made their way up the Mississippi River, and joined Georg Rogers Clark in the Illinois country. L.C. 978; Correspondence with Daniel J. Rupert, Kalamazoo, MI, 1988.

Notes to 1780

1) This is another example of exaggerating the enemy strength to explain English/Hessian losses.

2) In the Learned version Waldeck wrote as though he were with the troops. Actually he remained in Pensacola.

3) This may have been The Village, also known as Frenchtown, where Colonel von Hanxleden was killed in 1781.

4) The portion of the paragraph in italics was written in Latin.

5) The spelling of the names of the Indian chiefs may be in error as the manuscript handwriting is extremely difficult to decipher.

6) The 1779 Waldeck recruit shipment embarked on the Weser River at Beverungen on 2 April with 2 non-commissioned officers, 20 recruits, 2 batmen, 1 provost, and 1 wife. One recruit was left at Vegesack and one non-commissioned officer was left at Bremerlehe with the baggage, so that 24 Waldeckers boarded the transport *Joseph*, 253 tons, Captain Mapp, at Bremerlehe on 1 May 1779. There were also 106 men from Hesse-Cassel, Lieutenant Colonel von Horn, and his son Lieutenant Karl von Horn. It took the Waldeck recruits almost one year to reach the regiment in Pensacola. K.G. Davies (ed.), *Documents of the American Revolution, 1770-1783*, 21 vols., (1981), 16, 106; Library of Congress photo copy of Staatsarchiv Hamburg manuscript 10,897, Ritzebuttel, Abt. 7, Fach 6, G; L.C. 1003, 1, 105-107.

7) These officers were apparently on parole from captured Spanish ships.

8) The portion in italics was written in English.

9) Captain Pentzel was an excellent choice for this assignment as he had served as a cannoneer and bombardier with the artillery prior to being commissioned. Algemeen Rijksarchif, 's-Gravenhage, The Netherlands manuscript "Efficiency List (of captains and junior officers) of the 2nd Regiment of Infantry of Lieutenant General the Prince of Waldeck" (Nijmegen, 1 January 1773), Raad von State, inv. nr. 1944 II de Watteville.

Notes to Addendum

1) Even Steuernagel did not mention enlisted casualties, which were 13 killed and 19 wounded, including Waldeck soldiers Christoph Kussenbauer and Wilhelm Stoltz, who died 7 January, and Hermann Sievers, who died 9 January. Other Waldeckers wounded, included: Michael Goebel and Georg Jost, both seriously wounded, Sergeant Georg Embde, Fifer Friedrich Birckenhauer, Georg Kirschner, and Henrich Eisenberg. "Robert Farmar's Journal of the Siege of Pensacola", *The Historical Magazine*, (New York), 4 (1860), 171; L.C. 972, II, 167; L.C. 978.

2) During the siege of Pensacola, the garrison, including men at the Cliffs and naval personnel, totaled about 1,700 men, plus 1,500 Negroes and Indians. The losses were 150 killed and 105 wounded. The 7,000 Spanish and 3,000 French - Miranda puts the total at less than 5,000 - supported by a large naval force and an

immense artillery train, suffered 119 killed and 133 wounded, including Galvez. Waldeck forces at the surrender were about 350, including prisoners of Spain, or about 200 men at Pensacola. Losses among the Waldeckers were four killed and five wounded, plus a number of deserters. Maury Baker and Margaret Bissler Haas (eds.), "Bernardo de Galvez's Combat Diary for the Battle of Pensacola, 1781", *The Florida Historical Quarterly*, (Gainesville), 56, 1 (July, 1977), 196-197; Donald E. Worcester, "Miranda's Diary of the Siege of Pensacola, 1781", *The Florida Historical Quarterly*, 29 (January, 1951), 176; "Notes from 'An Account of the Surveys of Florida', (London, 1790), page 3"; and Farmar's Journal", 4 (1860), 171; L.C. 972, II, 167; L.C. 978; Robert R. Rea and James A. Servies, *The Log of H.M.S. Mentor, 1780-1781*, (1982), 176.

3) All the Waldeckers from the Pensacola garrison appear to have sailed back to New York on two ships. The *Santa Rosalia*, Captain Pedro Gatell, carried 113 persons, including 4 wives, 2 children, and 1 free Negress. The *San Pedro and San Pablo* carried 6 officers, 82 soldiers, 5 women, and 7 children. Archivo General de Indias, Seville, Spain. Information obtained by Dr. William Coker, University of West Florida, Pensacola, FL.

4) The 1782 Waldeck recruit shipment consisted of 1 officer, 134 men, and 13 women. It landed in Halifax, Nova Scotia, may have participated in an expedition to Penobscot, and returned to Germany from Nova Scotia after the war. L.C. 1002, 112.

5) Davies, *Documents, 19, 414.*

Bibliography

Conversation with Linda, Baroness von Dalwigk, Dalwigkstal, Germany, 4 November 1985.

Correspondence with Daniel J. Rupert, Kalamazoo, MI, 1988.

Manuscript Sources

ALGEMEEN RIJKSARCHIEF, 's-Gravenhage, The Netherlands, "Conduite Lisjte" or Efficiency Lists of captains and junior officers of the 2nd Regiment of Infantry of Lieutenant General the Prince of Waldeck (Nijmegen, 1 January 1773) Raad von Stade, inv. nr. 1944 II de Watteville.

ARCHIVO GENERAL DE INDIAS, Seville, Spain. List of Waldeck prisoners from the Pensacola garrison of 1781. Provided by Dr. William Coker of the University of West Florida.

COUNTY OF FRANKENBERG-WALDECK, Germany. Church Records of numerous churches, checked for birth information on men of the 3rd Waldeck Regiment.

LANDESKIRCHLICHES ARCHIV. Regensburg, Germany. Stroelein, Georgius Michael (comp.), "Ansbach-Bayreuth Military Church Book". Translated by Bruce E. Burgoyne.

NEW YORK PUBLIC LIBRARY. Steuernagel, Carl Philipp, "A Brief Description of the journey and about the Prince of Waldeck's Third Regiment in America from 20 May 1776 until the return from America in the year 1783" Translated by Bruce E. Burgoyne.

STAATSARCHIV Hamburg.   "Manuscript 10,897 Ritzebuttel. Abt VII, Fach. 7, vols, B and C and Amtsarch. Ritzebuttel, Abt VII, Fach. 6, vol. G".

STAATSARCHIV Marburg. "Fuerstlich Waldeckisches Kabinett", nrs. 972, 978, 1002, and 1003.

WALDECK GESCHICHTSVEREIN, Arolsen, Germany. "Lijsten Boek voor't 5de Battalillon Waldeck". Rosters of men of the 5th Waldeck Battalion serving in South Africa in 1804 to 1806.

Eighteenth Century America
Secondary Sources

AUERBACH, Inge, FRANZ, Eckhart, and FROEHLICH, Otto (eds.). *Hessische Truppen im Amerikanischen Unabhaengigkeitskrieg (HETRINA)*. 5 vols. Marburg, Germany, Staatsarchiv Marburg, 1972-1976.

BAKER, Maury and HAAS, Margaret Bissler (eds.). "Bernardo de Galvez's Combat Diary for the Battle of Pensacola, 1781", *The Florida Historical Quarterly*. 56, 1 (Gainesville, July 1977).

BING, Hermann. "Deutsche Soldaten im Amerikanischen Unabhaengigkeitskrieg", *Mein Waldeck, Waldeckische Landeszeitung*. 11 (Korbach, Germany, 1977).

BAURMEISTER, Carl L. *Revolution in America: Confidential Letters and Journals, 1776-1784, of Adjutant General Major Baurmeister of the Hessian Forces*. Edited and translated by Bernard A Uhlendorf. New Brunswick, NJ: Rutgers University Press, 1957.

CLARK, William Bell et al. (eds.). *Naval Documents of the American Revolution*. 8 vols. Washington: US Naval Department, 1964-1976.

DAVIES, K.G. (ed.). *Documents of the American Revo-lution, 1770-1783*. Colonial Office Series. 21 vols. County Dublin: Irish University Press, 1973-1980.

DE MARCE, Virginia. *German military Settlers in Canada after the American Revolution*. Sparta, Wisc: Joy Reisinger, 1984.

DOEHLA, Johann Conrad. *A Hessian Diary of the American Revolution*. Edited and translated by Bruce E. Burgoyne. Norman: University of Oklahoma Press, 1990.

DORNEMANN, William (trans.). "The Diary of Philipp Waldeck", *Journal of the Johannes Schwalm Historical Association, Inc.* 2, 3 and 4 and 3, 1 (Lyndhurst, Ohio, and Millville, PA, 1983-1985).

EELKING, Max von. *The German Allied Troops in the North American War of Independence, 1776-1783*. Translated and abridged by Joseph G. Rosengarten. Baltimore: Genealogical Publishing Co., 1969.

FARMAR, Robert. "Robert Farmar's Journal of the Siege of Pensacola", *The Historical Magazine*. 4 (New York, 1860).

FORCE, Peter (ed.). *American Archives, Fifth Series (July 4, 1776 - September 3, 1783)*. 3 vols. Washington: 1848-1853.

HAARMANN, Albert W. "The Spanish Conquest of British West Florida, 1779-1781", *The Florida Historical Quarterly.* 39, 2 (Gainesville, 1960-61).

Heads of Families at the First Census of the United States taken in the Year 1790 - New York. Baltimore: Genealogical Publishing Co., 1976.

MACKENZIE, Frederick. *Mackenzie Diaries, Diary of Frederick Mackenzie, Giving a Daily Narrative of His Military Service as an Officer of the Regiment of Royal Welsh Fusiliers during the Years 1775-1781 in Massachusetts, Rhode Island, and New York.* 2 vols. Cambridge, Mass.: Harvard University Press, 1930.

MOLLO, John and MC GREGOR, Malcolm. *Uniforms of the American Revolution, in Color.* New York: Macmillan Publishing Company, 1975.

"Notes from 'An Account of the Surveys of Florida', London, 1790", *The Historical Magazine*. 4 (New York, 1860).

Ortssippenbuecher. A series of genealogical books for places in Waldeck, Germany. Arolsen, 1938-present.

REA, Robert R. and SERVIES, James A. *The Log of H.M.S. Mentor, 1780-1781.* Pensacola: University Presses of Florida, 1982.

ROSENGARTEN, Joseph G. "A Defense of the Hessians" *Pennsylvania Magazine of History and Biography.* 23 (Philadelphia, July 1899).

STAEDTLER, Erhard. *Die Ansbach-Bayreuther Truppen im Amerikanischen Unabhaengigkeitskrieg, 1777-1783.* Nuernberg, Germany: Gesellschaft fuer Familien-forschung in Franken, 1956.

SUTHERLAND, Maxwell. "Case History of a Settlement", *The Dalhousie Review. 51 (Halifax, Spring 1961).*

TATUM, Edward H. (ed.). *The American Journal of Ambrose Serle, Secretary of Lord Howe, 1776-1778.* San Marino, CA: The Huntington Library, 1940.

TREVELYAN, Sir George Otto. *The American Revolution.* 3 vols. New York: Longmans, Green, and Company, 1905.

WALLACE, Paul A.W. *The Muhlenbergs of Pennsyl-vania.* Philadelphia: University of Pennsylvania Press, 1950.

WALLACE, Willard M. *Appeal to Arms, A Military History of the American Revolution.* New York: Harper and Brothers, 1951.

WORCESTER, Donald E. (trans.). "Miranda's Diary of the Siege of Pensacola, 1781", *The Florida Historical Quarterly.* 29, 3 (Gainesville, January 1951).

EVERYNAME INDEX

Other Heritage Books by Bruce E. Burgoyne:

A Hessian Officer's Diary of the American Revolution
Translated from an Anonymous Ansbach-Bayreuth Diary and the Prechtel Diary

Canada During the American Revolutionary War: Lieutenant Friedrich Julius von Papet's
Journal of the Sea Voyage to North America and the Campaign Conducted There

CD: A Hessian Diary of the American Revolution

CD: A Hessian Officer's Diary of The American Revolution

CD: A Hessian Report on the People, the Land, the War of Eighteenth Century
America, as Noted in the Diary of Chaplain Philipp Waldeck, 1776-1780

CD: Ansbach-Bayreuth Diaries from the Revolutionary War

CD: Canada During the America Revolutionary War

CD: Diaries of Two Ansbach Jaegers

CD: The Hessian Collection, Volume 1: Revolutionary War Era

CD: They Also Served. Women with the Hessian Auxiliaries

CD: Waldeck Soldiers of the American Revolutionary War

Defeat, Disaster, and Dedication

Diaries of Two Ansbach Jaegers

Eighteenth Century America (A Hessian Report on the People, the Land, the War)
as Noted in the Diary of Chaplain Philipp Waldeck (1776-1780)

Enemy Views: The American Revolutionary War as Recorded by the Hessian Participants

English Army and Navy Lists Compiled During the American Revolutionary War by
Ansbach-Bayreuth Lieutenant Johann Ernst Prechtel

Georg Pausch's Journal and Reports of the Campaign in America, as
Translated from the German Manuscript in the Lidgerwood Collection in the
Morristown Historical Park Archives, Morristown, New Jersey

Hesse-Hanau Order Books, a Diary and Roster: A Collection of Items
Concerning the Hesse-Hanau Contingent of "Hessians" Fighting
Against the American Colonists in the Revolutionary War

Hessian Chaplains: Their Diaries and Duties

Hessian Letters and Journals and a Memoir

Journal of a Hessian Grenadier Battalion

Journal of the Hesse-Cassel Jaeger Corps

Journal of the Prince Charles Regiment
Translated by Bruce E. Burgoyne; Edited by Dr. Marie E. Burgoyne

Most Illustrious Hereditary Prince: Letters to Their Prince from Members of Hesse-Hanau
Military Contingent in the Service of England During the American Revolution

Notes from a British Museum

Order Book of the Hesse-Cassel von Mirbach Regiment

CPSIA information can be obtained at www.ICGtesting.com
Printed in the USA
LVOW01s0228290115

424826LV00029B/519/P